SHANGHAI CONSPIRACY

THE SORGE SPY RING

MOSCOW • SHANGHAI • TOKYO

SAN FRANCISCO • NEW YORK

MAJOR GENERAL
CHARLES A. WILLOUGHBY

MacArthur's Chief of Intelligence 1941-1951

preface by

General of the Army Douglas MacArthur

THE AMERICANIST LIBRARY

Published by WESTERN ISLANDS ★ BOSTON ★ LOS ANGELES

SHANGHAI CONSPIRACY

A Western Islands book,
published by arrangement with the copyright owner.

Except for the omission of illustrations and line
cuts, this edition is complete and unabridged.

PRINTING HISTORY

E. P. Dutton edition published 1952
American Opinion edition published 1961
The Americanist Library edition published 1965

Manufactured in the United States of America

Published by
Western Islands
395 Concord Avenue
Belmont, Massachusetts 02178

CONTENTS

PART II   RICHARD SORGE'S OWN STORY AND KLAUSEN'S TESTIMONY   101

PART III   AGNES SMEDLEY AND THE WAR DEPARTMENT   193

PART IV   THE SHANGHAI CONSPIRACY   215

The Americanist Library

. . . reaches for its manuscripts to every corner of the earth, and to every era of man's culture. For the ideals represented by America at its best have been acclaimed alike by the Roman Cicero two thousand years ago; by the Frenchman Bastiat a hundred years ago; and by the Korean Syngman Rhee only yesterday.

. . . is published for readers of every clime and color and creed, and of every nationality. An American or a German or an Egyptian or a Japanese or an Australian; a Catholic or a Protestant or a Jew or a Mohammedan or a Buddhist; each alike can be or become a good americanist, in the fundamental meaning of that term which these volumes will strengthen and support.

. . . seeks to make readily available, in a uniform and inexpensive format, a growing series of great books that define many battle lines in the long war between freedom and slavery. The first fully recorded engagement in that war was between the constructive forces of Athenian individualism and the destructive forces of Spartan collectivism. Those prototypes find their recurrent spiritual reincarnation today in the bitter contemporary struggle between the americanist and the communist systems.

For the americanist, always and everywhere, education is the basic strategy, and truth is the vital weapon. It is the purpose of this series to supply searchlights and alarm bells, and weaponry and the will to win, for those who believe that Bryant's admonition must be heeded in every age:

> *"Not yet, O Freedom! close thy lids in slumber, for thine enemy never sleeps."*

Introduction to the Americanist Library Edition

The Kremlin has now confirmed the accuracy of General MacArthur's intelligence reports, 1947-1950, on the Richard Sorge spy case. However, press coverage of the sensational admission by the Kremlin that Sorge was "their man in Japan" was spotty. The New York *Times* article September 5, 1964, was prompt and was perhaps the most illuminating. The Washington *Post* piece dated October 1 (relayed via Bonn) was a copy of the British *Observer* story and was inaccurate regarding the details on how Sorge was trapped. The *Times* report read as follows:

Special to the New York Times

MOSCOW, Sept. 4—The Soviet Union acknowledged today that Richard Sorge, press officer at the German Embassy in Tokyo during World War II, headed a successful Soviet spy ring.

An article in Pravda, the Communist party newspaper, credited Sorge with having supplied information that enabled the Soviet Army to block the German forces driving on Moscow in the fall of 1941.

Sorge was arrested by the Japanese secret police and executed in 1944 after a trial behind closed doors.

The activities of the Sorge spy ring were first made public in a United States Army report prepared by Maj. Gen. Charles A. Willoughby, who was General Douglas MacArthur's chief of intelligence in the Far East command (1941-1951).

Foretold Nazi Attack

The Pravda article said that "many circumstances" had prevented the Soviet authorities from acknowledging earlier the links between Sorge and the Soviet intelligence system.

"Now the time has come to tell about the man whose name will be for future generations a symbol of devotion to the great cause of the fight for peace, a symbol of courage and heroism," the newspaper said.

Stressing the accuracy of the information supplied by

Sorge, Pravda said that in the spring of 1939 "he informed Moscow that the Hitlerites would invade Poland Sept. 1." This was in fact the date of the German attack, which touched off World War II.

"In April, 1941, Richard Sorge supplied valuable information about the preparation of a Hitlerite attack on the Soviet Union." Pravda continued. "He said 150 divisions were being concentrated at the borders of the U.S.S.R., supplied a general scheme of the military operations and in some reports, at first by one day off but later exactly, named the date of the attack, June 22." . . .

According to Pravda, Sorge informed Soviet intelligence two months before the Dec. 7, 1941 attack on Pearl Harbor that the Japanese were getting ready for a war in the Pacific and would not attack the Soviet Far East, as the Russians feared.

Troops Rushed to Moscow

This vital information, Pravda said, enabled the Soviet Army to shift urgently needed reinforcements from the Far East to help stop the Germans' advance at the gates of Moscow. . . .

Sorge was a grandson of Friedrich Albert Sorge, a German-American leader of the United States labor movement in the second half of the 19th century. Richard was born in 1895 in Baku, where his father, who was married to a Russian, was employed in the oilfields.

The family moved to Germany when Richard was 3 years old. He became a leftist while serving in the German Army in World War I and joined the German Communist party in 1919.

In the nineteen-twenties he emigrated to the Soviet Union, where he joined the intelligence service in 1929. After underground work in Shanghai, he showed up in Tokyo in 1933 as a German newspaper correspondent.

There Sorge won the confidence of the German military attaché, Eugen Ott, who upon assuming the ambassadorship in 1938 made Sorge press attaché and informal adviser. The head of the Gestapo's intelligence network in the Far East also maintained a close relationship with Sorge, who was regarded as a devoted Nazi.

The best coverage came from that unsung hero of the cold war, the Legislative Reference Service of the Library of Congress, and Mr. Sergius Yakobson, senior specialist for Russian affairs.

The American press generally seemed unaware of the

inner significance of the astounding Russian acknowledgement and its relation to current events, namely:

1. It confirmed the accuracy of MacArthur's reports, 1947-1950.

2. It exposed the spurious Washington attempts in highest quarters to repudiate and weaken these reports at the time of their publication.

3. The jurisprudential implications, then and now, are vast.

4. The reports identify 180 individuals, aliases and/or groups as associates of Richard Sorge, i.e. as juridical accessories. The list contains the top hierarchy of the American Communist party. Many of them are still alive and active today.

5. This group of accessories is responsible for the Communist takeover of China.

6. The leaders are pinpointed in exhibits 31-32 of the original G-2 report and in extracts from file cards: "Miscell. Records. Special Branch. Shanghai Municipal Police. Part II."

7. The ultimate result of the American-Communist conspiracy in China led to the collision between China and the United States in Korea.

8. This raises a moral issue: 134,000 killed, wounded or missing in the Sino-Korean War from 1950-1951 and the rising toll in Vietnam in 1965.

The observations of Robert Morris, former chief council for the Senate Internal Security Subcommittee, substantiate my views on these recent developments. I quote in part Dr. Morris' syndicated column "Around the World" devoted to this matter under the headline "Proof—and Indifference":

The belated Soviet announcement of Richard Sorge as its wartime spy in Japan and the simultaneous news report that H. A. R. Philby, former British diplomat is now employed by the Moscow press agency, Novosti, should spell out a conclusion that is just not being drawn in the 1964 political campaign.

The United States Senate Internal Security Subcommittee surveyed the activities of the Institute of Pacific Relations in the early fifties. It took the testimony of Maj. Gen. Charles A. Willoughby on his return from duty in Japan. General Willoughby courageously told the Senate that Richard Sorge had headed an international spy ring which, in the summer and fall of 1941, served Soviet cause by averting a Japanese attack on the USSR in support of the Nazi campaign in Europe. The abuse heaped upon General Willoughby by the press and government officials has rarely been equaled. The fact was that from his vantage point in the German Embassy in Tokyo, Sorge was able to tell Moscow that the vast Japanese military movements southward meant an imminent attack on the United States. Moscow did not alert Washington to the impending Pearl Harbor attack. . . .

A partial release of the MacArthur intelligence reports in 1949 by the late Secretary of Defense James V. Forrestal became a journalistic sensation but was repudiated by the Department of the Army. Indeed two hostile Cabinet members intervened personally on mass television programs and by means of press interviews. The details of these happenings were covered by me in a brief article in the *American Mercury*, January 1959.

Fragmentary official reports from Tokyo consisting of thirty-one "exhibits" from 1945-1947 were followed by a privately printed "digest" for the benefit of understaffed congressional committees. The title: *A Partial Documentation Of The Sorge Espionage Case*, Tokyo 1950.

In view of the sensational Soviet acknowledgement that Sorge was "their man in Japan," the MacArthur reports now stand as a proven authoritative analysis of Communist subversive techniques on a global scale. The Documentation *should, consequently, be exploited in service schools, universities and related government agencies.*

However, I find no evidence that this unique document has been used effectively except by the Central Intelligence Agency. Representative D. J. Flood (D., Pa.) made a test inquiry into the curriculum of the Inter-American Defense College. The results were negative, though the South American student body needs orientation on Communist techniques. The War College prefers civilian "lecturers on Communism" to this bona fide, professional military intelligence product, which has now been devastatingly vindicated.

The United States Information Agency spent approximately fourteen thousand dollars on printing a tailor-made, mediocre rehash on Communism when the Sorge *Documentation* was available for inexpensive offset reproduction at a fraction of that cost—not to mention the classical distinction between a "participating eyewitness report" and secondhand "academic generalities."

I urge the Sorge *Documentation* be given the full attention it merits by official agencies, both as a source of vital information and as a teaching weapon. And I resubmit this book, *Shanghai Conspiracy*, in its new edition to the American public.

PREFACE

By GENERAL DOUGLAS MACARTHUR

GENERAL WILLOUGHBY's book *Shanghai Conspiracy,* which includes the story of Richard Sorge, is of the gravest importance because it presents a clear delineation of a world-wide pattern of Communist sabotage and betrayal which is still being practiced today.

During our Occupation of Japan, military intelligence exercised limited civil functions in collaboration with the modernized Japanese police, in an alert against national and foreign communism. The story of Richard Sorge, Soviet master spy, falls into this category of security surveillance. It represents a devastating example of a brilliant success of espionage—its evolution, techniques, and methods. Elements of this Soviet-inspired conspiracy actually ranged from China and Japan into the United States, in the period 1931-50.

Over a period of years, there has been filed with Washington a most extensive documentation on the case, aggregating over a million words with hundreds of plates, photostats, and illustrations. Enormous efforts in translation and research have gone into it. It has been reviewed and authenticated by American lawyers, and is now being brought into focus by the Senate and House Committees on Internal Security and Un-American Activities.

Sorge's story did not begin or end with Tokyo but was only a chip in the general mosaic of Soviet Far Eastern strategy. It deals with a sinister epoch in the history of modern China and must be viewed against the vicious background of world conspiracy. Shanghai was a vineyard of communism for men and women of many nationalities who had no conceivable personal stake in China, but an almost inexplicable fanaticism for an alien cause—the Communist subjugation of the Western world. Here were sown the dragon's teeth that have since ripened into the Red harvest of today.

New York, January, 1952

DOUGLAS MacARTHUR

1

INTRODUCTION

Shanghai, 1935—Tokyo, 1945—New York, 1950

The British Police Commissioner, Mr. T. P. Givens, who knew too much ever again to enjoy real peace of mind, toyed with a curious piece of correspondence. This was China before the Japanese invasion of 1937 and Shanghai was the most important single piece of real estate in the Orient. While the National Chinese government felt that the hinterland (*Kiangsu*) was reasonably stable and quiet, the International Settlement Police knew better. Foreign agents had infiltrated more boldly. Everything pointed toward the Kremlin-controlled Third Communist International, secretly but increasingly more active in the area, under many fronts, ranging from labor- and maritime-workers unions to a crazy quilt of cultural, university, and social organizations, with some famous and even respectable names on their letterheads, including the venerated widow of Sun Yat-sen.

Mr. Givens had before him a letter from Mr. H. Steptoe, British Consul General, Shanghai, in which the Consul commented on the valuable work done by the municipal police in restricting the activities of Walsh and Koenig, during the period that these Comintern agents were in Shanghai. The letter, in part, follows.

. . . Broadly speaking the function of the Comintern is to act as the mainspring of an illegal conspiracy against international law and order. The function of the Police is to preserve that law and order, locally and as far as possible internationally and it will, in my opinion be a profound pity, if and when information concerning the presence of Comintern agents here is made available to the local Police from any source whatever the utmost endeavour is not made to discover everything possible concerning these people.

It may be, and in fact it is very often the case, that we do not, except in outstanding cases like the Noulens case, see the results of painstaking enquiry and watching at this end; but I would point out that the members of the Comintern like Walsh and Koenig are all highly trained and hand-picked men, sent out on their various missions only after intensive training. Their number is not legion; the Comintern is concerned with guarding their identity and their functions. If their identity can be discovered, personal descriptions obtained (and photographs where possible) their value to the Comintern is lessened, in fact it may become nil. Thus a shrewd blow is struck by the very hesitation which that body will have in again using them, and I will repeat that the number of trusted illegal and highly trained workers is not legion. If their functions on the spot can be ascertained, then knowledge of their method of work becomes available, the ramifications of the apparatus known and the chances of being able adequately to provide for internal security are enormously increased. In the case of Walsh we know that part of his functions was the penetration of various armed forces stationed here for the protection of the settlement. The result of your own raids bear mute testimony to the careful preparations which were made in this direction.

In watching Koenig as the Special Branch Officer so successfully did, they caused a complete breakdown in the liaison services of the Comintern of which he was the head. That the liaison can be built up again I will not deny, but every blow dealt, causes a pause (there is a definite one in Comintern activity here at present). The cumulative effect of the blows dealt, e.g. since the Noulens Case, I know is great and is causing much uneasiness in Comintern circles. . . .

This letter, dated January 19, 1935, is an almost perfect exposition of why intelligence reports, even those dealing with events that are chronologically old, remain valuable in the prosecution of the ceaseless cold war against Communist disturbers of the public peace.

The significance of this correspondence of "yesterday" is that it carries straight into "tomorrow"; the Walsh of Shanghai is Eugene Dennis, the Chief of the American Communist party, convicted in the Court of Judge Medina, in New York City.

Had the U.S. District Attorney known some of the data in the Shanghai police files, he would have had less difficulty in convicting Dennis in Judge Medina's court; by the same token, the learned Justices of the Supreme Court who later dissented on the appeal of the American Communist conspirators, might have concurred with the majority opinion had they clearly understood that Browder preceded Dennis, in China, and that their clandestine activities in Shanghai were under the direction of the Kremlin, the Comintern, and the 4th Bureau (Intelligence) of the Red Army.

The Shanghai police were on the track of a vast conspiracy to communize China, to overthrow Chiang Kai-shek, but the full extent of this international intrigue was not known even to them. Ten years later, Dr. Sorge was the first to describe, though hastily and guardedly, what he termed the "Comintern Group in Shanghai." Sorge's typewritten notes, more of a memoir than a confession, were picked up by MacArthur's intelligence service, as an incident of the Occupation of Japan. This incident became the springboard for a time-consuming investigative process, that started in Tokyo, with the records of Sorge's trail, and then moved backward to Shanghai and China in painstaking and expensive research, to trace the source of actions and individuals.

No details were known at that time. The interlocking relationships were not clear. The threat of the Soviets was discounted. The network of Red "fronts" and their traitorous character were not fully appreciated. It was left to MacArthur's intelligence service to disclose in complete detail one of the most striking chapters in the story of international treason, betrayal, and subversion.

Occupation Release of Political Prisoners

On September 22, 1945, General MacArthur established his headquarters in the Dai Ichi Building, the modern home of one of Japan's most important life insurance companies. The first phase of the Occupation began in the demobilization and disarmament of Japan's Home Armies of fifty odd divisions and over a million men and the repatriation of another five million from overseas.

The fata morgana of the Potsdam Declaration glittered and dazzled for a while before it was revealed in its Machiavellian realism. The jails were opened with the casual good nature of the American conquerers, and the victims of the *Kempeitai* and the "Thought Police" blinked their eyes in the unaccustomed glare of Western freedom. The released prisoners contained a sprinkling of political martyrs, the upper crust of prewar Japanese communism, not to mention a few bona-fide criminals, and a number of shadowy characters of uncertain nationality. An excited Japanese official advised me that the release list contained foreign espionage agents, the remnants of the Sorge espionage ring, in particular one Max Klausen, Sorge's radio operator. When Klausen became aware of G-2 surveillance, he vanished to Siberia via the Soviet Embassy.

The investigation required delicate handling. I took personal charge of the case though, at that time disarmament and demobilization of the Japanese war machine had priority in our attention. Some odd collateral circumstances aroused my curiosity. Service and Emmerson were temporarily on duty with the American Embassy. Nosaka Sanzo, the titular head of the Japanese Communist party then living in Yennan, the Chinese Communist capital, appealed to Emmerson as a "character witness" for admission to Japan via Korea. A Canadian diplomat was employed by our counterintelligence group as a "consultant" giving a foreign diplomat access to secret security files. The vagaries of the American intelligence service are great and astounding. I promptly terminated this extraordinary intimacy. I have since become a staunch supporter of a central intelligence agency which can put a stop to such absurdities, characteristic of routine military methods and the fruitless rotation of casual, uninformed amateurs. In that particular period, however, fraternization with Soviet Russia was a definitive policy of the Roosevelt regime and such matters then seemed hardly significant.

At the time of the liberation of the Sorge gang our counterintelligence was headed by Brigadier General Elliott R. Thorpe. This is the same Thorpe who later testified in behalf of Owen Lattimore, before the Tydings Committee. The impression created by this particular witness was that the Far East Command indorsed Lattimore. We promptly corrected this impression as unwarranted. Lattimore had not appeared prominently either during the war or in the Occupation period, consequently, there was no official basis for either favorable or unfavorable comment. Thorpe was not in a position to make such an "endorsement" and it was obvious that he had gone out of his way to do so.

Sorge Trial Parallels Canadian Espionage Case

From the point of view of national security, the discovery of direct links of the Sorge Spy Ring with American Communist operators, especially in California, required careful investigation. The process was leisurely and unobtrusive, since it was expected that the "liberated elements" would sooner or later pick up the thread with the mainland. Even more important and dramatic tendrils ultimately led to Shanghai and its International Settlement. It soon became apparent that the Sorge Ring was an integral part of the Third Communist International "apparatus" in a world-wide pattern of infiltration, subversion, and sedition, which had as its ultimate objective Soviet domination of the Far East. These matters so commonplace now were not fully understood in 1945.

When the Canadian Espionage Case with its shattering revelations by Igor Gouzenko became widely publicized by several government agencies, as a warning of subversive methods and techniques, I decided that the Sorge Case, though 10,000 miles away, was a complete parallel and should be reported to demonstrate an existing world-wide pattern and to induce FBI and U.S. Security Service investigation of certain American personnel involved. The wealth of documentation available in Japanese court records, not to mention other sources, offered complete and authenticated material. Lieutenant Colonel T. P. Davis of the CIS (Civil Intelligence Service) prepared an initial summary report, based on the Japanese Ministry of Justice pamphlets "Sorge Material: Parts I & II," published in April, 1942. Parts of this report were forwarded to Washington as early as 1946. In the manner of a Chinese tailor, who faithfully reproduces even the patches, the Davis study was employed by another Tokyo CIS writer, Dr. H. T. Noble, who added a certain popular touch to the manuscript. Noble's version was mimeographed, December 15, 1947, air-mailed to Washington and recommended for distribution to Military Service Schools, as instructional material, in view of the apprehensions aroused by the Canadian Espionage Case. G-2 Tokyo was not advocating public release of this material and consistently maintained that general publication was a matter for the Department of the Army. This position was firmly reiterated throughout 1948 when Washington intermittently negotiated for its release.

The Strange Case of Dr. Sanders Alias Gerold Eckelman

In March, 1948, one Gerold Eckelman, alias Dr. Fred Sanders, committed suicide in Tokyo. This man had acquired Soviet citizenship in 1946 and enjoyed the favor of the Soviet Embassy. G-2 happened to know a great deal about this individual. He had come under suspicion when he had sought the friendship of American soldiers, particularly those on duty with the Signal Corps: foreign agents blunder when they fool around signal communications and code personnel; as a sequel, counterintelligence surveillance was instituted immediately. A world-wide check revealed that Eckelman was born June 1, 1899, in Olsnitz, Germany, where he ultimately developed a police record. In a spotty itinerary throughout

the world, he operated in Shanghai, during the Sorge period
(1932), and appeared in the Sorge Records, probably as
"Alex" or "Jim." He followed Sorge to Tokyo but was picked
up by the Japanese police, on a civil charge and deported to
China in 1936. He next appeared in the United States, between 1936 and 1939, defrauding certain American firms of
considerable sums. He reappeared in Japan in 1940, as Dr.
Fred Sanders, with a false passport and counterfeit visa.
He then practiced medicine without a license and enjoyed
a surreptitious popularity as a discreet abortionist. He also
had numerous suspicious contacts with questionable German
and Russian nationals. In 1948 Eckelman was consequently
classified by the Occupation authorities as an "undersirable
alien" and ordered deported to Germany. The soviets were
obviously embarrassed. Dr. Sanders then committed suicide
under dramatic circumstances, though it is not quite certain
whether it was to escape deportation to Germany or to evade
a return to Soviet territory.

In custody of the military police, Sanders received permission to visit his house, accompanied by a young officer,
in order to obtain some additional clothing. He took a dose
of potassium cyanide instead. The panicky police officer summoned an ambulance and for some obscure reason, he stepped
outside, into the garden to unload his pistol, inadvertently
firing one round. American medical authorities took over
and cremated the deceased. The prostitutes of the neighborhood, to whom Sanders had been able to render occasional
assistance, started a rumor that he had been killed by the
MP. The Soviets added their own touch by criticizing the
speed of cremation, within eight to ten hours, suggesting
that it was done to prevent inspection by Soviet representatives, which might have disclosed bullet wounds.

Being a dull period, the local press took up this mysterious
case with reportorial gusto. The Canadian espionage record
had already aroused universal interest; the Tokyo correspondents suddenly remembered the Sorge Case.

Washington Negotiates for Release of Report: 1948

It was a foregone conclusion that the American press would
get the gist of the Sorge story eventually; the local correspondents had access to Court Records, if they cared to take
the trouble and expense of extensive translations, and some
popular Japanese magazine articles were available on the
subject. As a matter of fact, certain hints about the Sorge
Case appeared in the *Chicago Tribune* and *Plain Talk* months
before the War Department release.

Through their own elusive "pipelines" the Tokyo correspondents had become aware of the G-2 surveillance, since 1946, of the surviving members of the Sorge Ring, released from Confinement, and they frequently asked for a statement. We queried Washington but were told not to release information "since disclosure would reveal knowledge of espionage techniques."

However, the War Department soon reversed its position. On June 25, 1948, it cabled us that the State Department desired publication at the special request of the American Ambassador to the U.S.S.R. It will be recalled that American Embassy personnel in Moscow during this phase of the cold war were sporadically accused of espionage by the Soviets and they felt that a proved countercharge could be of value.

Apparently the story was getting "hot." G-2 Tokyo promptly drew certain conclusions and accurately anticipating possible protestations, requested FBI investigation of a number of individuals. Recognizing the risks involved in releasing the report G-2 Tokyo on July 12 warned Washington against "possible repercussions from persons involved only through indiscretions," and flatly stated, "this Headquarters does not desire to accept responsibility in a public release of the Sorge Spy Ring Case."

To protect Washington further in the event of public release, G-2 air-mailed on June 4, 1948, or August 17, 1948, sixteen (16) separate photostat copies of testimony by principal witnesses and defendants, in certified translations.

A period of official silence ensued, only punctuated by Drew Pearson's petulant reference to his competitors, the Alsop boys, suggesting that they had "the inside track" with the Secretary of Defense for a possible "scoop" on the Sorge report. Said Pearson:

. . . Forrestal had a significant conversation with two of his top men, Admiral Sid Souers, and General Al Gruenther. Forrestal said he wanted them to get him a top secret Army report on Communist espionage inside Japan. Because certain Americans were involved in pre-Pearl Harbor espionage, the report has been considered highly secret. "I want to give it to Joe Alsop" explained the Secretary of National Defense referring to one of the newsmen who had consistently defended the idea that Forrestal's continuation in office was essential to the nation. The Army promptly cabled General MacArthur asking if he had any objection. But although MacArthur at this writing had not replied, here are the main details of the top secret report which Secretary Forrestal wanted to give the press. The story is somewhat similar to that being unfolded before the N. Y. Grand Jury and the Un-American Activities Committee. Just as the Russians planted key men inside the U. S. Government, so they also began long before the war to plant key spies inside Japan. They began operating about 1934 and continued to 1941 .... When General MacArthur granted amnesty to Japanese political prisoners after VJ Day in 1945, he discovered the remnants of the Communist spy ring still in prison and turned them loose. From the Japanese Court records, his Chief of Intelligence General Willoughby, pieced together this amazing story of Communist intrigue. Note that some of the Japanese spy-leaders now head Japanese labor unions and one, Ito Ritsu, is presently a leading Communist ....

On December 8, 1948, the Secretary of Army actually queried Tokyo to obtain clearance for release to the Press of the "Sorge Spy Ring" Section of the CIS Periodical Summary No. 23, Dec. 15/47; Tokyo was incidentally reminded that some leakage about the case had already appeared in a few American periodicals.

GHQ Tokyo replied on the next day, reiterating its general position as previously stated on July 12, 1948 (*i.e.* release in Washington and not in Tokyo), and cleared the story. Like a string of Chinese firecrackers, the release set off a series of explosive reactions. The press took it up with noisy interest.

I was in charge of MacArthur's Intelligence and saw this drama unfold. In *Shanghai Conspiracy* I am giving the true story of the Sorge Spy Ring as revealed in the original report and in Sorge's own confidential memoirs.

PART ONE

THE SORGE SPY RING

The Original Tokyo Report: Far East Espionage

A powerful ring of Soviet spies was uncovered in Japan just before Pearl Harbor. Probably never in history has there been a ring more bold or more successful. Although most of the principals are dead, some are still at large. They can be expected to be secretly plying their trade at this very moment in various capitals of the world.

Though the work of Dr. Richard Sorge and his companions belongs to history, the methods of their work should serve as a clear warning for today and for the future. They concern not just the intelligence officer but every good citizen. Some of the implications are frightening. One begins to wonder whom one can trust, what innocent appearing friend may suddenly be discovered as an enemy.

For nine productive years a daring and skillful band of spies worked in Japan for their spiritual fatherland, Soviet Russia. Despite their widespread activity and enormous successes they went unsuspected and so undetected. Led by Dr. Richard Sorge, a German Communist posing convincingly as a loyal Nazi, this ring of spies almost succeeded in committing the perfect crime. Their discovery came through an accident and not through an error of their own.

While the personnel of the ring underwent numerous changes, a surprising number of men whom he had recruited originally for work in China became the core of his ring in Japan. Dr. Sorge, the head of the ring, and Ozaki Hozumi, his chief lieutenant, worked as spies for the Soviet Union in both China and Japan from 1929 to 1941. With the shift of major Soviet concern to Japan after the Japanese invasion of Manchuria in 1931, Dr. Sorge was ordered to cease his Shanghai operations, to go to Tokyo and set up a completely new network. Starting from nothing in a country which he never before had even visited, Dr. Sorge was able

11

to develop the most complete and successful espionage operation in Japanese history.

Sorge lived on intimate, trusted terms with the German ambassador and his staff; Ozaki Hozumi, his lieutenant, had a similar close relationship to Prince Konoye, thrice premier. From these perfect sources they drew a mass of information on every subject from politics to war and transmitted their intelligence to the U.S.S.R. by concealed radio, by courier, and through the Soviet Embassy. After June, 1941, their primary intelligence targets were Japanese plans and intentions for attack on the Soviet Union. As the German armies raced into western Russia, as great Soviet military formations were smashed and destroyed, reinforcement from the Siberian garrisons became vital. But the Red Army could not weaken their Siberian defenses if the Japanese Army would attack soon. Sorge was able to assure his superiors that there would be no attack: the Siberian divisions were entrained for the West and appeared on the Western Front for the successful defense of Moscow.

Through the years Sorge transmitted an enormous number of carefully analyzed intelligence reports from Tokyo to the Red Army's 4th Bureau. He was able to keep the Soviet Union fully informed on Japanese military and industrial potentials and intentions from 1933 to 1941. The Red Army always knew the status of current Japanese war plans, and could make its own plans and dispositions accordingly.

It is astonishing that despite Japanese deep suspicion of foreigners, their alertness to the remotest indication of espionage or Communist sympathies, despite the insularity of their country forcing couriers to enter or leave only through well-guarded ports, neither the Japanese civil police, the *gendarmerie* (*Kempeitai*), the special higher police (*Tokkoka*), nor any other Japanese security agency ever had the remotest suspicion of Sorge or any one of his gang of sixteen men and women.

The Sorge story concerns the individuals who composed the ring as much as what they discovered and how they operated. If we in the United States are to survive the Communist attack we must understand above all the minds and motives of the men and women who are willing to betray their own countries and blindly serve their Red masters.

Richard Sorge, Head of the Spy Ring

Richard Sorge, brilliant leader of this ring of spies, was born in Baku, in southern Russia, October 4, 1895. His father was a German engineer working for a German oil firm in the Caucasus and his mother is said to have been Russian. While Richard was still an infant his parents went to Berlin where the boy had the usual German education and grew up a patriotic son of Imperial Germany. However, even as a youngster, he seems to have been impressed by the memory of his paternal grandfather, Adolf Sorge, secretary to Karl Marx at the time of the formation of the First International.

Like many other patriotic students, at the beginning of World War I, Richard Sorge volunteered as a soldier, was wounded on the Western Front, and after long hospitalization, was discharged. In 1916 he re-enlisted and was wounded a second time on the Eastern Front. During his periods of convalescence and after the war he studied at the universities of Berlin, Kiel, and Hamburg, receiving a degree of Doctor of Political Science at Hamburg in 1920. For the next two years he worked intermittently as a schoolteacher and a coal miner and then in 1922 he began to write for newspapers and magazines. But even when he was teaching or digging coal, he was doing his best to convert his pupils and his fellow miners to the tenets of Karl Marx.

During the war while he was hospitalized, influenced in part by memories of his grandfather and in part by the impact of the Russian Revolution, Richard Sorge had begun the systematic study of Marxian literature and had converted himself. Immediately upon the formation of the German Communist party in October, 1919, Sorge joined the Hamburg branch. Many German soldiers who had served on the Eastern Front returned to their defeated country converts to the Communist cause, and Hamburg became a major center of German Communist activity. Possibly Sorge's maternal ancestry also slanted his thinking toward Russia. In later years he had a fluent command of Russsian, and it is likely that he first learned the language from his mother. He was a natural linguist and by the time he had become established in Japan he could converse easily in French, English, Russian, Japanese, and possibly Chinese.

Physically, Sorge was a big man, tall and stocky, with brown hair. His brow was creased and furrowed and his face was lined. As a Japanese acquaintance remarked, from a glance at his face you could tell he had lived a rough, hard life. There was an arrogance and cruelty to the set of his eyes and the line of his mouth. He was proud and overbearing, well-liked and deeply admired by those whose friendship he desired, but ruthless toward others and frankly detested by them. Many of his Japanese press colleagues saw him as the typically swash-buckling, arrogant Nazi and avoided him. He was quick-tempered, a hard drinker, and liked variety in women. In addition to having a wife in Russia and another, a schoolteacher, in the United States, he is known to have been intimate with some thirty women in Tokyo during his years of service. And yet despite his philandering, his quick temper, and his bouts of drunkenness he never betrayed himself. Though he lived on the most intimate terms with the members of the German Embassy staff, and drank heavily with them over a considerable period of years, none of them ever suspected that he knew a word of Russian.

Sorge began his professional Communist career in 1924. By that time he had made such an excellent reputation among German Communists and was so respected by Soviet leaders that he was summoned to Moscow. He resigned from the German Communist party, joined the Russian and became an agent of the Comintern, at that time a body of considerable importance in world Communist affairs.

Among Sorge's sponsors to the Russian Communist party and the Comintern were Dimitry Zakharovich Manuilsky, still member of the Central Committee of the Russian Communist party, and Solomon A. Lozovosky, currently Deputy Commissar of Foreign Affairs under Molotov, and also a member of the Central Committee. Naturally, even after he joined Red Army Intelligence his Comintern friends maintained their personal interest in him. It is reasonable to assume that Stalin, too, knew of Sorge's operations since they were so valuable and completely unique.

For three years Sorge worked for the Comintern at its Moscow headquarters, presumably learning the business, but in 1927 he went abroad to begin his hazardous career of field agent. Using the cover of an obscure German magazine, he spent two years in the Scandinavian countries and Great Britain as a special representative of the Intelligence and Organization Bureau of the Comintern. His job was to collaborate with the local Communist parties in the collection, evaluation, and transmission of information on labor problems and Communist activity. In part his job seems to have been to give advice and encouragement to local Communist organizations.

These were the early days of Soviet intelligence and the Russians were giving their intelligence agents the dual mission of espionage and Party activity. Sorge became convinced of the error of this practice, and upon his return to Moscow in 1929, made strong representations that it be changed. He pointed out that wherever Comintern and Soviet intelligence agents were associated with local Communist party officials, if the latter were arrested, the Comintern agent would also find himself in the hands of the police, and the entire intelligence net would be broken. He urged that intelligence and party activity be divorced completely, and that intelligence agents abroad be instructed to have nothing to do with local Communist parties.

Perhaps his superiors in the Comintern were not sympathetic to these suggestions, but Red Army Intelligence was. Sorge requested relief from duty with the Comintern and transfer to Red Army Intelligence, and the request was granted. For the remainder of his dangerous life he was attached to the 4th Bureau of the Red Army General Staff, the supreme intelligence agency of the Soviet Army.

Russian Communist Party Dominates Comintern

Sorge's testimony as to the identification of the Russian Communist party with all other national Communist parties is a useful refutation of the claims of the gullibles who persist in viewing such organs as the American Communist party or the Japanese Communist party as separate entities. Among other things, Sorge said:

The Russian Communist Party has become more influential than the Guidance Section of the Comintern. Today the actual spearhead of the Communist Party Labor movement is the Communist Party in Russia. Formerly the Guidance Section of the Comintern was independent in every respect. It consulted the leaders of the Russian Communist Party only occasionally on special problems. Later these consultations became more frequent until today (1942) it is no longer possible for the leaders of the Comintern to act independently of the Russian Communist Party . . . as they once did under the leadership of Zinoviev. Unity between the Guidance Section of the Comintern and the Russian Communist Party was achieved when the superiority of the Russian Communist Party was recognized. . . .

. . . But of course this extraordinary position of the Russian Communist Party is not a permanent one. If Communist parties gain power in other countries the center of gravity will again shift from the Soviet Union to the Comintern. The preeminence of the . . . Russian Communist Party is temporary. Nevertheless, for the past 10 years, today (1942) and for the next decade its preeminence cannot be questioned.

. . . The shifting of the . . . leadership of the

revolutionary labor movement from the . . . Comintern
to the Russian Communist Party can be traced in my
own career. All of my activity at first was connected
with the Comintern. Later I came to work directly
under the Soviet Union. This change did not mean that
. . . (the) members of my group had alienated themselves from the Communist movement as a whole. It
meant only that we had transferred our activity from an
international movement to . . . the development of the
Soviet Union. This activity has worked for the economic
and political stability . . . and the defense of the Soviet
Union from . . . outside attack.

. . . It must be remembered that my intelligence work
in China and Japan was entirely new and original. . . .
This is particularly true about Japan, because I was the
first man and the only man ever able to carry out this
kind of an assignment successfully for such a long period
of time. All of my orders and instructions came from
the 4th Bureau of the Red Army. The Comintern gave
me no orders. . . .

Somewhere along the line Sorge developed a profound
interest in the Far East. Although he had not previously
studied or been trained in Asiatic affairs he became convinced that China and Japan should become the area of his
specialization. In 1929 after his return from Northern Europe,
and his transfer to the Red Army's 4th Bureau, Sorge was
directed to go to Shanghai to help in developing, and then
to direct, a China intelligence net. The expulsion of Borodin
and Galen, with their followers, and the arrest, imprisonment, and execution of numerous Communists, both Russian
and Chinese, throughout China during the previous year must
have badly shaken the Comintern's net as well as that of the
Red Army. Sorge's recommendations that the Soviet intelligence agent should have nothing to do with local Communist
party groups must have had a particular appeal to the directors of Red Army Intelligence just at this time because of
the disaster which had overtaken their agents who had been
identified with the Communist wing of the Chinese Nationalist party. Sorge proceeded to China under strict orders not
to associate with the Chinese Communist party and not to
engage in any Communist activity of his own. His primary
mission was to secure intelligence on Japanese activity, intentions, order of battle, and operations in China. His secondary mission concerned strictly Chinese affairs.

Richard Sorge in Shanghai

Sorge went to Shanghai in January, 1930, with the cover of correspondent for the German *Soziologische Magazin*. Shanghai was a free and easy place, all sorts of odd characters were drifting in and out and seemingly it was not thought essential to have a substantial cover to operate successfully.

Three agents of the 4th Bureau went to China together; "Alex," not otherwise identified; Dr. Richard Sorge; and a certain "Weingart," a German wireless operator. After about six months "Alex," the chief of the mission, left, presumably to return to Russia, and Sorge became head of the ring whose headquarters were at Shanghai but which covered most of China, being especially active in Hangchow, Nanking, Canton, Hankow, Kaifeng, Tsinan, Peiping, and Manchuria. Sorge traveled extensively; read widely and deeply on Chinese and Japanese politics, history, and culture; studied the two languages and came to be unusually well-informed on Asiatic affairs.

Sorge recruited and developed a ring of spies in China. We know the names of sixteen of them, but probably there were more. Three principles which guided them are noteworthy: (1) While the group was highly cosmopolitan there seems not to have been a Russian among them. (2) While every member of the group was either a Communist party member or strong sympathizer, they avoided association with the Chinese Communist party. (3) They did not function as a group, and few of the members knew who the others were, or even were aware of their precise mission or whom they were working for. They knew they were working for the Cause, but not the chain of command.

Some members of the ring are identified today only by their first names or by cover names, such as "John," "Paul," and "Jacob." We know that "Jacob" was an American journalist, but not much more. The three Chinese members we know only by the common Chinese surnames of Chang, Wong, and Li. The five Japanese, a German named Max Klausen, and an American woman we know well.

Agnes Smedley, American-Soviet Spy

The American, Miss Agnes Smedley, has been one of the most energetic workers for the Soviet Cause in China for over twenty years. She was one of the early perpetrators, if not the originator, of the hoax that the Chinese Communists were not really Communists at all but only local agrarian revolutionists innocent of any Soviet connections. This concocted tale has had enormous effect in molding American opinion on China, both private and official, and has bemused American writers for twenty years. Miss Smedley in her five books and innumerable articles, other Communist writers, and numerous liberal innocents have continued to spread this point of view till today high American government officials find it difficult to accept any other. It should be noted that Miss Smedley's writings are used as source material by most writers and commentators on China, many of whom admit that she may have been a Communist sympathizer but nonetheless feel that she was one of the few writers on China who had plumbed the depths of truth because for so long she had lived with and thrown in her lot with the suffering Chinese. The harm has been done, but perhaps it could be mitigated if now it becomes generally known that she was a spy and agent for the Soviet government.

Miss Smedley worked closely with Dr. Sorge as a member of his ring from late 1930 until he left China. Presumably in the past she had been a Comintern agent, though we do not know whether she had transferred to Red Army intelligence, as had Sorge, or whether by some special arrangement she continued with the Comintern and yet worked with Sorge. In the light of Sorge's strong stand on the necessity for separation of Soviet intelligence and Comintern-Communist intelligence, however, it is likely that Miss Smedley too had been transferred.

The climax and greatest achievement of Sorge's career was his work in Japan, but several of his Tokyo associates first joined Sorge in Shanghai, and they deserve careful study. Without Ozaki Hozumi and Max Klausen, Sorge could never have achieved his success in Japan. He met and developed these men in Shanghai.

Ozaki Hozumi, Sorge's Major Assistant

Sorge's most valuable single associate in Japan was to be Ozaki Hozumi, a well-known journalist and commentator on Chinese affairs.

Ozaki Hozumi, second son of a journalist from Gifu Prefecture, was born on May 1, 1901. His father moved the family to Formosa to become editor of the Taiwan *Nichi Nichi Shimbun,* and it was in Taihoku that Hozumi grew up and finished Middle School. He later attended and was graduated from the Tokyo First Higher School (College)

and the Law School of Tokyo Imperial University, taking
his degree in 1925. Any graduate of *Ichi-Ko* and *Teidai*
knew that his classmates would become leaders of Japan's
business, professional, and governmental worlds. The men of
the class of 1925 at *Teidai* while not yet at the top by 1940,
were holding positions of great responsibility throughout
Japan, especially in the bureaus and ministries of the Imperial government. Any young man as brilliant as Ozaki
Hozumi was certain to make and keep many close friends
who would know almost everything there was to know and
who would be glad to share their knowledge with a trusted
confident.

Following his graduation from Tokyo Imperial University,
Ozaki spent a year of postgraduate reading, chiefly in economics and sociology. Then, following in his father's foot-
steps, in May, 1926, he joined the staff of the Tokyo *Asahi
Shimbun*. He was transferred to the *Osaka Asahi* in November, 1927, and was sent to Shanghai as a special correspondent of this great paper in November, 1928. He remained in China for three years, during which time he met
and worked for Sorge, returning to Osaka in 1932. In the
autumn of 1934 he was transferred again to Tokyo, where
he joined an *Asahi* staff research group devoted to a study
of Oriental affairs, the East Asia Problems Investigation
Society (*Toa Mondai Chosa Kai*). He came to be known
as one of Japan's leading experts on Chinese affairs and
wrote widely on this subject in a variety of magazines. He
often wrote in English for *Contemporary Japan*, and was
admired for his contributions to the Institute of Pacific
Relations, especially after he had attended the Yosemite Conference of that body in 1936 as one of the Japanese delegates.

In July, 1938, Ozaki resigned from the *Asahi* to become
unofficial adviser to the Cabinet (*Naikaku Shokutaku*) under
Prince Konoye. With the fall of the first Konoye Cabinet,
in January, 1939, Ozaki resigned this post, but in June he
became unofficial adviser (*Shokutaku*) of the Tokyo office of
the South Manchurian Railway. Being more an empire than
a railroad, the SMR conducted extensive research on all
Manchurian problems, and particularly on all Russian and
Chinese factors that affected Manchuria. Ozaki's SMR
assignment was invaluable to a man who wanted to learn of
Japan's plans and capabilities for a war with the Soviet
Union.

Ozaki originally developed his interest in the Chinese and
his hostility to Japanese militarism while he was a boy in
Formosa. While he was in college in Tokyo he began reading
Japanese leftist literature, which was published in consider-

able quantity after World War I, and he also became absorbed in the German philosophers, who fascinated him. He was deeply moved by the first mass arrest of Japanese Communists, in June, 1923, when he was twenty-two years old and a university student. After the earthquake three months later he was greatly disturbed by the arrest of the whole family of Morisaki Genkichi, who ran the Agrarian Movement Society (*Nomin Undosha*) and by the cold-blooded murder of Osugi Sakae, the anarchist leader, and his common-law wife and nephew by a gendarme (*Kempeitai*) captain. At the university he began studying Marx, Engels, Lenin, and many books on China. Gradually his sympathies drifted toward communism and so to the Soviet Union, although he never became a member of any Communist party. In Japan we find, as was found in Canada, that party sympathy is enough to develop a high-class agent and spy. Party membership is not necessary, and no one should be led astray by the absence of Party cards.

After Ozaki reached Shanghai he soon became associated with a left-wing Chinese literary group, the Creation Society (*Sozo Sha*) to whose magazine he contributed under pseudonyms. He also became associated with leftist-minded Japanese students at the East Asia Common Script School (*Toa Dobun Shoin*) and with the Chinese Communist Youth League. Through these contacts he came to know the advisers and leaders of the Chinese Communist party in Shanghai.

Now and then Ozaki visited the Zeitgeist Bookshop on Soochow Creek, in Shanghai, and became well acquainted with the proprietress, a Mrs. Wiedemeyer. Late in 1929 or early in 1930 this woman introduced Ozaki to Miss Agnes Smedley, at that time correspondent for the *Frankfurter Zeitung*. From this meeting dates Ozaki's career as a Soviet agent, though it was some time before he himself was aware that such a change had occurred. Since it was Miss Smedley who recruited Ozaki, it is reasonable to assume that she had recruited other Soviet agents before and has recruited many others since.

A deep and genuine friendship quickly developed between the Japanese journalist, Ozaki, and the American Communist journalist, Agnes Smedley. Ozaki met Miss Smedley at many places besides the bookshop, and as they exchanged ideas and discovered the depths of their mutual understanding, Miss Smedley told Ozaki that she was a Communist. Since he had already reached the conclusion that he too was a Communist in spirit he gladly agreed to her suggestion that they exchange information. From his *Asahi* and other Japanese connections, Ozaki had much to tell Miss Smedley that the Communists wanted to know.

In the fall of 1930 a Japanese member of the American Communist party, Kito Ginichi, who had come to Shanghai via Annam, became a frequent caller at Ozaki's office. How Kito discovered Ozaki we do not know, but it is reasonable to assume that Miss Smedley was the connecting link. Almost from the start Ozaki knew that Kito was a Communist. Soon after Kito's first visit he asked Ozaki if he would like to meet an American journalist named Johnson. Ozaki put him off without a definite answer and consulted Miss Smedley, who cautioned him sharply against any further mention of this "American." Some days later, however, Miss Smedley reopened the subject and said she herself wished to introduce Ozaki to "Johnson." She arranged the meeting at a restaurant on Nanking Road, and over a leisurely dinner Ozaki talked with a tall, stocky man who spoke English with a European accent. Although Ozaki had not been told that "Johnson" was a Comintern agent he assumed as much since he knew both Miss Smedley and Kito were Communists. It was not till six years later that Ozaki learned Johnson's real name. In 1936 when Ozaki returned from America as a Japanese delegate to the Yosemite Conference of the Institute of Pacific Relations, a Dutch delegate introduced him in Tokyo to "Johnson." The Dutchman, however, called him Dr. Richard Sorge.

Obviously Sorge had been fully satisfied with Ozaki's loyalty through the checks and recommendations of Miss Smedley and Kito, for at their first meeting Sorge asked Ozaki to collect and supply him with information on the internal Chinese situation and on Japanese policy toward China. Ozaki consented without hesitation. His consent was not connected with any specific knowledge of the Comintern or of the group with which he was to be associated. As for the 4th Bureau of the Red Army General Staff, he never heard of it till after his arrest in 1941 when the police interrogators began asking him about it. He was completely indifferent to all matters of organization. He agreed to help "Johnson" because he was convinced that he would be doing something worth while in cooperating with an intelligence group connected in some way with the Soviet Communist International.

From this time until he left Shanghai in February, 1932, Ozaki met "Johnson" and Miss Smedley two or three times a month at various restaurants or at Miss Smedley's apartment. Ozaki did not have assignments on specific subjects, but rather the three friends engaged in lengthy discussions of current news, to which Ozaki was able to contribute the

Japanese point of view, as well as an acute and analytical mind. He had a very wide knowledge of Asiatic affairs, and through his *Asahi* connections could give information on an extensive amount of current topics. Following these discussions, Sorge would come to final conclusions which he would incorporate in reports sent back to the U.S.S.R. As will be seen, this practice came to be more clearly developed after he reached Japan. Ozaki knew none of the other European members of the Sorge group aside from Miss Smedley. He couldn't decide whether Miss Smedley ranked above or below "Johnson" although he believed that Sorge was the more important since he acted with more authority. Among his Japanese friends in Shanghai he was aware that three— Funakoshi Hisao, *Shanghai Mainichi* reporter; Kito Ginichi; and Mizuno Shigeru, student at *Toa Dobun Shoin*—were involved with the ring, but he had no precise knowledge of their activities. Actually, in addition to these men there were two other Japanese members. These were Kawai Teikichi, reporter for the *Shanghai Weekly,* and Yamagami Masayoshi, correspondent for *Rengo Tsushin.* These men will be described later in connection with their work after Sorge was established in Japan.

Ozaki himself introduced Kawai to Sorge, who took him into the group on condition that he sever all connection with his Communist associates. After the Japanese attack on Manchuria in 1931, Sorge asked Ozaki to get some trustworthy agent to investigate conditions there. Kawai Teikichi was his choice. Miss Smedley already knew Kawai. In 1932 when Ozaki was recalled to Japan by the *Asahi* he recommended Yamagami Masayoshi, the *Rengo* man, as his substitute, but Yamagami refused to serve and Funakoshi Hisao, reporter for the *Shanghai Mainichi,* took the post.

When the *Asahi* ordered Ozaki back to Osaka, Sorge wanted him to quit his job and stay in Shanghai, but Ozaki pointed out that if he left the *Asahi* his chief information source and hence his major usefulness would be lost. After he returned to Japan he had no communications with "Johnson," but he did correspond with Miss Smedley. When Miss Smedley wrote asking him to meet her in Peiping he left at once, sailing from Kobe on December 25, 1932. Miss Smedley wanted him to join a new intelligence agency which she was organizing in North China, presumably to cover developments in Manchuria, but Ozaki refused, and after recommending Kawai Teikichi in his place, returned to Japan. He took with him the translation rights to all of Miss Smedley's books, and ultimately published her autobiographical novel, *A Daughter of the Earth,* in Japanese as *Onna Hitori*

Daichi Wo Yuku (A Woman Walks the Earth Alone). He used his pen name, Shirakawa Jiro, under which he had often published leftist articles in Shanghai. For more than a year he did not hear from Miss Smedley, who was in a sanitarium in Southern Russia. In the summer of 1934, however, she wrote him again, and on her way from America to Shanghai in September of that year she stopped to see him in Japan. By this time Ozaki was Sorge's major assistant in Tokyo. Sorge warned him that it was dangerous to correspond with such known Communists as Miss Smedley; it might well arouse police suspicions where none existed and so bring about the betrayal of their whole operation. Ozaki never communicated with Miss Smedley again.

Ozaki was a prolific writer, and became extremely well known in Japan as an expert on Chinese affairs. His many signed articles in *Central Review* (*Chuo Koron*) and his five books on China, the last, *Strength of the Great Powers in China* (*Ajia Ni Okeru Rekkyo No Chikara*) published in 1941, give no hint of his Communist sympathies. It is amazing that a man could feel so deeply on the subjects of China, Japanese militarism and communism, could write so much and so widely, and yet never betray himself to the vigilant Japanese censors and Thought Police.

Max Klausen, Sorge's Radio Operator

One more member of the Sorge ring in China must be mentioned. When Sorge reached Shanghai in 1930 he found another German, Max Gottfried Friedrich Klausen, also an agent of the 4th Bureau, who had the rank of major in the Red Army. Klausen had come from Moscow the year before and already had had considerable experience as operator of secret radio stations. That was his role in Sorge's ring, and in Japan Klausen was to become Sorge's chief communications link with the Soviet Union.

Klausen was a heavy-set, coarse-featured German, not well educated and the last conceivable suspect as a successful agent of the Red Army. One sensed at once that Sorge and Ozaki were brilliant, but Klausen was not the type of man even the suspicious police were likely to associate with the brilliant journalist, Richard Sorge. Actually Klausen was never the intelligent operative; his role always was in communications.

Max Klausen was born in February, 1899 on an island off the coast of Schleswig-Holstein, the son of a poor shopkeeper and bicycle repairman. His mother died when he was only three. After finishing school Max first helped in his father's shop, and then was apprenticed to a blacksmith while attending a trade school in the evenings. Here he laid the foundations of a very considerable mechanical knowledge which in the end built for Sorge a radio transmitter so small it could be carried in a brief case and yet so powerful it could reach Vladivostok from Tokyo with the greatest of ease.

In 1917 Klausen was drafted and served in the German Signal Corps, being assigned to a radio unit on the Western Front. After his discharge in 1919 he wandered through a number of unrelated jobs, including that of guard at a reform school, until in 1921 he began going to sea out of Hamburg. It was at Hamburg, spiritual home of both Sorge and Klausen, that the latter was converted to the Communist cause. The defeat and postwar confusion, heavy Communist infiltration into the maritime unions with their propaganda and agitation, unemployment and despair, all left their mark on this stolid young man. In 1927 he joined the Hamburg Branch of the German Communist party.

Part of Klausen's later account of his experiences is worth repeating:

> During my early youth I had no interest in political affairs, but after my enlistment in the army, I met many soldiers, particularly among my immediate superiors, who were imbued with Communistic thought and who were engaged in Communist propaganda. Army life . . . was favorable to the spread of the doctrine. Thus, the young men in our group were gradually attracted to the ideology by our seniors. . . .
>
> When the war was over, after many of the seniors left the barracks, Communist sentiment was on the wane. . . . It had been the wish of my father that I return home to my job with the blacksmith. The second influence in my political life was this man, who was a follower of the Volks Party. Under his guidance I became a Communist sympathizer.
>
> In 1922 when all mechanics throughout the country went on strike, I was working aboard a steamer. As a Communist sympathizer I became a picket. All sailors at that time were members of the Seamen's Section of the All German Transportation Labor Union, which was one of the official organizations of the Social Democratic Party. Of course, I, too was a member of the union. But in 1922, when the German Seamen's Union was formed by Communist elements, I joined.
>
> Germany was in an extremely difficult economic condition, with more than six million unemployed. The

government was entirely at a loss what to do. . . . I came to feel that the only doctrine which could save the German people from their misery was communism. When I visited Soviet Russia aboard the S.S. *Neptune* and witnessed the fine equipment of Russian industry, I became firmly convinced that communism would promote the happiest society in the world. Since by this time the German Communist party has been organized as a legitimate political party, I made up my mind to become a member and to engage in Communist activity. Upon my return to Hamburg from this voyage, I applied for membership in 1927.

My application was not accepted immediately. For the first six months I was listed as a marine-cell member. I was assigned as a lecturer to argue the party platform with sailors on my ship. After my initiation I was examined by Karl "Lesse," the leader of the union. Having passed the test I formally became a member of the Communist party.

Klausen must have made an excellent impression for sincerity and devotion to party principles. Only the next year a Soviet operative known to Klausen only as "George," upon the recommendation of "Lesse," invited him to join an international espionage group as a radioman. Klausen readily accepted the invitation, and in February, 1929, he went to Moscow, where he joined the 4th Bureau of the Red Army General Staff as a radio operator.

Klausen received only a brief indoctrination, and then was ordered to Shanghai to serve as radio operator for the Bureau's China Unit. Before leaving, Klausen received a ticket to Harbin and $150 in American money. He was shown a photograph of a man called "Mishin," who was to be his Shanghai contact. He was directed to go to the Palace Hotel in Shanghai, sit in the lobby with a newspaper in his left hand and a pipe in his right. When the "Mishin" of the photograph came up and spoke to him he was to give the password, "Regards from Erna."

In due time Klausen sat in the lobby of the Palace Hotel and gave "Mishin" Erna's regards. He then went with "Mishin" to the latter's home where he was given two rooms on the third floor, and received instructions from "Mishin" in radio technique. Finally, "Mishin" took him to meet the head of the China unit, a German named "Lehman" who also used the alias of "Grevitch." Lehman told Klausen that he was to replace a renegade Pole, named Goble, who had seceded from the group. From this date to 1933 Klausen worked in various parts of China under the command of Lehman; then of "Alex," presumably a Russian; of Richard Sorge; and finally of "Paul," who previously had been subordinate to Sorge.

Together "Constantin Mishin" and Max Klausen built a short-wave radio receiving and sending set and maintained contact with another station known as "Wiesbaden." This was the same station which subsequently received his signals from Tokyo. Klausen never was positive whether "Wiesbaden" was Vladivostok or whether it was Khabarovsk, but he believed it was the former. Considering that later Moscow was designated as "Munchon," the alliteration suggests Vladivostok. It is noteworthy that in this operation as well as the later one in Japan, the geographical and national cover of Germany and Germans was used throughout. Even the Russian language was never used, and before coding messages always were written either in German or English.

After getting the Shanghai set in operation Klausen assembled the parts for another set and sent them to Harbin in the care of a French diplomat who kindly smuggled them up there. In August, 1929, Klausen himself went to Harbin to assemble a set, and at the Hotel Moderne he met another agent named "Benedict." "Benedict" introduced Klausen to the chief of the Soviet agents in Harbin, "Gloemberg-Ott." An American vice-consul, Tycho L. Lilliestrom, allowed "Gloemberg-Ott" to use two rooms of his residence, and it was there that Klausen set up his illegal radio set. There is some reason to believe that Lilliestrom also supplied information to his guest.

Klausen was able to get back to Shanghai in October, 1929, where he continued with his illegal radio activity under the cover of his work as a garage mechanic. In January, 1930, "Lehman" directed Klausen to go to the Anchor Hotel where he would meet a friend. This friend truned out to be "Josef Weingart," a German, whom Klausen had known earlier in Hamburg, and who had just come to China to join the group. A few days later Weingart introduced his old friend Max to Dr. Richard Sorge.

After his return to Shanghai, Klausen moved to a boarding house where a widow, Mrs. Anna Wallenius, a White Russian, was living. She was then thirty-one. Her husband had died four years before, and she had been making a living first as a seamstress and subsequently as a practical nurse at the Shanghai Isolation Hospital. Both she and her late husband, a well-to-do Finnish tanner, brother of that General K. Martti Wallenius of the Finnish Army General Staff who headed a Finnish Military Mission to Japan in 1937, had suffered cruelly in the Russian Revolution. Like most other "Whites" they managed to reach China with little more than their lives, and Anna never recovered from her bitter and intense hatred of all things Bolshevik.

Anna little guessed when she first met the new boarder that she was also meeting an ardent professional Communist and Soviet spy. She took Max for a good, steady automobile mechanic with a decent income. The poor woman fell in love. Max too seemed to have loved her, for in later years he suffered many inconveniences and even jeopardized his career with the Party in order to keep her with him. Here was a strange union of personal love with mutual hatred of each other's ideals. That it lasted through the years, through terrors and dangers and prison, is testimony to its strength and power.

Anna became suspicious of Max's conduct only a few days after they had been "married." She was his common-law wife for several years before he was allowed to legalize the union. He constantly went on unexplained errands at night but he quieted her fears by assuring her he was active in an anti-Nazi society. Only in 1931 or 1932, a year or two after their "marriage" she finally discovered that the headquarters of this anti-Nazi society was in Moscow. By then she could not bring herself to leave Max.

Years later Klausen told the Japanese court that Anna had never lost her hatred for communism. She had consented to help him only out of fear of punishment from Moscow, and also because he continually rewarded her with valuable and desirable presents. For example, he gave her a $2,000 fur coat, expensive dresses, and frequently U.S. currency in small denominations. Answering the court's question as to whether their marriage had borne fruit, Klausen said neither love nor money could persuade the woman to become pregnant by a Soviet spy. Through the years Anna complained bitterly that Max had married her because he needed her for camouflage. "News correspondents like Sorge can afford to remain single," she said, "but a businessman like Max needs cover." She scoffed at what she called her husband's dreams of paradise. The court gave considerable weight to this testimony in passing sentence.

Klausen worked in various Chinese cities as directed by his chief. He put up sets in Canton and Mukden, in addition to those in Shanghai and Harbin. For some reason he was unable to raise "Wiesbaden" from Canton. In August, 1933, Klausen left Mukden, via Harbin, for Siberia and the long train ride to Moscow. Originally he was directed to travel with a specified woman agent but Max refused point-blank to travel with any woman but his Anna, and finally he was permitted to take his wife instead of the other woman. Anna thought they were bound for Germany, a belief corroborated by their receipt of German passports in Harbin. On the first night they were in Moscow, however, the Klausens were robbed of all they possessed, including their passports. Perhaps the 4th Bureau was doing a little checking. In any case Max soon appeared in the uniform of a Red Army officer, which he continued to wear as long as they were in Moscow.

After a six week's vacation at Odessa, Klausen entered a radio school for advanced training. Suddenly he was transferred out of the school, and ordered to one of the German republics on the shores of the Volga "as punishment for a record of inefficiency in China." It will be remembered that this was the beginning of the Russian purges, when thousands of Communists were passing from honor to disgrace overnight, and then as mysteriously being restored to the good graces of the Party. It seems that Klausen was a victim of the same hysteria.

For nearly two years Klausen remained in this provincial center, mending shoes, ploughing fields, and taking part in Party propaganda programs. In the spring of 1935, he was recalled to Moscow by order of General Voroshilov to meet "Lehman," Sorge, and "Weingart," with all of whom he had worked in Shanghai. Sorge was in search of a good radio operator to replace an incompetent he had with him in Tokyo. He invited Max Klausen to join him. Later Klausen told the Japanese court, "From childhood I had heard nothing but evil of Japan. I detested especially Japan's invasion of Manchuria. Therefore, I gladly consented to go to work for Sorge there." He soon set off to join Sorge, who had been working in Tokyo for nearly three years.

Sorge Organizes His Ring in Japan

In China, Dr. Sorge's primary intelligence mission had concerned Japan. Probably when they first sent him to Shanghai the directors of the 4th Bureau had him in mind for later operations in Tokyo. Having successfully completed his apprenticeship, Sorge was now ready to undertake the most difficult assignment at the hands of the Red Army.

Richard Sorge returned to Moscow in December, 1932, and received orders to proceed to Tokyo to organize and operate a completely new espionage ring. Although the Japanese were still in the early stages of their campaign to conquer Manchuria they already had invaded the Soviet sphere of influence. Japanese and Russian antagonisms were old and deep. Japanese ambitions for Siberian territory were common knowledge. Japanese forces had evacuated Vladivostok only a decade before, but perhaps they felt stronger now. What were Japanese intentions and capabilities? As Japanese troops approached and finally reached the Soviet-Manchurian border there always was the possibility of armed explosion. Did the Japanese government or the Japanese Army intend to precipitate and exploit such explosions into general war?

Sorge's mission was to discover the answers to these questions and to find new answers as conditions changed. In 1933 in the midst of the first five-year plan and the bitter internal struggle over forced collectivization, the Soviets were in no condition for war with Japan. Subsequently, with the rise of a powerful Nazi Germany there was the constant possibility of a war on two fronts. Perhaps in Tokyo Sorge could discover the answers to the questions of both German and Japanese intentions.

Sorge's job was to paint the big picture. Any Japanese information which he could discover on order of battle, troop movements or military installations and equipment would be welcomed. His primary mission, however, concerned intelligence at the highest level, the top secret plans of the Japanese Army and government.

Sorge laid down four conditions for this assignment which were accepted by his superiors: (1) He was to have no relations of any kind with the Japan Communist party or its known members. (2) He must be supplied with a Caucasian assistant neither Russian nor German. (3) He must be supplied with a high level Japanese assistant. (4) He must have as little contact with the Soviet Embassy as was conceivably possible, which meant that except in emergencies he would use his own channels of communication.

Sorge Establishes Cover

Sorge left for Berlin in May 1933 to establish his cover. In Germany he secured assignments as special correspondent in Japan for the *Frankfurter Zeitung,* the *Bergen Kurier,* the *Technische Rundschau* and the *Amsterdam Handelsblatt.* He applied for membership in the Nazi party, which had just seized power under Adolf Hitler, and his credentials were accepted without question. How he secured those excellent covers remains a mystery. The key newspaper was the *Frankfurter Zeitung,* whose Shanghai correspondent was a concealed Communist and Soviet agent, Miss Agnes Smedley.

Having just seized power the Nazi party and the Gestapo had not yet acquired the efficiency and thorough national coverage they were to develop later. Nevertheless, there must have been a Soviet agent in a responsible post at Gestapo files. When check was made in 1941 highly derogatory information was turned up at once, yet in 1933 Sorge's applications for Party membership and for travel abroad as a correspondent went unchallenged. In due course, after he reached Tokyo, he received his Nazi party card. Seemingly, in the following years until 1941, when Berlin received a frantic inquiry from the Gestapo man in Tokyo, it never occurred to anyone to run a file check on Dr. Richard Sorge. Even when he was appointed to a post in the Tokyo Embassy in 1939, his Party card was considered sufficient evidence of his loyalty. The lessons of this experience are obvious.

With his Nazi loyalties established and having an excellent journalistic cover, Dr. Sorge proceeded to Japan via the United States and Canada. In America he met with some American agents of the Soviets before catching his ship at Vancouver, B. C.

Dr. Richard Sorge first reached Yokohama on September 6, 1933. There seemed nothing unusual about this German journalist and the water police quickly let him ashore. Not long afterward Sorge found a house in Tokyo, at No. 30 Nagasakamachi, Azabu-ku, Tokyo, a good neighborhood, and settled down to covering Japan for his various newspapers. He made himself known at the German Embassy and the German Club and was readily accepted by the German community as well as by his colleagues of the press.

Branko de Voukelitch, Yugoslav Communist

Meanwhile, that extraordinary international organization, the Comintern, at the request of the Red Army, began picking up unsuspected agents and moving them around the world. The evidence regarding world-wide Comintern card lists and controls produced at the Canadian spy inquiry is corroborated by the evidence of the Sorge trial. The Red Army needed some spies in Japan of a certain type and category. In due course, the Comintern agents in France and the United States received orders. Men who were complete strangers to each other and who had never heard the name of Sorge began packing their bags for Tokyo. While others came along in due course, the two key figures were

Branko de Voukelitch and Miyagi Yotoku. Voukelitch traveled from Paris, Miyagi from Los Angeles.

Branko de Voukelitch was a Yugoslav, living in Paris with his wife, Edith, later described by Miyagi as a "dull woman, good only for cover." De Voukelitch was tall and heavy-set, had brown hair and carried himself in such a manner as to give the impression to the Japanese that he was a German. Branko was born in Serbia in 1904 where his father was an officer.

After finishing high school in Zagreb he studied art for a time and then entered the University of Zagreb to take up architecture. After two years, in 1926, he went to Paris, abandoning the arts for law at the University of Paris. Before completing his course, however, he went to work for the Compagnie Generale d'Electricité. It was during this time that he met Edith, a Danish woman of whom we know little, and married her.

De Voukelitch became interested in Marxian movements during his student days in Zagreb. In 1924 he was arrested as a member of the Zagreb Marxist Students' Group. From about the year 1925 he participated in the Croatian independence movement (against Yugoslavia) which had the support of Communist elements. It was not until January, 1932, however, that he formally became a Communist. He had met some former comrades of the Zagreb Marxist Students' Group in Paris and through them joined the Party. It is not clear whether this was the French or the Yugoslav party.

In March, 1932, de Voukelitch's Croatian friends introduced him to a mysterious "Baltic Woman Olga," who persuaded him to join a so-called "Red International Intelligence Organ" in Paris. He joined the Party and became a Soviet agent almost simultaneously. The Soviets seem equally able to use men as agents who either are not Party members at all, providing they are willing to make every sacrifice for the Party's cause, or who hold Party cards on which the signatures are scarcely dry. The previous interests and convictions of the man concerned rather than formal Party allegiance seem to determine his selection.

De Voukelitch first heard that he would be sent abroad from an unnamed Russian Jew, who told him he was to be assigned to duty either in Japan or Rumania. Having received permission from "Olga" to take his wife with him on this mission, he sent Edith to Denmark for a short course in physical education to give her a legitimate occupation should she need a cover when they got abroad. As it turned out her occupation as housewife was sufficient to disarm Japanese suspicion.

De Voukelitch received his travel orders to Japan in October, 1932. He was appointed special correspondent in Tokyo for the French picture magazine *La Vue* and for the Yugoslav daily *Politica*. Branko, Edith, and their small boy sailed from Marseilles on December 30, 1932. Proceeding along the tourist route through the Red Sea, and stopping briefly at Singapore and Shanghai the new journalist and his family landed at Yokohama on February 11, 1933. After staying temporarily at the Imperial Hotel, de Voukelitch found a place at the Bunka Apartments in Hongo-ku, probably the best apartments in Tokyo.

Since Sorge had not yet arrived, de Voukelitch had time to get started on his newspaper career, free of the need to engage in subversive activities. He had been told how to get in touch with "Bernhardt," Sorge's radio man, however, and met him as "Olga" had told him to do. After Sorge reached Tokyo in the fall "Bernhardt" introduced Voukelitch to him. At the first meeting Sorge used the name of Schmidt, an odd precaution since Branko knew he was there to work for him, and in any case both being journalists they were bound to meet at press conferences and other places where Branko would learn his true identity.

This was a long term project, and Sorge was in no hurry to get started till his machine was functioning smoothly. He needed agents, a considerable net of them, adequate radio and courier communication, a darkroom, and good outside contacts.

The German Embassy was Sorge's major target, but he had no more immediate entree than any other German journalist and less than those who represented the all-powerful DNB agency. But through the man's wife he did know an assistant German Military Attaché, Lieutenant Colonel Eugen Ott, then on duty in Nagoya with a Japanese artillery regiment. Sorge had chanced to know Mrs. Ott when she was a wife of an architect in Munich, years before. Rumor has it that Mrs. Ott was quite radical in her views and even that she was a Communist, though there is no positive evidence on this point. Either directly or through Mrs. Ott, Sorge met the Colonel, and gradually a strong friendship developed between this officer of the Reichswehr and the unsuspected Red Army agent.

Ott was out of symathy with the Nazi program, but he carried out the orders of his government. He had arrived in Japan in 1933, after being transferred out of Germany by higher ranking officers who feared for his safety in the Nazi purges then under way. Whatever Ott knew or thought about Germany, he knew almost nothing about Japan, and he was delighted to find in his new friend, Richard, an extraordinary fund of information on the Japanese, on Japanese politics and trends, as well as a source of sage advice. When Ott was promoted and moved to Tokyo his friendship with Sorge deepened and their meetings came to be more and more frequent.

From the very first Sorge began his campaign for acceptance at the German Embassy. Simultaneously he was developing his organization. The de Voukelitch family moved out of the Bunka Apartments in November to a private house in Sanai-cho, Ushigomo-ku. Sorge needed more privacy. Branko, an enthusiastic amateur cameraman, had a darkroom built in his house for his hobby. Subsequently, documents were photographed there and microfilm was prepared for transmission to Shanghai or the Soviet Embassy. It was at this house that "Bernhardt" built his clumsy radio transmitter during April and May, 1934.

Miyagi Yotoku, Artist and Spy

The Comintern continued to move its men across the world to aid their man Sorge. The exact process through which the Comintern supplied men to the Red Army is not known in the Sorge case. It is possible that "Olga" worked for the 4th Bureau, and that de Voukelitch was recruited directly for Red Army intelligence, but Miyagi Yotoku, in Los Angeles, had no connections with the 4th Bureau. Clearly, he was recruited by the American Communist party and the Comintern, though he came to be an agent of the Soviet Army, 4th Bureau. Miyagi never knew precisely for whom he was working. It is most significant that Miyagi, Ozaki, and many others had merely the vaguest ideas as to what agency they worked for. All they needed to commit treason was a general knowledge that the Communists wanted their services and that in some manner their information was being relayed to the spiritual homeland of all Communists.

The name of Miyagi Yotoku must be added to those of Sorge, Ozaki, de Voukelitch, and Klausen to complete the list of the top level operatives in Tokyo. Miyagi, a Japanese who had lived in the United States since 1919, and who was a member of the American Communist party, was the Comintern's choice to meet Sorge's request for a Japanese assistant. Sorge personally brought Ozaki into the ring later, but Miyagi was the man who was sent to him officially. Miyagi too was invaluable, although considering his previous history, it seems strange that Red Army Intelligence should have thought of him as a particularly useful agent.

Miyagi Yotoku was a native of Okinawa, born February 10, 1903. Like many Okinawans his father had migrated, first to Davao and then to California, where he worked on a farm near Los Angeles. The senior Miyagi returned to Okinawa in 1920 and died in 1938.

The boy, Yotoku, was brought up by his maternal grandparents. After finishing elementary school in 1917, he entered a teacher training institute, but was forced to quit in 1919 because of illness. He had tuberculosis, which was to plague him for the rest of his short life.

Miyagi joined his father in California in June, 1919, and for two years went to a school near Brawley to learn English. For the next four years he was attending art schools first in San Francisco and later in San Diego, being forced to interrupt his work by that bothersome lung. He graduated from the San Diego Art School in 1925, but worked on a farm near Brawley for about a year before he could put his art training to much use. From November, 1926 until 1933, Miyagi ran a restaurant, the "Owl," in Los Angeles' Little Tokyo in partnership with several Japanese friends: Tabo Kenden, Matayoshi Jun, Kochi Shinsei, and Nakamura Koki. He began to paint and to his delight soon made enough from his pictures to support himself independently of the restaurant. In the summer of 1927, he married Yamaki Chiyo, a woman who figures little in this record.

Miyagi's bachelor quarters were inadequate for his married life, and soon he and his bride went to live at the Los Angeles home of a Japanese farmer, Kitabayashi Yoshisaburo. Years later Mrs. Kitabayashi was to become a minor member of the Sorge ring.

In the case of each of these agents the question of motivation as well as of action is of great importance. After his arrest Miyagi testified freely. His testimony portrays him as a rather confused young man of strong social conscience but of uncertain belief. Yet despite this uncertainty a Comintern agent had merely to ask him and he gave up his security in Los Angeles to go to Tokyo to betray Japan, to risk and then to lose his life.

"There was a time in my boyhood when I was a pure and simple nationalist, but even then I detested the tyranny of the Japanese bureaucracy. Doctors, lawyers, bankers, and retired officials were wont to come . . . from Kagoshima, and they became moneylenders and exploited the local farmers. I detested these people because my grandfather taught me never to bully the weak. Likewise he taught me Okinawa history, comparing . . . (our) glorious period . . . with the present semi-colonial status. . . . I believe that my grandfather's severe criticism of this . . . tyranny and of the poverty of the Okinawa people first turned my mind to political questions."

In America, Miyagi had many discontented friends and with them he began to read Marxian literature. Of this period he said: "I do not say that I was not influenced by my friends and by the books which I read, but I was more affected by what I saw: the inconsistency of American capitalism, the tyranny of the governing classes, and above all the inhuman discrimination against the Asiatic races. I came to the conclusion that communism was the cure for all these ills."

It will be noted that Miyagi arrived in California at the height of the anti-Japanese agitation as well as during the period of the Russian Revolution. It is likely that he suffered keenly from the discrimination against all Asiatics, but especially against Japanese, then common in the State of California, and in turn looked to the embattled armies of Lenin and Trotsky as the hope of a free and happier society.

Although Miyagi did not join the Communist party in those early days he was close enough to it to know a great deal about its activities. He and his friends at the Owl Restaurant organized a study group in 1926 to discuss social problems. The parallel with the Canadian study groups is striking. After the second or third meeting they were joined by some Communist leaders: Takahashi, an American professor of Russian whose name is reported as Herbert Harris, and a Swiss called Fister. These men gave lectures to the earnest group. Gradually other Communists came to attend the meetings, but there was also an increase of non-Communist members. By this time the informal study group had become a club with the name Society of the Dawn (*Roimei Kai*).

The club split in 1927 in a dispute between Communist and non-Communist members. The Communists left to form a new association, the Class War Society (*Kaikyu Sensen Sha*) but Miyagi, who had not yet wholly become a Communist in his own thinking remained with the *Roimei Kai*. The *Kaikyu Sensen Sha* expanded to become the Labor Society (*Rodo Kyokai*) in 1928, and began publishing a magazine, *Class War* (*Kaikyu Sen*) and a weekly newssheet, *Labor News* (*Rodo Shimbun*). The California Branch of the American Communist party set up a Los Angeles headquarters at about this time and the Labor Society (*Rodo Kyokai*) joined at once. Soon afterwards when a Japanese section of the American Communist party was organized in San Francisco, *Labor News* (*Rodo Shimbun*) came to be published there.

Miyagi had a good general knowledge of all these developments, but remained on the outside. He joined his first Communist front organization in 1929 when the Proletarian Arts Society was formed by Akagi Tetsu and a Yoshioka under the auspices of the Labor Society (*Rodo Kyokai*). Many of the members were his friends, such as: Kemmotsu, editor of *Labor News;* Mrs. Kitabayashi, his landlady; and his wife, Chiyo.

Political activity by foreigners in the United States aimed at the change and overthrow of American institutions was an illegal act. Kemmotsu Teiichi and Kobayashi Isamu were arrested in San Francisco and Horiuchi Tetsuji and Yamaguchi Einosuke in Los Angeles in 1929. The American Communist party sent Yano Tsutomu from New York to continue their work. The Japanese section of the Party, however, was very seriously disrupted in 1930 when a large number of Communists were arrested during the Party's general meeting at Long Beach. Seven of these arrested were deported to Hamburg, under guarantee to the German ambassador, instead of to Japan. Miyagi believed they made their way to Russia once they had reached Germany. Although these deportations broke up the Japanese section of the Party, it was reconstructed in 1931, and although all Japanese were welcomed a special drive was opened to get nisei members who could legally take part in political movements. Among the new members joining the American Communist party at this time were Miyagi Yotoku and Mrs. Kitabayashi.

Miyagi had been a formal member of the American Communist party for a little over a year when Yano and another Comintern agent, whose name is unknown, called on him. They asked him to go to Tokyo for a month to serve as a Comintern agent. Nothing was said about the Red army. It is clear that Yano was an agent of the Comintern, although possibly the man with him represented the other branch. They told Miyagi to call on a Comintern agent then in Los Angeles named Roy for instructions. Possibly this was the same Roy, an East Indian member of the Comintern, who served with Borodin in China in 1927. Miyagi seems to have made an early call, but he put off his departure from month to month because, as he said, he was busy with his painting. Probably, also he was reluctant to leave his home in the United States and to risk the dangers of Tokyo. There was nothing in his record to present him as a heroic figure or even as a potentially dangerous spy. Perhaps that was why he was selected from the many Japanese Communists in California.

Finally in September 1933 Roy demanded that Miyagi start off at once. Either out of ignorance or else to hasten him along, Roy promised that he would be back in Los Angeles in no time. Roy gave him $200 for expenses, and a one dollar bill which he was to show to a man who would meet him in Tokyo carrying another note with a consecutive number. He was to watch the want ads in the Japan *Advertiser*. When he saw one asking for Ukiyoe—a Japanese print—he was to answer it. If the man he met through the advertisement had this other dollar bill he should follow his instructions.

Miyagi could postpone his duty no longer, and soon left for Japan. Since he was expecting to return soon he left all his personal possessions, as well as his wife, Chiyo, in America. He was never to see them again.

Miyagi reached Tokyo in October, 1933. Although they had yet to meet, all of Richard Sorge's top level aides were now in Japan. Miyagi settled down adjusting himself to the life of Tokyo which was entirely new to him, while he daily read the Japan *Advertiser*. De Voukclitch finally inserted his ad from December 14 to 18: "Wanted to buy Ukiyoe." Miyagi answered the advertisement and a few days later Branko de Voukelitch and Miyagi Yotoku met for the first time at the advertising agency Issui Sha, and compared dollar bills.

Early Days of the Ring in Tokyo

The chief links in the ring were now established: Dr. Richard Sorge, the leader; Branko de Voukelitch, the "neutral" press contact man; Miyagi Yotoku, the innocent Japanese artist; and a shadowy and inept figure, the radio operator, "Bruno Vendt," alias "Bernhardt." The task now was to create a simple means of communication with the ring, and to establish Japanese and other contacts who would assure a flow of worthwhile information. The Soviet Embassy could be counted on to supply a steady stream of information on Japan: Sorge's group had to produce something different and more important.

De Voukelitch introduced Miyagi to Sorge near the end of December, 1933, at the Ueno Art Gallery. At first the conversation was general, but after four or five meetings Miyagi realized that Sorge's assignment was intelligence rather than Communist propaganda, and that he was expected to help. When Sorge made a formal proposal in January,

1934, Miyagi consented with some reluctance. His Communist affiliation had prepared him abstractly for work for the Soviets but his previous experience had not prepared him practically or psychologically to become an agent in Japan. His account of his hesitation is interesting.

"It was some time before I could decide to join Sorge's group. If I had been in the United States my position would have been different, but what would be the position of a Japanese working in Japan? Especially, was this not a contradiction of myself since I had been interested in racial emancipation? I made up my mind to participate, however, when I realized the historical importance of the mission, since we were helping to avoid war between Japan and Russia. At first I meant to get out of the business as soon as I could find someone to replace me, because I had no training for this kind of work. As time went on, I realized that there was nobody who would be willing to do the job. So I stayed on, although I knew well that what I was doing was illegal and that in wartime I would be hanged."

Both Miyagi and Ozaki satisfied their consciences in their betrayal of their country by the argument that they were working secretly to avert a war which would be a catastrophe for both Japanese and Russians but which could be avoided only by flow of significant intelligence on Japanese war plans to the Soviet Union. By corollary they came to the conclusion that if war came despite their best efforts, the fundamental interests of the common people would be served by a Soviet victory.

Sorge's immediate contacts were through normal press channels. He had come to Japan with letters of introduction to Japanese prominent in government service, such as Shiratori Toshio, a career diplomat who years later was to be a defendant at the Tokyo War Crimes Trials, and Debuchi Katsuji, another career diplomat with long and friendly experience in the United States. Sorge's Nazi party membership was sufficient to give him entree to the German Ambassador, Herbert von Dirksen, and to other officials at the embassy, while his own qualities proved sufficient to assure that he would be invited to return.

As Colonel Eugen Ott rose to major general and from assistant military attaché to military attaché and finally to ambassador, Sorge's access to the best German information in Japan became established. Ott found Sorge's information and advice invaluable and needless to say the 4th Bureau in Moscow, through Sorge, found Ott's information even more invaluable. With the passage of years Ott came to show his official documents quite freely to Sorge, to exchange views and to keep him informed. Similarly, the Military Attaché, the Air Attaché, the Naval Attaché and the Gestapo chief attached to the embassy from 1940—Colonel Jospeh Meissinger—came to trust and rely on Dr. Richard Sorge. Only the Naval Attaché seems to have doubted him, and not on any suspicion of Soviet affiliations but because he didn't like him. Naturally it took many years for Sorge to arrive at this incredible position of trust at the German Embassy, but by 1939 he had traveled the full route. After the outbreak of the European War, Ott designated Sorge as press attaché of the embassy, putting him on the German payroll, and giving him the strength of official position. Most mornings after Sorge had pounded out the press releases on the progress of the war in Europe, he joined the ambassador over late breakfast. Sorge had much to give the ambassador in the way of Japanese gossip and fact, and in turn the ambassador had much to tell Sorge. He showed Sorge the instructions from home and his proposed replies. The other chief members of the mission followed the ambassador's example, the officer closest to Dr. Richard Sorge, Soviet spy, being none other than Colonel Meissinger of the Gestapo. On occasion Sorge memorized the essentials of these documents and conversations, and sometimes he recorded the documents with his ever present camera. Like de Voukelitch he was an incorrigible amateur camera enthusiast.

After 1939, with his office at the German Embassy, and in effect a part of that embassy's intelligence organization, Sorge's position was perfect for learning everything about Japan, its capacities and intentions, that was known to Japan's ally Germany. There was much unknown to the German allies, however, and this information Sorge had to gather in other ways. After the signing of the Tripartite Pact on September 27, 1940, however, the Japanese Army and Navy General Staff discussed their problems far more freely with appropriate members of the German Embassy. These embassy officers frankly asked Sorge for his opinions. Indeed, Sorge had been a primary architect of that Axis Pact. General Ott had felt so indebted to Sorge for his work in the development of the Tripartite Pact that he intended to have Sorge present at the official signing in Tokyo. Hitler's special representative, Dr. Heinrich Stahmer, who had come over from China to complete the treaty, however, objected, and Sorge was not present. Stahmer had no suspicions of Sorge's integrity. At most he must have been jealous of sharing credit with a relatively unknown and minor figure. There is nothing more ironical in the history of the Sorge ring, however, than Sorge's part in bringing on the Tripartite Pact which inevitably hastened the war.

This highlighting of Sorge's successes skips over his early and most difficult years when he was slowly establishing himself and his ring. As newspaper correspondents Sorge and de Voukelitch attended the press conferences of the Foreign Office and the Board of Information, had friendly access both to Japanese and foreign press circles where there was always a great deal of general information to be picked up, and indeed had trustful friends in various consulates and embassies. De Voukelitch was particularly successful in his outside conquests. According to his testimony he had many intimate talks with the British Military Attaché, Major General Francis S. Piggott. He was very close to the Reuters man, James M. Cox, who had ready access to the British Embassy before he jumped from a window at Kempeitai Headquarters in July, 1940. By 1938 de Voukelitch had become a Havas man himself, acquiring more standing and more contacts. He heard the prevalent views and news of the French Embassy either directly or through his colleague, chief of the Havas Bureau, Robert Guillain. And through the likeable and thoughtful Joseph Newman of the *New York Herald Tribune,* who had easy access to Eugene H. Dooman, Counselor of the American Embassy, he kept in touch with American activities. Since each embassy was working hard to collect information on Japan, as well as to keep in touch with the views of their home governments, Sorge was able to gather and evaluate the views of the German, American, French, and British embassies, in Tokyo. Naturally, only at the German Embassy could he get documentary evidence and secret plans, but the information from the embassies opposed to the Axis served as a very useful check against the conclusions reached by the Germans.

Most of the records of the interrogation of De Voukelitch are lost, and it is not possible properly to assess his contribution to the ring. It is possible that de Voukelitch showed greater courage under pressure than any of the others, since even in the extant material and the summaries of the procurators, which we have in full, not much information is attributed to him. His early death in prison raises the question of torture. He was only forty-one when he died, and the record does not show that he was physically below par before his arrest. It is very possible that he was firm in his refusal to talk, and was treated accordingly.

Sorge sharply criticized de Voukelitch and all of his assistants excepting Ozaki in talking with the prosecutors and the police. Perhaps he hoped to help them by minimizing their work, but it is more likely that his words were a reflection of his own arrogance. He had this to say of Branko: "De Voukelitch came to Japan for the express purpose of becoming a member of my intelligence group. At the same time he was, like myself a press correspondent, to cover his espionage work. While I found my newspaper work irksome because intelligence was my real job, de Voukelitch spent more and more effort on his reporting and repeated to me everything he heard with no sense of discrimination. He left all evaluation to me."

Edith de Voukelitch was a dull sort of woman, and Branko soon tired of her. After playing around the Tokyo bars he finally met Yamazaki Yoshiko, and fell in love with her. She spoke English fluently and seems to have been quite attractive. She soon became Branko's mistress, and according to the Japanese police was not indifferent to the attentions of Dr. Sorge. Presumably, Branko did not learn of this lapse.

Edith and Branko separated in July, 1938, and Yoshiko came to live with him. Branko persuaded Edith to divorce him; the divorce became effective on December 18, 1939, and Branko married Yoshiko in January, 1940. It seems certain that this was a liaison of romance and passion, and that Yamazaki Yoshiko had nothing to do with espionage, or even any suspicion that it was going on. The Japanese Higher Special Police convinced themselves of this. In making such judgments they were not likely to err on the side of kindness.

There is no doubt that Edith de Voukelitch came to Japan knowingly as a Soviet spy, within her limits helped her husband, and through him helped Dr. Richard Sorge in espionage for the Red Army. She left the ring not because of disillusionment with communism and the U.S.R.R., but because her husband, Branko, preferred to live with another woman.

Edith was not permitted to leave until Sorge had received permission from Moscow. Presumably she made pledges which the Soviet authorities felt were adequately binding before they allowed her to leave the ring and Japan. The accounts of her payoff differ. Just before she sailed Sorge gave Klausen $500 for her but he never delivered the money. This was the cause of a violent quarrel between Max and de Voukelitch. A Japanese police report claims, however, that the Russians already had paid her off with $5,000 to which Sorge had added $1,000 on his own responsibility while Klausen had added a bit more.

Sorge's Intelligence Targets

While Sorge was in Japan he received specific instructions on intelligence targets. He received his general instructions, however, before he left for Moscow in August, 1933, and while he was in Moscow again for twenty days in 1935. The subsequent outbreak of the European War changed the specific but not the general questions. Overriding all was the problem of whether Japan planned to attack the Soviet Union, and if so what were her capabilities. The following seven points, derived from Sorge's replies to his interrogation, cover these targets:

1. Japan's police relative to the U.S.S.R. following the invasion of Manchuria. Did Japan intend to attack the U.S.S.R.? After 1939 this target became overriding.

2. Organization, armament, order of battle of the Japanese Army and Air Force, with special attention to military preparations in Manchuria.

3. Japanese-German relations. The Soviet government early estimated that close German-Japanese relations were inevitable, to the detriment of the Soviet Union. Increasingly after the signature of the Anti-Comintern Pact heavy emphasis was placed on this question.

4. Japan's policy and activity in China.

5. The development of Japan's relations and policies toward the United States and Great Britain. Before the "Manchurian Incident" the Soviets seemed to have estimated that Japan might attack the U.S.S.R. with support from the United States and Great Britain. Subsequently this question became closely related to Japan's capabilities for attack on the U.S.S.R. as related to her war in China and her program of southward advance.

6. Detailed observation of the role played by the Japanese Army in political affairs, since the Soviets estimated that fundamental foreign policy would be based on army decisions.

7. Systematic observation of the operations and growth of Japanese heavy industry, as well as its branches in Manchuria.

Sorge amassed an amazing amount of material on these questions, and at the most critical time was able to inform his superiors that Japan did not intend to attack the U.S.S.R. but instead would move South. He served, however, as a high level evaluator of information, not merely as a transmitter of undigested facts submitted to him by his agents. After gathering together facts, opinions, and estimates from a wide range of sources—the German Embassy, the British Embassy, and the American and French Embassies and the Dutch Legation, the Japanese War Ministry, the Imperial Cabinet, common household gossip, the press and magazines —Sorge sorted them out. Often he asked the opinions of Ozaki and Miyagi. Having come to a conclusion, usually he would test it in conversations with the German Ambassador and the military, air, and naval attachés of the embassy. He had a high respect for their judgments since they were professional soldiers charged with evaluating just such information for the guidance of the German government.

Meanwhile, de Voukelitch would be discussing the same problems with his newspaper friends who had access to the American, French, and British embassies, who were well informed themselves and who could often get a semiofficial view from their diplomatic contacts. Only after he had milked dry every source, had weighed and counterchecked did Sorge write his careful dispatches to Moscow. Some of these he sent out over his radio circuit, some on microfilm by courier to Shanghai, some to the Soviet Embassy.

Precautions Used by Sorge Ring

Sorge limited his own contacts within the ring to de Voukelitch, Ozaki, Miyagi, the radio operator, who was Max Klausen after 1935, and from the period 1936 to 1938 to Guenther Stein. He met those people frequently at restaurants and bars like the Rheingold, the Fledermaus and Lohmeyer's, or at his own home. For years these meetings appeared natural since three of the group were journalists with common professional interests.

It was only after 1940 when police surveillance became more rigid that Sorge began meeting the men secretly. When they met at Sorge's home the members of the ring had to adopt the usual practices of changes of cabs at distant addresses, while Sorge manipulated his porch light as an all clear signal.

Some of the precautions observed by the group, chiefly relating to the radio, were tabulated by Klausen as follows:

All members must have a rational occupation as covers.

Members must have no traffic with Japanese Communists or Communist sympathizers.

The radio cipher must be altered by the use of different scramble numbers with each sending.

The transmitter must be dismantled, packed in a case, and moved after each operation.

Messages must be sent from different locations, never from any one house over a long period.

Liaison with "Moscow men" must be carried out in the utmost secrecy with no mention of names on either side.

Each member must have a cover name. Real names must never be mentioned in radios or conversations.

Place names must be disguised in code, such as "Wiesbaden" for Vladivostok and "Munchen" for Moscow.

Documents must be destroyed immediately after they have served their purpose.

Never under any circumstances must a Russian be admitted to the circle.

Similarly, Ozaki discussed his technique and listed the following nine precepts as a guide for any intelligence agent:

Never give the impression that you are eager to obtain news: Men who are engaged in important affairs will refuse to talk to you if they suspect that your motive is to collect information.

If you give the impression that you have more information than your prospective informant he will give with a smile.

Informal dinner parties are an excellent setting for the gathering of news.

It is convenient to be a specialist of some kind. For my part I am a specialist on Chinese questions, and have always received inquiries from all quarters. I was able to gather much data from men who came to ask me questions.

My position as a writer for newspapers and magazines stood me in good stead.

Because I was often asked to lecture in all parts of Japan I had an excellent chance to learn general trends of local opinion.

Connections with important organizations engaged in the collection of news are vital. I was affiliated with the *Asahi Shimbun* and later with the South Manchurian Railway.

Above all you must cultivate trust and confidence in you on the part of those who you are using as informants in order to be able to pump them without seeming unnatural.

In these days of unrest you cannot be a good intelligence man unless you yourself are a good source of information. You can achieve this only after constant study and wide experience.

Sorge's Personal Views on Espionage Operations

Sorge has made some shrewd observations on the techniques of espionage, which are probably standard Soviet training methods and as such universally applicable.

1. *Mental attitude of spies.* ". . . A shrewd spy will not spend all his time on the collection of military and political secrets and classified documents. Also, I may add, reliable information cannot be procured by effort alone; espionage work entails the accumulation of information, often fragmentary, covering a broad field, and the drawing of conclusions based thereon. This means that a spy in Japan, for example, must study Japanese history and the racial characteristics of the people and orient himself thoroughly on Japan's politics, society, economics, and culture. Today, the Emperor of Japan is closely encircled by political, army, naval, and economic blocs, and it is necessary to cultivate contacts with the members of those blocs in order to obtain reliable information. Similarly, contacts with foreigners are essential.

"I was able to draw definite conclusions through conversations with acquaintances in various fields only because I knew Japan. Had I not known it, there would have been nothing to serve as a basis for my judgment."

2. *Women and espionage work.* "Women are absolutely unfit for espionage work. They have no understanding of political and other affairs and I have never received satisfactory information from them. Since they were useless to me, I did not employ them in my group. Even upper class women have no comprehension of what has been said by their husbands and are, therefore, very poor sources of information. This does not apply merely to Japanese women; in my opinion, no woman in the world has the aptitude for espionage work. The woman whom I employed in China was merely a co-worker of her Chinese husband. Smedley had a good educational background and a brilliant mind and fit in well as a news reporter, but as a wife her value was nil. In short, she was like a man. I might add that cultivation of intimate relations with married women for purposes of espionage will arouse the jealousy of their husbands and hence react to the detriment of the cause. In the final analysis, espionage operations must be performed by a man with a good education and a keen mind."

3. *Espionage operations.* "Money is a prerequisite to espionage work. It was essential to our operations in Japan, but the amount that I spent was quite enough. Indiscriminate

spending might have led to detection, and there was no urgent need for it because our group was held together by strong ideological ties.

"Wireless is the best possible means for short-range communication because it is difficult to locate a transmitter by means of detection apparatus.

"There is no school or agency in Moscow which functions exclusively for the purpose of training espionage agents to be sent to foreign countries. Men who possess the essential attributes — character, education, technical knowledge, and experience—are selected and sent out on assignments.

"The wireless communications school in Moscow develops wireless technicians for the Red Army; only a few of its graduates are used for espionage operations.

"As stated above, there is no special school for training future espionage agents and, consequently, there is no basic procedure that must be observed. The espionage agent must cope with each exigency as it arises; in other words, he must adapt himself to his individual circumstances.

"Since conditions vary in each country, adaptability is a basic requirement for the man engaged in espionage work. He must acquire a complete knowledge of the situation within the country to which he is assigned and operate cautiously in the light of that knowledge.

"That completes my general observations."

4. *Precautions while operating in Japan.* "It is difficult to set up operational procedures for foreign, particularly Caucasian, agents entering Japan. I have, however, drawn the following conclusions from my observations.

"Legitimate cover is absolutely essential to an agent. I worked as a news reporter and found that the foreign correspondent is conveniently situated for the acquisition of information of various types, but that he is closely observed by the police. I believe that, in Japan and China, the best thing an agent can do is to become a big merchant. A man clever enough to take up espionage work as a career in the first place would not forsake his career for business, and, even if he did, the chances are that he would not succeed. Generally speaking, the mercantile class is made up of men of average or less than average intelligence, and the agent who assumes such a cover would be quite safe from detection by the police. Moreover, as a merchant with extensive business connections (which he would utilize as sources of information), he could associate with people of various classes without arousing suspicion.

"Because of the difference in race, it is extremely difficult for a foreign agent to operate in Japan, and well-qualified Japanese assistants are absolutely necessary. I must admit that I owe my immense success to Ozaki and Miyagi. Enlistment of qualified Japanese assistants is not an easy matter, but the Soviet Union enjoys an advantage because, through communism, it can recruit on an ideological basis, while other world powers must attract agents with promises of monetary reward, political advancement, etc. The United States may, for example, extend promises of admission to the country and comfortable living, while Great Britain may divulge valuable information as a reciprocal gesture and in this way increase his value to the Japanese government.

"I shall outline, as they occur to me, the numerous precautions I observed in Japan against the police.

"I did not engage in any special activities for several months after arriving in Japan because I felt that new foreigners would be placed under observation. I met Aritomi Mitsukado, a reporter on the *Jiji Shimpo,* at the German Embassy shortly after my arrival. He was exceedingly eager to cultivate my friendship and found a room for me at the Meguro Hotel. I believe he had told the manager of the hotel to watch me, because the manager intimated to me that he had once been a Japanese Army spy. On another occasion, Aritomi introduced me to a former left-winger who spoke Russian. The man spoke to me in Russian but I pretended not to understand him. Aritomi, in my opinion, operated on orders from the Metropolitan Police Board, frequenting the German Embassy and investigating German nationals. He came to assist me when I moved to Nagata Cho in Azabu Ku, but stayed away from me after that. We met by chance at the Imperial Hotel once.

"The following facts warned me that I was under surveillance by the police:

I was being watched by Aritomi Mitsukado.

My maid and laundryman were frequently questioned by the police.

I was constantly watched by policemen, even at the Imperial Hotel.

A Japanese translator employed by the German Embassy was questioned by the police.

I was watched by either plain-clothes men or Kempei, even at restaurants.

My house had been searched and my brief case examined during my absence on a trip to China.

"I believe the foregoing is standard police procedure for all foreigners; I was not the only foreigner under suspicion.

In view of the foregoing, I endeavored to make my movements known; that is, I went openly to the German Embassy and the Imperial Hotel, and when I went to Homoku I made it a point to return with souvenir matches from the houses and restaurants I patronized. Whenever I had to make long trips, I left all my valuables at the German Embassy so that no incriminating evidence would be discovered if the house were searched during my absence. The embassy staff were aware that the homes of employees and other foreigners were being searched and they willingly took care of property. Once when I returned from a trip, Ambassador Ott asked me whether my house had been subjected to a "house cleaning," and, in reply, I told him that I had entrusted all my valuables to Wennecker.

"I might add that I employed an old woman as housemaid and had her commute to work; one of the reasons for this was to withhold from her the identities of the guests I received during the night."

5. *Operational objectives.* "In Japan, information concerning the Army was the most difficult to obtain; next was information concerning the Navy. Had I not enjoyed access to the German Embassy, I would have had no alternative to the cultivation of sources within the armed forces. This would have been extremely difficult, since it would have been necessary to use Japanese agents for the work. I might have succeeded had I tried, but it would have been a difficult operation.

"The information most easily obtained in Japan was that concerning domestic policies and foreign affairs. It was not nearly as hard to come by as news concerning the armed services. In fact, there was a tendency to publicize even confidential information concerning governmental and foreign affairs. Upon obtaining information on Japan's domestic policies, one could draw a general estimate of the military situation, because military policy and domestic policy were inseparable. Information concerning government policies was most easily obtained through the upper classes, who could not dodge the issue if one challenged them to a debate; it was impossible for them to feign ignorance under such circumstances. Also, if one revealed some information concerning Germany, he would be obligated to divulge a certain amount of confidential information concerning Japan.

"News reporters have the easiest access to information and can secure it with the least amount of effort. Even confidential matters are disclosed to them.

"It is difficult to maintain absolute secrecy on political matters. Public information is essential to the government;

public information and politics go hand in hand. For example, to ascertain how Germany will react to the occupation of French Indo-China by Japanese troops, the Japanese government must discuss the matter with the German Ambassador, and the discussion will lead to the guess that Japan is preparing to occupy French Indo-China. Thus Japan cannot consult German officials for their opinion unless she states her case first.

"It is erroneous to think that information is procured exclusively through careless talk.

"Rumors precede every important happening in Japan, and by piecing them together one can predict the nature of impending events. For instance, when rumors concerning German-Japanese negotiations began to circulate during the weeks preceding the Anti-Comintern Pact, I investigated them (although I had already obtained authentic information from the Germany Embassy) and hit upon one concerning the past. When rumors have it that a close tie-up between the Germany Embassy and the General Staff has been effected, a thorough investigation is bound to reveal that military negotiations are under way.

"Every major occurrence in Japan is preceded by widespread rumors. Since the Japanese are given to rumor-mongering, it may be said that information is easy to obtain in Japan. I can state from personal experience that the Japanese, like the Chinese, are curious about secrets that do not concern them in any way and are given to spreading rumors.

"When 'Haak,' the German special envoy, came to Japan, he informed me that Soviet agents had been posted outside the homes of Military Attaché Oshima, Foreign Minister Ribbentrop, and Special Service Chief Canaris, that they had even taken pictures during secret negotiations for the Anti-Comintern Pact, and that he had served as a go-between among the three officials so that the negotiations could continue without further Russian detection. As I have noted earlier, Oshima, Ribbentrop and Canaris were being watched as a result of my reports to the Soviet authorities. As soon as 'Haak' told me what had happened, I reported it and I believe he, too, was watched thereafter.

"One must refrain carefully from careless talk and not reveal secrets to any outsider, even one's most trusted friend."

Liaison Between Members of the Spy Ring

Procedure Employed to Establish Contact Between Two Unacquainted Agents:

"I employed the following methods to establish contact with unknown agents while operating in Europe, the United States, China, and Japan. Some of them I evolved myself and others were specified in orders. In any case, the time, place, and method of contact were decided upon and made known to both sides prior to the meeting.

"The simplest method used was to locate a person whose appearance and dress matched a given description at a specified time and place and engage him in a prearranged conversation.

"The conversation would be: 'I heard that you had arrived in Shanghai. I am so-and-so. I was asked by so-and-so to extend his regards to you.' If the person were the person I was to contact, he would reply, 'I am so-and-so. I also was asked by so-and-so to extend his regards to you.'

"Each knew the prearranged names to be given. The meeting place was a hotel, a restaurant, etc.

"A somewhat more complicated form, an elaboration upon the above procedure, was used to ascertain the other party's identity more definitely.

"To the question, 'Do you know Mrs. Ott?' the answer would be, 'I know Mrs. Heruma Ott.' In this case, to the simple reference 'Mrs. Ott,' the reply of the other person had to be, in full, 'Mrs. Heruma Ott.'

"An even more complicated form was to use the spelling of a name. For instance, if I asked, 'Do you know a person called Ram?' the other party would reply, 'Doesn't his name end in Say?' That is, by a combination of the two, the name Ramsay would result.

"Another form was to show a peculiarly torn calling card to the other person, who would produce the other half of the card. By putting them together, one made certain that the other person was the proper contact. On some occasions, I made sure that the other person was the right man by producing a dollar bill bearing the serial number 112235 and having him show me a dollar bill bearing the serial number 112236.

"Another method I might take:

"When I met another man, I would take out my tobacco and say, 'I brought a special brand of tobacco with me because I heard that this is the only brand you smoke. Please have one.' He would then hold out his tobacco and say, 'I brought the brand of tobacco you like. Please have one,' thus completing the contact.

"Another method was to carry a book and say, 'This is a very interesting book. The most interesting part is on page so-and-so.' The other would then reply, 'I found page so-

and-so most interesting.' The page numbers would be prearranged.

"If I said, 'I must go to such-and-such a store to buy a certain thing,' the other man would say, 'I too must go to such-and-such store to buy a certain thing.' In such a case, the stores adjoined each other and the articles to be purchased had been prearranged.

"Or, while talking about an art gallery, I would say, 'I like so-and-so's paintings,' and, in reply, the other person would say, 'I like so-and-so's painting.' The artists' names to be mentioned would of course be prearranged.

"Once I made a contact in a record store by asking, 'Would you like to help me find such-and-such a record?' I did not name the record in full, but the other party gave the name in full in reply, saying, 'I shall help you find so-and-so and such-and-such a record.'

"At other times, I made contacts by buying theater tickets and managing it so that the other person would be seated either to my right or left in the third seat away from me (either to the right or left.)

"I made contacts by arranging meetings at specified counters in department stores, where I would buy handkerchiefs and the other party stockings.

"I made contacts by going to a restaurant where I would order one special dish and the other party another, and we would enter into a discussion of them.

"At times, I would be in a restaurant holding an odd-shaped pipe and the other man would be there with a large cigar. The cue was to light and begin smoking at the same time after each had become aware of the other's presence.

"I made contacts in restaurants by folding a newspaper I was reading in a special peculiar way when the other party entered.

"I also used the colors of wrapping paper, gloves and neckties, and the manner in which a pipe or cigar was held as cues.

"At times, when there were no prearranged place and time, I used newspaper advertisements.

"Again, if I knew the other party's name and the hotel where he was staying, I would telephone him and then go to see him.

"In summation I would say that the Japanese police were interested too much in little things and not enough in big ones. It seems to me that they were wasting their time with little things of no value. At any rate, I believe the wrong counterintelligence methods were in use in Japan.

"The best countermeasures against spies is not to make

everything a secret, but to change incessantly whatever the spies want to find out. If that is done, they will eventually get tired of seeking the information and give up."

Forged passports. "When I went to the Soviet Union via the United States from Japan in 1935, a Communist party contact man in New York gave me a forged passport. I used it to go to Moscow and destroyed it in Holland on my return trip. I used a forged passport because I did not want my real passport to show that I had been in Soviet Russia. Prior to that, when returning to Moscow from Scandinavia, I had also used a forged Scandinavian passport. In neither of these cases did I forge the passport; contact men gave them to me. I do not know, therefore, whether or not there is a special section in the Comintern which makes forged passports.

"I used my real passport twice to go to Moscow; once when I first went there from Germany in 1924 and once when I returned from China via Siberia in 1933.

"The passport I received in the United States was not new. It was an old one that had belonged to someone, but it bore my picture and description. The nationality was given as Austrian and the name was long and outlandish; I have forgotten it now. An Austrian visa had been stamped on it, so all I had to do in Paris was to get Czechoslovakian, Polish, and Russian visas. I had to go through the regular procedure just like any other traveler; I was not given any special privileges when I went to apply for my entrance and exit visas at the Soviet Consulate.·

"When I was buying a ticket at a steamship office preparatory to going to Europe with the forged passport, I found that I had forgotten the outlandish name on it and had to take it out of my pocket to refresh my memory.

"When I was leaving New York, I had a suit tailored, giving the tailor my real name, and on my return trip I went to the same tailor and gave him the name in the forged passport. The tailor remembered me and noted that my name was different, but he was not interested in the change and made the suit for me. People in the United States do not think it strange if the same man uses two different names.

"In this respect, the British are rather strict and their passport inspection is thorough. It is said that England knows more about spies than any other nation in Europe, but I am not in a position to make a definite statement because I have made no special study of the subject.

"I shall give an illustration of how loosely everything is done in the United States. I did not pay my exit tax and forgot to get a stamped receipt when I went on board the ship for Europe. Just as the ship was about to sail, a customs officer found out about it, and it looked as though he were going to take me off the ship, but I slipped him fifty dollars and the matter was dropped at once. Things are very flexible in the United States."

Klausen Comes to Japan

Sorge early decided that "Bernhardt" was not suitable for the delicate Japanese assignment. In the summer of 1935 he went to Europe, nominally to renew his contract with the *Frankfurter Zeitung,* but actually to attend the Comintern congress of that year in Moscow, to report to his superiors, and to receive their instructions.

He went to New York on his regular German passport, but while there a man called at his hotel room with a new passport already visaed for the U.S.S.R. Sorge went directly to Moscow; it is not clear whether he went to Berlin at all, but presumably he must have gone to maintain his cover. In Moscow he interviewed his associate of China days, Max Klausen, and selected him to replace the disgraced "Bernhardt." Sorge then returned to Japan, one story says, by air on the first Junkers flight from Germany to Tokyo.

Max Klausen, the radio operator, received his travel orders in July, 1935 from the chief of the 4th Bureau, General "Olitsky," and from the Chief of the Far Eastern Section of the 4th Bureau, "Kalin." In September he bade farewell to Anna, who was to meet him later, and started out with three passports in different names, one Italian, one Canadian, and one his own German passport. These changes of identity seem to have been intended to escape the interest of counter-intelligence agents while he was traveling in Europe. Klausen described this part of his trip as follows:

"There are hundreds of passports of different countries at Headquarters. All are genuine because they have been duly purchased by the Soviet government from their rightful owners. Only the names and the photographs are false. Before my depature I received instructions as to the use of the passports and was given U.S. $1,800. I proceeded to Le Havre via Leningrad, Helsinki, and Stockholm. At the Swedish capital I purchased an American seaman's certificate and set out for New York aboard the *Boston.* Upon my arrival I had my own German passport renewed at the German Consulate and booked in at the Hotel Lincoln because I had been instructed to do so. There I received a call from a man who said his name was 'Jones.' 'Jones' asked me if I needed money. I refused the offer. I did not discover whether he was a member of the Soviet Embassy or a member of an intelligence group."

Klausen arrived in Yokohama aboard the *Tatsuta Maru* on November 28, 1935. He had intended to continue to Shanghai, where he expected to meet Anna, marry her, and bring her to Japan. He was short of funds, however, and had to postpone that trip.

Anna had a very frightening time in Russia before she managed to get to Shanghai, but her experiences do not affect the main Sorge story. It was not until July, 1936 that Max was able to meet her in Shanghai, give marriage notice at the German Consulate, and then return in August to marry her. He took Anna back to Tokyo, where she served as a minor and somewhat unwilling member of the ring.

Before their separate departures from Moscow, Sorge and Klausen had arranged to meet on Tuesday evenings at the Blue Ribbon Bar near Sukiyabashi, Tokyo. On the day after Max got to town, however, they chanced to meet at the German Club. Naturally, they passed this off as their first introduction, but were spared any further pretense of not knowing each other. Klausen replaced "Bernhardt," and settled down to making himself a cover.

At first Klausen tried to set up an export-import business, but this failed. Then he established the firm of M. Klausen Shokai (M. Klausen & Co.), with offices in the Karasumori Building, Shiba-ku, Tokyo. M. Klausen Shokai made and sold printing presses for blueprints as well as fluorescent plates, and almost immediately began to make money. Among its customers were such firms as Mitsubishi, Mitsui, Nakajima, and Hitachi, as well as munition factories, the Japanese Army and the Japanese Navy. While Klausen was manufacturing machinery for the Army's blueprints, Sorge was getting the finished blueprints of the Imperial government. By February, 1941, Klausen had done so well that he reorganized his firm as a joint stock company capitalized at 100,000 yen of which he contributed 85,000 yen. He even established a branch at Mukden, with a working capital of 20,000 yen. In fact, Klausen was doing so well, and making so much money that his earlier convictions of the perfection of communism were shaken, especially as Anna was always poking fun at his dreams of pie in the sky whenever she wanted a new fur coat. But in the meantime his business not only was a personal cover but also a perfect cover for the financial transactions of the ring. He bought and sold abroad, and there was nothing irregular in his receipt of drafts from New York or San Francisco or Shanghai for his bank account.

Guenther Stein, British Journalist

Guenther Stein, a member of the ring, is a man about whom too little is known. Stein was a German Jew who seems to have become a British citizen. He represented the *Berlin Tageblatt* as a correspondent for a time, but in 1936 came to Japan as correspondent for the *British Financial News*. His specialty was economic and financial affairs, and his small book *Made in Japan* often is used as an authoritative source on prewar Japanese commerce and industry. During World War II, Stein was a war correspondent in China, based in Chungking. Late in 1944 he was one of a group of six who visited Yenen, and one of two correspondents whose accounts of Communist China were published as books. His *Challenge of Red China,* published in America in 1945, has the outward appearance of the thoughtful reporting of a serious, objective analyst who is neither pro- nor anti-Communist, but who only wants to discover the underlying truth. His book has been very effective in perpetuating the legend that Chinese Communists are not Communists and are not in any way connected with the Soviet Union. Like Miss Smedley, Guenther Stein was a Soviet agent, and one can be certain that neither of them was publishing the truth about Chinese Communists.

Because he was no longer in Japan when the members of the Sorge ring were arrested, the Japanese police did not go very deeply into Stein's antecedents and complicity. That he was a top level member of the ring is clear, but we do not know how he got into it. Klausen suggested that Sorge recruited Stein after he arrived in Japan, but the speed with which Stein put his home at Klausen's disposal as a radio station makes it likely that he was a party to Soviet espionage before he met Sorge in Japan. We know also that Stein made at least one courier run to Hong Kong in 1937, and that sometimes he served as Sorge's deputy in dealing with Ozaki.

Guenther Stein had a woman friend, a Swiss correspondent, Margit Gantenbein, whom he married in Hong Kong in July, 1938. Sorge testified that ". . . because she was a friend of Guenther Stein we did things for her, and indirectly she did things in favor of our work." It appears that she supplied information to Stein, who passed it on to Sorge, but she seems to have acted knowingly. Sorge went on to testify: " . . . [when] she stopped at Yokohama on her way to Hong Kong to marry Guenther Stein I had de Voukelitch meet her at the ship . . . although I don't remember the details. I believe it was because I didn't want to talk to her myself. . . . I did meet her just for a moment however at a Foreign Office banquet held at the New Grand."

After Stein left Japan for good, Sorge was ordered to have no further contact with him. Consequently, although both men were in Hong Kong in 1939, when Sorge was on a courier run, they did not meet. As Sorge said, "I didn't meet him, although I had heard from other correspondents that he was in the city."

While it could mean that Stein had broken from his Soviet connections, this is an unlikely interpretation. Sorge and Ozaki were also ordered to have nothing further to do with Miss Smedley, after they were working in Japan, although she was heading a Soviet espionage ring in Peiping and was working as faithfully as ever for the Cause. The chances are that after Stein's work took him away from Japan he was separated from further connection with the ring in Tokyo, as a security measure, but that he continued to help the Cause in Hong Kong and every other place that he moved. Whether his romance with Margit, compounded of journalism and espionage, developed into a lasting marriage is not known.

The Japanese Agents: Rings within Rings

Sorge had rings within a ring. The outer ring consisted of the principals: Sorge, Ozaki, de Voukelitch, Miyagi, Stein, and Klausen. Sometimes Sorge dealt directly with each of these men, although often he dealt with one through another. He was trying, of course, to reduce the number of contacts to reduce the risks. For example, on at least four occasions he dealt with Ozaki through Stein, and similarly he dealt with Stein through de Voukelitch and with de Voukelitch through Stein. On occasion his contact with Miyagi was through Ozaki and on occasion this contact was reversed and he dealt with Ozaki through Miyagi. Although he knew her, Sorge seems not to have dealt directly with Stein's friend, Margit Gantenbein but instead she probably funneled her modest bits of information to Sorge through Stein. Similarly Anna Klausen received her orders through her husband, and Edith de Voukelitch was dealt with through her husband, Branko.

Within this outer ring were two lesser rings, one maintained by Ozaki and one by Miyagi. The members were not entirely unknown to each other, but where possible they were kept separate. This was the strictly Japanese part of the Sorge ring at the popular level, as contrasted with Ozaki's high level contacts in the government. Ozaki and Miyagi met on natural and plausible grounds since Mrs. Ozaki who never once suspected her husband, wanted her daughter to have painting lessons. Every Sunday Miyagi called at Ozaki's house to instruct the latter's daughter in the gentle art of color. The growing friendship between her husband and the artist and his frequent social calls were nothing to arouse the suspicion of Mrs. Ozaki or anyone else.

Lesser Rings of Ozaki and Miyagi

The Japanese in Ozaki's ring were: Funakoshi Hisao, member of the China Research Institute; Kawamura Yoshio of the *Manchurian Daily News;* Kawai Teikichi, former China correspondent, member of The China Research Institute, and latterly employed by the Japan Reclaimed Paper Co., Ltd.; and Mizuno Shige, formerly a student in Shanghai and employed in Kyoto.

Those in Miyagi's little ring were: Kitabayashi Tomo, a Seventh Day Adventist and teacher in a sewing school; Koshiro Yoshinobu, a soldier; Dr. Yasuda Tokutaro, physician; Taguchi Ugenda, having minor contacts at the War Ministry; Yamana Masazane, expert on agricultural affairs; Kuzumi Fusako, employed by the Social Mass Party (*Shakai Taishuto*) but with access to the Cabinet Information Bureau; and Akiyama Koji, who worked as a translator. In addition both Ozaki and Miyagi had many friends and contacts whom they exploited, but none of these belonged to the ring.

While perhaps none of these people were essential to the success of Sorge's mission of discovering Japan's war plans, they did help a great deal. What they learned was screened through either Miyagi or Ozaki, and subsequently assessed by Sorge in his conversations with the experts at the German Embassy. To see the Sorge case in its fullest ramifications it is necessary to know of these lesser spies, to understand who they were and why they turned traitor.

There is a thread common to most of their lives: residence abroad. The exaggerated claims of Japanese militarists as to their benign conduct in China could not be concealed from Japanese who lived there or from others who lived in America and read the papers. These minor agents were both antimilitarist and pro-Communist; they seemed to labor under a misapprehension that one was a corollary of the other. The readiness of these Japanese subjects to commit treason may surprise those who believe that the Japanese people possessed unique and fanatical patriotism which permeated the whole nation. Although in the famous Canadian spy case presumably loyal Canadian and English citizens as quickly and as readily agreed to betray their countries on behalf of the Soviet Union, no parallel can be drawn between the repressions of militaristic Japan and the freedoms of democratic Canada and England as breeding grounds for disloyalty. What the Japanese, Canadian, and English traitors had in common was a fanatical faith in the purity of intentions of the Soviet Union. The lesser individuals of the Ozaki and Miyagi rings within the Sorge ring present a wide variety of backgrounds and motives, yet all of them ultimately found themselves working for the Red Army Intelligence.

Funakoshi Hisao, China Operator

Funakoshi Hisao, who served as a China representative of Dr. Sorge until his arrest in 1942, was a newspaper reporter. He had beeen born in Okayama Prefecture in 1901, and left Waseda University in 1925 without graduating to go to Tsingtao. By March, 1927, he had reached Shanghai as a reporter for the *Shanghai Mainichi,* but soon joined the staff of the news agency known as Rengo Tsushinsha, becoming manager of their Hankow and Tientsin branches successively. For two years, from 1935 to 1937, he represented the *Yomiuri Shimbun* in Tientsin. From 1938 to 1941 he was an unofficial adviser to the headquarters of the Japanese Army at Hankow. Obviously, such a man was in an excellent position to get information on Japanese order of battle, troop movements, intentions, and capabilities in China.

Funakoshi became interested in communism in Shanghai, where he was a member of Ozaki's discussion group in 1929. In 1930 he joined the secret Communism Research Society (*Kyosan Shugi Kenkyu Kai*) of which Kawai Teikichi was a fellow member. In March, 1932, Kawai asked him to replace a Yamagami Masayoshi as liaison man between Japanese groups and a Soviet spy ring. Funakoshi seems readily to have accepted this invitation, so Kawai introduced him to Dr. Richard Sorge and Miss Agnes Smedley, who were then active in Shanghai espionage. For the next six months Kawai met Sorge every five days to pass the information he had collected. When Sorge was recalled, he introduced Funakoshi to "Paul," to whom this

Japanese reported regularly till his transfer to Hankow in February, 1933. From Hankow Funakoshi continued to supply information on the Japanese Army, through another Japanese, Nozawa Fusaji. In November, 1936, Funakoshi established the China Problems Investigation Institute (*Shino Mondai Kemkyo Jo*) to which such Soviet agents as Nakanishi Ko, a member of the postwar House of Councillors, and Ozaki Shotaro made monthly reports. The Japanese police learned of Funakoshi from members of the Sorge ring. They arrested him in Peiping on January 4, 1942 where he was still operating his China Problems Investigation Institute. Sentenced to ten years' imprisonment after trial in Tokyo, Funakoshi died in jail on February 27, 1945.

Kawai Teikichi, China Adventurer

Kawai Teikichi, who introduced Funakoshi to Dr. Sorge, was born in 1900 and was graduated from Meiji University in 1925. He constantly moved from job to job never holding any one very long. In March, 1928, he went to China, where he managed to hang on as a reporter for the *Shanghai Weekly* from 1930 to 1932. He ran a bookshop in Tientsin for a time in 1933, but then started on his round of jobs again. For a time in 1939 he was employed by an army intelligence agency, the Osako Special Duty Organ (*Osako Tokumu Kikan*). He returned to Japan in 1940, where Ozaki got him a job with the Japan Reclaimed Paper Company, Ltd. (*Dai Nippon Saiseishi KK*).

Kamai became a Communist at Shanghai in 1928. He joined the Leftist Literary Society (*Sayoku Bunkensho Kai*), most of whose members were also members of the Communism Research Society (*Kyosan Shugi Kenkyo Kai*). In this group among others he came to know Komatsu Shigeo, Hidaka Tameo, Tejima Hiroo, Funakoshi Hisao, and Mizuno Shigo. The last two men worked in the Sorge ring until the end.

When Kawai joined these men in forming the Sino-Japanese Struggle Group (*Nishi Toso Domei*), very naturally he came under the suspicion of Japanese police agents at Shanghai. Kawai moved to Peiping until the heat was off. He was back in Shanghai in 1931, and while working in a secondhand bookstore he received instruction on the proper collection and assessment of military and political information from Mizuno Shige, Hadaka Tameo, Tejima Hiroo, and Sakamaki Takashi. In October, 1931, he met Ozaki who introduced him to Sorge and Miss Smedley, who soon added him to their group. Sorge sent him to Manchuria which the Japanese Army had just invaded, to gather military information. From this time Kawai was very active in North China and Manchuria, living variously in Harbin, Mukden, Peiping, and Tientsin, and passing a great stream of information to Sorge, to his successor "Paul," to Ozaki, to Ozaki's successor—Funakoshi Hisao—at Shanghai, and to Miss Smedley in Peiping. For a time he worked closely with Chinese spies.

Kawai returned to Tokyo on a trip in 1934 and saw Ozaki, who seems to have been his idol. Since Kawai's connections with the Chinese spies had ended and he had no known connections with Communists, Ozaki felt he could be sent back to Tientsin safely. He returned to Tokyo again in 1935, however, and worked for Miyagi for a time before being sent back to China. His final homecoming was in 1940.

While he was in Japan, Kawai was chiefly useful as a source on Japanese nationalist movements because of his connections as a young man. He was much more useful in China.

Miyagi's judgment of Kawai is interesting. He told the prosecutor, "Kawai was introduced to me by Ozaki. He was . . . a China adventurer (*Shina Ronin*). Whenever he was short of money he ran to Ozaki, who gave him cash. . . . Because of Ozaki's important position and the high caliber of the men who called on him I thought it might embarrass Ozaki to have Kawai dropping into his office. After consulting Sorge, I suggested that henceforth I look after Kawai; Sorge approved and told me to train the man to work for me. I gave him 60 yen or 100 yen every month. By May, 1940 I had discovered that Kawai had no firm convictions so I sent him back to Ozaki.

"I could not trust Kawai fully because the standard of his comprehension of communism was low and because his private life was scandalous. He seemed to admire Ozaki tremendously, however. . . . I made many attempts to find him a job, but the man hated work. In the end Ozaki placed him in the paper company in May, 1941."

Kawai was arrested on October 22, 1941. He was sentenced to ten years' imprisonment, but was released on October 10, 1945, and now is at large.

Mizuno Shige, High Caliber Spy

A higher caliber man among these lesser spies was Mizuno Shige, who was born in 1909. After graduating from middle school in Kyoto he entered the East Asia Common Script School (*Toa Dobun Shoin*) in Shanghai in 1929. Almost immediately he became involved in Communist groups. By October, 1930, he had helped set up a cell of the Chinese Communist party at the school and took a leading part in a student strike. In December he was detained for ten days by the Japanese consular police for distributing pacifist handbills to some Japanese naval cadets, and in January, 1931, he was expelled from the school.

The Sorge group must have been keeping a watchful eye on all potential Japanese Communist agents. Mizuno met Ozaki in October, 1930 and the next April was introduced by a Formosan Communist to Kito Oinichi, the Japanese Communist from America. Kito sounded him out and was apparently satisfied, for in May, 1931, Kito introduced Mizuno to Dr. Richard Sorge. Soon thereafter, Mizuno was gathering military and political information for the Sorge ring. His work was cut short, however, when he was arrested in August, 1931 by the Shanghai police and handed over to the Japanese consulate. He was deported to Japan, not for espionage but for Communist agitation at his school, where he had been active even after his expulsion.

In Japan, Mizuno was employed by the Ohara Social Problems Research Institute (*Ohara Shakai Mondai Kenkyo*), possibly a Communist cover organization. He renewed his friendship with Ozaki there after Ozaki returned to the *Asahi*. He was arrested again in 1936, charged with taking part in the attempted reconstruction of the Japan Communist party. Apparently the police didn't have much of a case against him, for he soon was out, went to Tokyo and got a job with the Oriental Society (*Toyo Kyokai*). In Tokyo he teamed up again with Ozaki, who introduced him to Sorge in January, 1937 and to Miyagi in July. Thereafter he worked continuously for the Sorge ring, gathering news on social and political questions in general and on the Kyoto region in particular. His subsequent employment in the Showa Study Society (*Showa Kenkyu Kai*) from 1936 to 1939, and his part in the compilation of a yearbook for the Great Japan Youth Association (*Dai Nippon Seinen Dan*) assisted him in his work with Sorge. In connection with his job he was able to write lengthy reports on the Great Japan Youth Party, the Black Dragon Society, and the reorganization of the old-line political parties in 1940. He, it was, who reported on the equipment and movements of the 16th Division in July, 1939, and the 116th Division in August, 1940.

Miyagi had this to say of Mizuno:

"I never gave him any money. He was more closely connected with Ozaki and he had a regular job. If he ran short of money, I think Ozaki helped him out. I wanted to use him for more important work, in fact, I wanted him to take my place in Tokyo in order that I might travel about the country. Sorge and Ozaki, however, did not approve of the idea, so nothing came of it."

Mizuno was arrested on October 17, 1941. He was given a prison sentence of thirteen years. He died in Miyagi Prison on March 22, 1945.

Koshiro Yoshinobu, Soldier Turned Traitor

Koshiro Yoshinobu was a soldier, a corporal, the only military man in Sorge's ring. In a country like Japan even a corporal could discover a great deal which is unknown to civilians.

Koshiro was born in 1909, graduated from Meiji University in 1935, and spent most of the rest of his free life in the army. He was drafted in March, 1936, and sent to Manchuria. After the outbreak of the China War in July, 1937, his unit was sent to the North China front and fought at Suiyuan. He was made corporal in November, 1938, and was returned to civil life as a reservist. Almost immediately, however, he was called up again, was sent to Manchuria and then to Korea, but was back in the inactive reserves in March, 1939. He had time enough to get a job in a paper shop, to get married and to father a child before he was called up again in July, 1941, when he was sent to South China. He was still on duty in China with his unit when he was arrested on April 11, 1942. He was given a dishonorable discharge in January, 1943, in order that he might be tried in a civil court. The verdict of that court was fifteen years' imprisonment. The court was cheated by the defeat of Japan, and Koshiro was released by order of American authorities on October 8, 1945.

Koshiro became interested in communism while a student at Meiji University through the influence of a neighbor named Kiotake Yasumasa. Years later, in May, 1939, while Koshiro was between wars this neighbor introduced him to Miyagi.

Miyagi told Koshiro that he was an agent of the Comintern, and asked the reservist to supply information on military affairs and troop movements through his army connections. Koshiro seems to have agreed at once and showed no hesitation to commit treason. Between May, 1939 and July, 1941, during his short period of civilian life, Koshiro supplied Miyagi with information on the Nomohan battle, the defense plans for Manchukuo, the distribution and equipment of troops, and the quality of various weapons. He also secured classified manuals of the Japanese infantry, engineers, and air force as well as other military publications. Miyagi developed such confidence in him that he recommended him to Sorge for designation as a Soviet agent. Sorge approved and transmitted his *curriculum vitae* to Moscow for consideration.

Miyagi's account of Koshiro gave a clear picture of this Japanese soldier turned traitor. He said:

"Koshiro Yoshinobu required no financial help because he lived with his father. I met him in the spring of 1939 after he had been discharged from the army. He impressed me as frank and straightforward, yet reserved. I thought he would become a good helper after training and consulted Sorge as to his future. Sorge agreed to give him about 100 yen a month if he were willing to work for us.

"In May, 1939, when Koshiro came to see me, I said: 'If a war should break out between Russia and Japan it would mean a great sacrifice not only on the part of the farmers and laborers of both countries but also on the part of the whole Japanese people. To avoid such a tragedy that is to say a Russo-Japanese War, I am sending various data on the situation in Japan to the Comintern.' I asked Koshiro if he would help me by telling what he knew about the army and by obtaining military information from his friends. I told him that he would be paid. Koshiro did not say clearly whether he would help; he only smiled and replied that he did not know many secret matters. He declared that I did not have to worry about money because he had savings.

From that time Koshiro began to tell me things, and I gave him about fifty yen a month. When he took trips for me I paid him more. I intended to train him for a couple of years and then make him an independent member of our group. Meanwhile, I thought it would be convenient to have him employed in some office where he would have access to military information. I thought the War Ministry; if possible the Mobilization Bureau would be a good place, but before I could arrange it, he found a job at the Hakushin Sha through a friend of his father's.

"Of course, I consulted Sorge about my plans, introduced Koshiro to him, and had the boy's *curriculum vitae* sent to Moscow. To let the headquarters be informed of his share in our business I always mentioned his name in reporting information which came from him. We called him 'Miki' as a cover name. He was an eldest son, however, with both parents living. Moreover, he married soon after his discharge, and later a baby was born. All of these circumstances made him unsuitable for intelligence work, so I had to change my mind."

Kuzumi Fusako, Female Communist

Kuzumi Fusako was one of the two women in the ring in Japan, although there had been several women in China. This woman, born in 1888 in Okayama Prefecture and graduated from a girls' high school in 1912, was the divorced wife of a Christian minister and the mother of two daughters. After her divorce in 1920 she became associated with various left-wingers and Communists congregating around Waseda University, in Tokyo. By August, 1921, she became the common-law wife of a leading Communist, Mitamura Shiro, and active in the Communist labor movement. She joined the Party in November, 1927, and became a member of the Hokkaido District Committee.

Mrs. Kuzumi was in prison from April, 1929, until June, 1934, along with other Communist leaders. Just before her release she read in the papers of the recantations of several prominent Communists, including that of her husband, Mitamura, so she did likewise. Subsequently, however, she backslid into the Communist movement and was mentally prepared when she met Miyagi in March, 1936. Miyagi confided that he was a Comintern agent, and asked for her help. She began to collect information on the February 26, 1936, Incident, the Social Mass Party (*Shakai Taishuto*), the All Japan Federation of Labor (*Zen Nippon Rodo Sodomei*), the Great Japan Youth Party (*Dai Nippon Seinen To,*) and similar subjects.

Kuzumi Fusako was arrested on October 13, 1941, and received a sentence of eight years at hard labor. She was released by the Americans on October 8, 1945.

Kitabayashi Tomo, the Weak Link

Mrs. Kitabayashi was the other woman in this case. She had been Miyagi's friend since his early days in Los Angeles, where she had gone with her husband, Yoshisaburo, in 1920. She had added to her income in Los Angeles by teaching dressmaking, and later found this a useful device for picking up gossip in Tokyo. Mrs. Kitabayashi had joined the Proletarian Art Society in Los Angeles in 1931, along with Miyagi, and soon was persuaded to join the Japanese group of the 13th Branch of the American Communist party. Tomo had another type of conversion in 1933, when she joined the Women's Christian Temperance Union and the Seventh Day Adventist Church. She continued to be friendly with Miyagi, however, and saw him in Tokyo soon after her return in 1936. She taught dressmaking in the Los Angeles Seamstress's School in Tokyo until her husband Yoshisaburo, came back to Japan, when she joined him at Kokawa, Wakayama Prefecture, in December, 1939.

When Miyagi asked her to collect information in April, 1938, she agreed, although she suspected that he was a Comintern agent. Her gossip from the sewing classes and the Seventh Day Adventist Church, which she attended, could not have been very important for Dr. Sorge. It seems strange that Miyagi risked disclosing himself to her. Of course, he had known her well in America, and had lived at her home for several years. As it turned out, it was this risk which undid the whole conspiracy. The Japanese police arrested her and her husband on September 28, 1941. Yoshisaburo was found innocent, but Tomo was convicted and sentenced to five years in prison. She was released, with reduction of time for good behavior, at the end of her term, and died since the end of the war.

Akiyama Koji, the only Mercenary

Akiyama Koji was the only member of the ring who didn't work for love of the Cause. According to Miyagi, Akiyama had little interest in causes, and less interest in Miyagi's use of his work. So long as Miyagi kept paying him a modest sixty to a hundred yen a month, Akiyama asked no questions and translated into English anything that Miyagi gave him.

Akiyama was born in 1889, and after finishing a middle school in Kanda Ward, Tokyo, he taught in a primary school. In 1914 he entered Rikkyo University, but before graduating went to America as an employee of an export firm. In Los Angeles he attended night classes at a high school, at the Los Angeles Polytechnic School, and the California Business College, where he was graduated in 1923. For the next ten years, until his return to Japan in 1933, he worked in a bookshop.

Back in Tokyo Akiyama had trouble getting a job till he met Miyagi, whom he had known in America. Miyagi offered him a job translating documents into English, which he gladly accepted. He did not suspect that Miyagi was passing these translations to a foreigner until 1938 or 1939, but he was not deterred even then. After all he had to eat, so he kept the job.

Miyagi commented on Akiyama:

"Akiyama was not a suitable kind of man for intelligence work. I never intended to draw him into our group, but I found him useful for he was ready at hand to translate anything I gave him. He was not interested in social problems, however. I consulted Ozaki in 1939 in hope of obtaining a special translator, but we could not find a satisfactory man. Therefore, I continued to use Akiyama.

"Of course, Akiyama knew I was a Communist, but he never fully understood how secret or important my work was...."

Akiyama was arrested on October 13, 1941 and was sentenced to seven years in prison. He was released on October 10, 1945.

Yasuda Tokutaro, Medical Informant

Yasuda Tokutaro, a physician, was born in 1897, and was graduated from the Medical School of Kyoto Imperial University. While still a medical student he was introduced to Marxian literature by a professor of the University, Kawakami Hajime. He received his M.D. in 1930.

Dr. Yasuda was directed leftward by a cousin who raised him, Yamato Senji (a labor leader, who was assassinated in 1929), by Professor Kawakami, and by Mrs. Kuzumi Fusako. He first became active in the Communist movement when he joined the Proletarian Scientific Research Institute (*Puroretaria Kagaku Kenkyo Jo*) and other Communist front organizations.

Miyagi Yotoku called on Dr. Yasuda in January, 1935, as a patient. In March of the next year Kuzumi Fusako told Dr. Yasuda that Miyagi was a Comintern agent, so that when Miyagi asked his help in September, 1937, the doctor was quite ready to answer his questions. He was able to contribute information chiefly on the state of medical supplies and gossip on troop movements picked up from his patients.

Dr. Yasuda was arrested on June 8, 1942. He was sentenced to two years' imprisonment, but was given a five years' suspension of execution. After the war he ran unsuccessfully for the Lower House of the Diet from Kyoto, on the Communist ticket, is now living in Tokyo and reminiscing of the great days when he was a member of the Sorge-Ozaki ring.

Kawamura Yoshio, Shanghai Contact

The only member of the ring about whom almost nothing is known is Kawamura Yoshio. This man, the chief of the Shanghai office of the *Manshu Nichi Nichi* (*Manchuria Daily News*), was Ozaki's Shanghai agent. Kawamura was arrested on March 31, 1942, and brought to Tokyo for trial. It was established that Kawamura, then aged thirty-two, had been accepted by Sorge as a member of the ring. He was able to supply information on Manchuria because of his job. Unfortunately, however, Kawamura died in jail soon after his arrest, and it was not possible to develop his case with the thoroughness of the others.

Yamana Masazane, Agrarian Expert

The ring's agrarian contact was Yamana Masazane, son of a Hokkaido farmer. He was born in 1902, and his formal education ended with primary school. He became a member of the Hokkaido League (*Hokkaido Rengo Kai*) of the Japan Farmer's Union (*Nippon Nomin Kumiai*) and developed a lifelong interest in agrarian movements. For a time he worked in Manchuria. Through acquaintance with Communist party leaders, including the present Secretary General Tokuda Kyuichi, he became a Communist and joined the Party in November, 1927. After being arrested on March 15, 1928, he was sentenced to five years hard labor for violation of the Peace Preservation Law. He joined Kuzumi Fusako after his release from prison, and through her met Miyagi in March, 1936. At Miyagi's request he agreed to gather information on rural and agrarian questions. Miyagi describes him as follows:

"Yamana had served a sentence for participating in some Communist affair. He was introduced to me by Kuzumi Fusako soon after he came down from Hokkaido. She asked me to help him find a job. I did not intend to use him in connection with our group except to learn something about Japan's agrarian problems, but after he became connected with the Current Politics Society (*Jisei Kai*) and began to bring me news about political and economic affairs I started to make use of him. . . . I began to pay him about sixty yen a month, from the spring of 1936 until the beginning of 1938. When he made trips . . . I paid his expenses.

"I tried to find Yamana a regular job but was unsuccessful. He never told me where or how he lived. We met either at my boardinghouse or at some restaurant in Tokyo.

Some time in 1938 I realized that Yamana wanted to cut his connection with me. I wanted to find out why, so I visited his house which I happened to know at that time. I saw at once that he wanted to leave me because of a woman and that I could not stop him. Soon after that Yamana found a job with an agrarian union. . . . [and not much later] . . . found employment with the Eastern Society (*Tohokai*). He took trips to Karafuto, Hokkaido, Aomori, Akita, Miyagi, Fukushima, Toyama, Ishikawa, and many other places. I wanted to organize a group of my own with members in Tokyo, Magoya, Osaka, Kyushu, Hokkaido, and Hokuriku but I couldn't find the proper people. I thought Yamana could be one of them, but he wanted to lead an easy life and I had to give up the idea."

The police arrested Yamana on December 15, 1941. He was sentenced to twelve years at hard labor, but was released by American order on October 7, 1945.

Taguchi Ugenda, Minor Informant

One of the less useful members of the ring was Taguchi Ugenda, who was introduced to Miyagi by Yamana. Both Taguchi and Yamana were from Hokkaido, and both were members of the Japan Communist party.

Taguchi, born in 1902, finished the Hokkaido Middle School, studied for a time at the Oriental University (*Toyo Daigaku*) but transferred to Meiji Gakuin in 1924. Without graduating he left Meiji to go to Sapporo where he joined a labor union affiliated with the Japan Labor Unions Conference (*Nihon Rodo Kumiai Hyogikai*). He joined the Japan Communist party in December, 1927, a month after Yamana, and was arrested along with Yamana and many other Communists on March 15, 1928. He was sentenced to three years' imprisonment, but with time off for good behavior was out by November, 1929, when he came to Tokyo and promptly met Miyagi. At Miyagi's request he began reporting on Hokkaido, chiefly on economic matters such as oil, coal, and the food supply.

Miyagi remarked of this agent, "I did not intend to enlist (his) help in the beginning because Kuzumi Fusako described him as a 'formalist' unsuitable for espionage. He had already arranged to set up a peat factory in Manchuria. According to my standards he was not a genuine Communist because he was going to Manchuria to make money. He was always hot after some sort of queer enterprise."

After they had the principals, the police soon unearthed Taguchi. They arrested him on October 29, 1941. The court sentenced him to thirteen years in prison, but he, too, was released by U.S. Army order on October 6, 1945.

Nakanishi Ko, Postwar Diet Member

Nakanishi Ko, Diet member, supposedly an expert on China, former chief editorial writer for *Mimpo* and leading member of the Japan Communist party, was associated with Ozaki but does not seem to have been a member of the Sorge ring. He led a Soviet spy ring in China, but his career and his activities so frequently crossed those of the Sorge ring, both during the China and Japan days, that he deserves special mention. The records of his trial in Tokyo after 1942 have not been available, so that it is not possible to give a full account of his espionage activities, but a great deal is known from police records and from his own statements since the end of the war.

Nakanishi, who was born in Mie Prefecture in 1910, went to Shanghai after graduation from middle school in Japan and attended the East Asia Common Script School (*Toa Dobun Shoin*) at which Mizuno Shige was a fellow student. There he joined the Chinese Communist Party's Young Communist League, the Chinese Communist party, and several Communist front organizations, such as the Japan-China Joint Struggle League (*Nishi Toso Domei*), along with Mizuno he took an active part in the Communist-led student strike at his school in 1930, and like Mizuno was arrested by the Japanese consular police for subversive activities. While no evidence is available to prove the point, it is reasonable to assume that not only Mizuno but Nakanishi, too, came under the observation of the Sorge ring at this time, and that his first acquaintance with Ozaki dates from this date.

Nakanishi returned to Japan in February 1932, and immediately joined the China Problems Research Society of the Proletarian Science Research Institute, a Communist-front organization. In April he was arrested and detained for forty days before being released. He then returned to his native Mie Prefecture, where he was active in a secret agrarian reform movement. By June he had gone to Osaka to enter the Ohara Social Problems Research Institute (*Ohara Shakai Mondai Kenkyu Jo*) to work on labor problems. Mizuno, too, worked for this society. Nakanishi only stayed with the Ohara organization till November, 1933, when he looked around for a new job with wider opportunities.

The Investigation Department of the Dairen office of the

South Manchurian Railway employed Nakanishi in May, 1934, and he continued to work for this organization in various offices until his arrest in June, 1942. He served twice in Dairen, once in Tientsin, and longest of all, in Shanghai. Progressively he advanced in rank and pay and responsibility. At this time the South Manchurian Railway, working closely with the Kwantung Army, was investigating a wide range of subjects from the transportation potential of the Trans-Siberian Railway and the capacities of Siberian military bases to the economic and political situation in China. With the progress of the war in China the SMR extended its offices to the chief cities in occupied China, employing over 1,000 men in the investigation branch alone. Naturally, this organization became a primary target for Japanese Communists, and being staffed entirely by civilians it was easier to enter than the Army Intelligence agencies. Out of the 1,000 men about thirty were Japanese Communists, either sympathizers or Party members, who organized their own investigation body so that the results of the research of this intelligence agency came to be at the disposal of the Chinese Communists and the Soviets. Close liaison seems to have been maintained with both. Since the end of the war Nakanishi has boasted that he received a secret commendation directly from Mao Tse-tung, political leader of the Chinese Communist party, for his superior espionage work in Shanghai.

Nakanishi took an active part in the China Problems Research Institute, which was headed in Peiping by Funakoshi Hisao of the Sorge ring. It is reasonable to assume that Funakoshi and Nakanishi worked closely together, and that he was in frequent touch with Agnes Smedley, who headed a branch of Soviet espionage to Peiping for a time. It is not believed, however, that Nakanishi was directly a part of the Sorge ring in Japan. The fact that the Japanese Higher Special Police decided, after lengthy interrogation, that Nakanishi was not a member of the Sorge ring supports this assumption.

One of the lesser members of the Sorge ring informed on Nakanishi Ko. Since Funakoshi Hisao had been arrested on October 22, 1941, while Kawamura Yoshio was not arrested till March 31, 1942, it is possible that the latter was the one to betray Nakanishi, since Funakoshi had full knowledge of him. The Tokyo Metropolitan Police sent special agents to Shanghai in the spring of 1942 to uncover a large group of Japanese Communists who were suspected both of being members of the Sorge ring and of supplying information directly to the Chinese Communists and to the Soviets. On

June 16, 1942 they arrested nearly a hundred men, and held about twenty for prosecution. Nakanishi Ko was one of these who was brought to Tokyo. He was not tried for over three years, not until the prosecutors believed they had secured all the information he possessed. He was tried on September 11, 1945 before the Tokyo District Court, the prosecutor demanding the death penalty for this Japanese subject who had committed treason. On September 28, 1945, the court sentenced him to life imprisonment. This was after the Japanese surrender, and Nakanishi was released from prison on October 10, 1945 under the American order for the release of political prisoners.

While Nakanishi was in prison he wrote a twelve-volume history of the Chinese Communist party, and since the end of the war has become famous not only as an exponent of communism but as an expert on the Chinese Communists. He had joined the Japan Communist party and is one of its best known writers and propagandists. From February, 1946 to August, 1947 he was chief editorial writer of the newspaper *Mimpo,* and simultaneously was a director of the China Research Institute. Nakanishi ran for the upper house of the Diet in the 1950 elections and won a seat in the House of Councilors becoming one of eight Communist party members in the Japanese Parliament.

Communications and Finance

Dr. Sorge used three channels to communicate with the U.S.S.R.: (1) by concealed radio, (2) by special courier, and (3) through the Soviet Embassy. The last channel was too dangerous and he did not resort to it until the very end.

After Klausen arrived one of his first acts was to dispose of the clumsy radio set made by his predecessor and to make a new sending and receiving set. Most of the parts he bought in different shops on the Ginza, while those which it was difficult or dangerous to buy, such as short-wave transmission coils, he made himself from copper pipe. Altogether, during the next six years he remodeled or built three transmitters and three or four receivers with a maximum range of about 2,500 miles. He built them at the homes of different members of the ring. He operated his sets at various places at safe distances from each other, making frequent changes in location. His set was so small that it could be, and was, dismantled and carried in a large brief case. Once he had walked away with his brief case, there was no evidence in the house of his illegal acts except the reasonably innocent appearing permanent outlets. Klausen assumed that

Japanese direction finders could not locate his sender more accurately than within a radius of two square miles. By dismantling his set after each operation and storing it in some distant location he guarded against being caught in a house-to-house search. After his arrest, Klausen discovered that Japanese stations had intercepted many of his messages, but had been unable to decipher them or discover where they came from.

Klausen always used the second story of a wooden Japanese house for his radio station. The houses which he used in irregular sequence were:

Guenther Stein
  Hommura-cho Azabu-ku
  Feb. '36-Oct. '37
Max Klausen
  Shinryudo-cho, Azabu-ku
  Mar. '38-Oct. '38
de Voukelitch
  Sanai-cho, Ushigome-ku
  May '38-Oct. '41
Max Klausen
  Hiroo-cho, Azabu-ku
  Aug. '38-Sep. '41
Edith de Voukelitch
  Kami-Meguro, Meguro-ku
  Mar. '39-Aug. '41

Codes and Ciphers

At first Sorge coded and decoded all messages to "Wiesbaden." In 1937 or 1938, following a motor accident which put him in the hospital, he taught the cipher to Klausen. Messages were in English or German, but the code was a numerical one screened through the pages of the *Statisches Jahrbuch Für Dan Deutsche Reich*. Since most Germans in the Far East had copies of this year book, possession of it would not have aroused suspicion.

Although Japanese stations at home and in Manchuria had been intercepting long series of ciphers for a good many years, they had been unable to get any hint of their origin or meaning. While the call letters indicated Chinese amateur stations this did not satisfy Japanese radio intelligence. Greatly perplexed, they continued to gather a mounting pile of messages, so that when Sorge and his gang were arrested, Japanese intelligence quickly assumed they had discovered their source. They set themselves to break the code. It is not clear whether Klausen helped them in the beginning, but soon he told them the whole story and gave them every assistance. Naturally, the decoded copies of these messages came to be among the most damning pieces of evidence in the trials.

The location of the Soviet receiving station, presumably lying within a radius of 2,000 kilometers from Tokyo, remains a complete mystery; it was never revealed to the radio operators.

Klausen believed it to be Vladivostok, Khabarovsk, or Komsomolsk. Among themselves, the ring referred to the station as Wiesbaden.

According to data collected by the Communications Ministry, the general direction of the station was the Shanghai area before 1940 and the Soviet Far East thereafter.

Arrangement of Contact Time

In the days before the China Incident, when the volume of communications was still relatively small, all radio contacts were initiated by the Russians, who notified the ring as to the time of the next contact on each occasion.

The code employed to announce the details of the next contact was built around the phrase *"Morgenstunde hat Gold im Munde"* (a well-known German saying having the same meaning as "The early bird catches the worm"). The first 21 letters were divided into sets of three to represent the days of the week.

Monday	M	T	T
Tuesday	O	U	G
Wednesday	R	N	O
Thursday	G	D	L
Friday	E	E	D
Saturday	N	H	I
Sunday	S	A	M

Thus, Wednesday was spelled RNO.

The code form for the notice of the next contact was written with the day of the week followed by the Greenwich Meridian Time in 24-hour units added to the day of the month to confuse outside listeners. For example, suppose the next contact was scheduled for 1500 hours on Tuesday (the 16th). Since 15 plus 16 is 31, it would be written OUG 31. As the date was known to fall on the following Tuesday, the receivers had no difficulty decoding the message. Contacts were made at least once a week. This code was not incorporated into the text but attached at the end of the message. In 1938, after the outbreak of the China Incident, Klausen asked that contact be made between 1500 on odd days and Sundays and 1000 the following mornings (Tokyo time). Further details were arranged by the Moscow authorities as follows:

"Starting August 1, we will be standing by for messages from you during the first 15 minutes of every hour."

The reason for operating only between 1500 and 1000 hours was that daylight hours were avoided as much as possible because of poor atmospheric conditions.

After the spring of 1941, the schedule of odd days and Sundays was discontinued and irregular transmission was resumed.

Klausen says that atmospheric conditions were best at sunset and sunrise. He usually worked between the hours of 1600 and 1900, often for four-hour stretches.

The number of transmissions and the number of words dispatched were approximately as follows:

1939	60 times	23,139 words
1940	60 times	29,179 words
1941	21 times	13,103 words

Call Signals

The call signals consisted of five components:

Tokyo   AC (1 number) (2 letters)
Soviet   XU (1 number) (2 letters)

To avoid discovery, the last three were changed constantly as follows: The third component of the Tokyo call signal was derived by adding the month to the date plus two and taking the unit figure of the resulting sum (the figure in the 10 column was discarded).

Couriers

In addition to sending radio messages, Sorge sent a great volume of material by courier, usually in the form of microfilmed documents, chiefly of his own analyses but often actual German or Japanese texts. On occasion some shadowy "Moscow" men appear to have made direct contact with Sorge or Klausen in Tokyo, and to have taken away material. But until 1939 liaison with Moscow was conducted chiefly in Shanghai and Hong Kong. Most of the members of the group, including the reluctant Anna, served as couriers at various times. In April and July, 1936, and again in 1939, Max Klausen took documentary microfilm to Shanghai where he exchanged them for cash and sometimes microfilm, with a stranger who gave a prearranged recognition signal. Once when they projected some of the received microfilm on a wall in the home of de Voukelitch they found that letters from Mrs. Sorge in Russia had been included with the official material.

On these trips, the men found it easy to string the film cartridges on a cord and to hide the improvised belt under their clothing. It was even easier for Mrs. Klausen to hide them. Since she was a former resident of Shanghai, the Japanese police did not think it strange that she should wish to visit her old home from time to time.

In 1937 Richard Sorge took films to Shanghai and Guenther Stein took some to Hong Kong. In October, 1937, and again in November, 1938, Anna went to Shanghai. Anna refused to go at first, but was persuaded by the threat of punishment by Moscow. Orders for her first trip came from Sorge, for the second direct from Russia. Each time Anna carried about thirty film cartridges, hidden in her seemingly ample bosom. She delivered them to men she met at the Sun Sun Department store, a bookstore on Bubbling Well Road, in the lobby of the Cathay Hotel and on the sidewalk of Avenue Haig. Each time she received some five thousand U.S. Dollars ($5,000) which she deposited to Max's account with the Hong Kong and Shanghai Bank, Ltd. Subsequently, Max transferred the money to Tokyo by bank draft.

By 1939 Sorge decided it was too dangerous for members of his ring to travel to China as messengers. The intensification of the war in China so increased the suspicion and scrutiny of Japanese intelligence agencies that the risks had become disproportionate. Subsequently, with the severance of economic ties between Japan and the United States, it became too difficult to secure funds through American banks. In 1939 Sorge radioed a request for establishment of liaison in Japan. Instructions soon came for Klausen, "Two tickets with higher numbers for Fritz. One with a smaller number for liaison man." Soon afterward, Max found two tickets for the Imperial Theater in his mail box at the Tokyo Central Post Office. He took Anna to the show and sat in the low-numbered seat. In the darkness he passed to his right-hand neighbor thirty-eight film cartridges of photographs of documents from the German Embassy. In return his neighbor passed him $5,000.

Klausen's neighbor turned out to be the Soviet Consul in Tokyo, Helge Leonidvitch Vutokevitch. The following April Klausen and Anna attended the *All Girls Opera* at the Takarazuka Theater, where Max handed over another thirty rolls of film and received in return U.S. $3,000 and 2,500 yen. Not long after this pleasant entertainment Vutokevitch returned to Russia and was replaced by Viktor Sergeyevitch Zaitsev, a Soviet Embassy official, who used the cover name of "Serge."

"Serge" met Klausen about ten times, chiefly in Max's office. He was brief and to the point. Sorge was present at the meetings only once. Klausen recorded the meetings in his diary as, "S-TR," for *"Serge Treffen"* meaning "Met Serge." Early in 1941 during one of his visits at Max's office, Serge listed the Sorge ring as he himself knew it:

Name	Alias	Code Name
Richard Sorge	Ramsay	Fix or Inson
Branko de Voukelitch	Gigolo	_____
Ozaki Hozumi	Otto	Invest
Miyagi Yotoku	Joe	Intelli
Dr. Woidt	_____	Kommersant
Viktor S. Zaitsev	Serge	_____
Max Klausen	Fritz	_____

Aside from the information on the aliases and code names, this list is significant chiefly as showing what part of the ring was known to the Soviet espionage agent attached to their Tokyo embassy. It is also significant that this Soviet consul listed himself as a member of the ring.

Money

This extraordinarily bold and successful spy organization cost the Soviet Union practically nothing. Even so they tried to cut down their expenses and in 1940 directed that part of the profits from M. Klausen Shokai should go into the ring. Perhaps they were only wisely trying to forestall the possible apostasy of Max Klausen which his growing wealth was likely to bring about.

The total cost of the Sorge ring was estimated at about 3,000 yen a month. This was an expenditure of considerably less than U.S. $1,500 a month to pay for the extremely valuable work of nearly twenty agents. Since with one exception they all worked for love of the Cause and not for money their monthly pay was merely to cover living and travel costs and not to compensate them for their work. Ozaki, for example, never received a penny for himself, and was actually out of pocket, since he supported some of the agents under him. Sorge, de Voukelitch, and Klausen, of course, had regular incomes from their work, but still they had extra expenses. Klausen was the treasurer, and about once a year he submitted a statement of income and expenses to Sorge, who had it photostated and a copy sent to Russia. During Klausen's service as treasurer from 1936 till October, 1941, he received U.S. $24,500 and 18,300 yen through the couriers, plus about $10,000 in bank remittances, a total of about $40,000. Certainly the information which Sorge sent after June 22, 1941 was worth many millions of dollars to the Soviet Union. Since it had a profound effect on the Soviet deployment of troops, and hence on the stopping of the Germans at the most critical phase of the war its total value is incalculable.

International Reports of Sorge and Ozaki

Sorge sent an immense amount of soundly evaluated intelligence to the U.S.S.R. over the years. Under interrogation from memory alone Ozaki described more than fifty reports and Klausen another fifty. The decoded radio messages added much greater detail.

From 1933 to 1935 Japanese activities in Manchuria, centering around the Chinese Eastern Railway in which the Soviet Union had a half interest, very naturally were of much concern to Moscow. Based on reports made by Ozaki, Miyagi, and then German Ambassador, Dr. Herbert von Dirksen, Sorge was able to report that Japan would not fight the U.S.S.R. over the question of the Chinese Eastern Railway, would devote herself to the development of heavy industries in Manchuria, and would discuss a nonaggression pact with the Soviet Union. In fact, as Sorge was able to report on the basis of information secured through Miyagi and Ozaki in 1935, the Japanese government placed more stress on the China problem than on that of the Soviet Union and any possible advance to the North. The German-Japanese Anti-Comintern Pact of 1936 looked like the real thing, but Sorge was able to report from excellent German Embassy sources that although the Germans had wanted a military pact it was being limited to an anti-Comintern pact because of Japanese reluctance to have trouble with the U.S.S.R.

Sorge made full reports on intentions and operations in North China after July, 1937, as well as on the nature of Japanese mobilization. He transmitted Ozaki's estimate that Japan would fail in her plan to solve her North China problem by a fast campaign and that the war was bound to develop into a long struggle. Throughout the rest of the China War Sorge kept a steady flow of fundamental information to the U.S.S.R.

Sorge Paves Way for Soviet-German Pact

The European picture was very black in the spring of 1939. The U.S.S.R. had a choice of negotiations either with the Anglo-French bloc or with the Germans. After they had learned from Sorge that the Germans had proposed to Tokyo, with the support of Ambassador General Oshima Hiroshi, an alliance directed against the U.S.S.R. and Great Britain, but that the Cabinet, the navy and the Zaibatsu were all opposed to such an alliance and had blocked it, the Soviet government itself entered into the famous, and disastrous, nonaggression pact with Nazi Germany in August, 1939. It was the signature of this pact, securing Hitler's Eastern frontier, which precipitated the Second World War by the invasion of Poland.

At the time of the Nomonhan Incident, in the summer of 1939, when the Red Army and the Japanese Kwantung Army engaged in a full-scale, local war, the Red Army was able to learn Japanese intentions. They learned what units were being dispatched from what parts of Manchuria, as well as what reinforcements would come from Japan. Above all, they learned that the Japanese government did not intend to exploit this incident, but intended to settle it locally, and the Russians conducted themselves accordingly. Aside from his sources in Tokyo, Sorge was able to get a good on-the-spot report from de Voukelitch who as a correspondent was taken to Nomonhan as the guest of the Japanese Army. The Japanese assessment of their lessons at Nomonhan especially their need to mechanize all their forces and develop armored divisions on the German model, was transmitted by Sorge on the basis of information gathered both by the German Embassy and by Miyagi.

On February 16, 1940, Sorge sent a reliable account of Japanese output of munitions, aircraft, and motorcars, along with a report on the factories making these materials as well as iron and steel. From time to time, he brought these figures up to date. In August, 1941, he reported on Japanese petroleum resources, a top secret bit of information of the most vital importance in estimating both Japanese war plans and capabilities. He reported that there was in storage in Japan sufficient petroleum for a two years' use by the navy, half a year by the army, and half a year by the nation at large. His sources were the German Embassy and Miyagi.

The crucial year was 1941. After earlier general reports, on May 20, 1941, Sorge flashed the urgent warning that the Reichswehr would concentrate from 170 to 190 divisions on the Soviet border and on June 20 would attack along the whole frontier. The main direction of the drive would be toward Moscow. It will be recalled that this attack did occur on June 22. Naturally, thereafter, the answer to the question of Japanese attack from the East became the most vital mission of the Sorge ring. All questions, whether of Japanese-American relations, the war in China, or internal politics were subordinated to answering that basic question. Without a sound answer the Red Army could not draw on their Far Eastern Army for use in the West, and, as the event showed, only a massing of limitless reserves made possible the stopping of the violent German thrusts.

Sorge could not come by the answer immediately, partly because it had not been decided definitely by the responsible Japanese authorities. Naturally, Ambassador Ott was urging the Japanese to enter the war and distract the Russians on their Eastern frontier. Sorge was able to report on July 2, immediately after the Imperial Council of that date, that the Japanese government had decided to push southward into French Indo-China and seize various bases. Meanwhile, while adhering to their neutrality treaty with the U.S.S.R., in view of the possibility of war with the Soviet Union, they would mobilize their whole forces. Late in July Sorge reported that a few troops from the Tokyo-Osaka areas had been sent south, but that to advance into Thailand and Malaya they needed 300,000 men. So far there were only 40,000 men in Indo-China.

Ozaki Keeps Finger on War Pulse

Sorge's estimates of late July and early August, based on information supplied by Ozaki, Miyagi, and the German Embassy, showed that one million new men had been mobilized, that the great majority had been sent to China or further south, and that only a small proportion were being sent to Manchuria. By the end of August he reported that the German Embassy had lost hope of Japan's joining in the war against Russia in 1941, and on the basis of Miyagi's information he reported that the Kwantung Army did not want to fight the Red Army that year. While the decision might be changed if the Russians were crushingly defeated in the West, reported Sorge, the progress of the German Army had been too slow to encourage the Japanese government which was devoting its attentions to negotiations with the United States and to a probable thrust southward.

Sorge maintained a steady watch and reported on United States-Japanese negotiations during the summer and fall of

1941. His information was full and accurate, since Ozaki was so close to Konoye, the key man in the negotiations. During early October Sorge reported on the third mobilization, completed in mid-September, and subsequently that men from 25 to 35 years old had been called up. He also reported that the mobilization in December and January would be greater than in the previous year. While he did transmit Prince Konoye's optimistic views, he informed his superiors that the Japanese Navy planned to move south if Japan did not receive a satisfactory reply by the first week in October. "The next two or three weeks will be the most crucial with respect to Japan's advance to the south."

By October 15 Sorge had transmitted his final sober conclusions that the Japanese had decided to move south and that there now was no serious danger of an attack by the Kwantung Army across the Siberian frontier. He felt that his mission was completed and drafted a dispatch suggesting his recall to the Soviet Union; Klausen argued that this request was premature, and the message was never sent.

Ozaki's Contacts and Methods

Next to Sorge, Ozaki Hozumi was by far the most important member of the ring. During his years on the *Asahi,* to which his contributions were prolific, he firmly established his reputation as a China expert. In recognition of his abilities he was transferred to Tokyo in 1934 and was appointed to the East Asia Problems Investigation Society (*Toa Mondai Chosa Kai*) within the *Asahi* for the study of China problems. He added to his reputation by numerous signed articles on China affairs in such popular magazines as *Central Review* (*Chuo Koron*), to the English language *Contemporary Japan,* and by his five books, from *China Facing the Storm* (*Arashi Ni Tatsu Shina*) in 1937 to *Strength of the Great Powers in China* (*Ajia Ni Okeru Rokkuo No Chikara*) in 1941.

In April, 1937 Ozaki became a member of the China Section of the Showa Study Society (*Showa Kenkyo Kai*) sponsored by Prince Konoye Fumimaro. The head of its China section was Kazami Akira, who soon became chief secretary of the first Konoye Cabinet in June, 1937. Ozaki then succeeded Kazami as head of the China section but he didn't lose touch with Kazami. Immediately after a cabinet meeting to discuss policy on the outbreak of the China Incident at Marco Polo Bridge on July 7, 1937, Ozaki called on Kazami at his office. Ozaki warned Kazami that Japan's attitude and decisions would decide whether this affair would develop into a second world war. Kazami refused to take this gloomy prophecy seriously, and remarked, "Our minds are made up, don't worry!" so Ozaki went on to see Ushiba, Konoye's private secretary, where he repeated this warning. He then published his conclusions in an article, "The Nanking Government," appearing in *Chuo Koron* in September, 1937.

By the next summer Japan was hopelessly bogged down in the China War. As a war measure, the Foreign Office set up a special investigative agency in Peiping to study political, social and economic conditions in North China. Kazami, now in a more somber frame of mind, wished to retain a China expert in Tokyo as an adviser, and chose Ozaki Hozumi. In this manner Ozaki, secret Communist and Soviet spy, first came to hold official position as Unofficial Adviser to the Cabinet (*Naikaku Shokutaku*) from July, 1938 until the fall of the government the following January. Perhaps because his pessimism coincided with that of the Konoye group he was not suspected of being other than a loyal Japanese.

As cabinet adviser, naturally, Ozaki had access to important state documents, of which he made the best use for Dr. Sorge. Even more important than his official positions was his close association with two old friends of college days at the Tokyo First Higher School. Ushiba Tomohiko and Kishi Michizo were both private secretaries to Prince Konoye, three times premier of Japan. Around those two men was centered the "Breakfast Group," sometimes called the "Wednesday Group," an informal discussion society of bright young men around Prince Konoye. Ushiba and Kishi found it pleasant and informative to invite writers, journalists, professors, and other stimulating persons to dinner to draw out their opinions on current subjects. All conversation was off the record and the baleful Thought Police do not seem to have listened in. When dinners became inconvenient these men met at breakfast, hence the name "Breakfast Group." At first the meetings were held twice monthly. From 1939 to the autumn of 1941, they met every Wednesday, giving the group its second name. During the first Konoye Cabinet they met at Ushiba's home, but later had breakfasts at the Mampoi Hotel. From April, 1939 until November, 1940, they met at Saionji's home. From then until so many were pulled in by the police that there was no quorum to meet, they assembled at the premier's official residence back of the Diet Building.

After the fall of the Konoye Cabinet on January 4, 1939, had deprived Ozaki of his official link with the cabinet he was appointed as adviser to the South Manchurian Railway and attached to the Investigation Section of the Tokyo Office. He continued to hold this post till his arrest. Since the South

Manchurian Railway was interested in every activity in Manchuria and Siberia, Ozaki was in an excellent position to learn anything that might become known to any Japanese. The railway was closely controlled by the Japanese and Manchurian governments, so that for practical purposes Ozaki was an intelligence officer of these governments with a special assignment to study Manchuria and Soviet affairs. After early 1940 the Information Section of the SMR exchanged information freely with the Information Section of Mitsui Bussan Kaisha, so that Sorge's target of Japanese heavy industry was amply covered.

Although Ozaki used all of his sources for the gathering of information for Sorge, and utilized his intimacy with highly placed friends to obtain documents and news, he never passed on undigested information. He stored up his knowledge, weighed it against other relevant data, and made a preliminary evaluation. He discussed his conclusions with officials, his associates, and friends, and with the members of the Breakfast Club. He presented only final evaluations in answer to Sorge's questions, although from time to time he did borrow some document to be photographed by de Voukelitch before he returned it to its proper owner. Frequently, when some friend would ask his opinion, he asked for the basic documents to study before he could render sensible advice. These documents he often took to his home, and since he was entitled to receive them in line of duty no one thought anything about it. Sometimes, officials like young Saionji Kinkazu would give him top secret information to get his reaction, because he trusted so greatly his judgment and integrity.

During his trial Ozaki gave the following description of his activity:

"If you ask me for special points of my technique, I would say that my activity was characterized by a total lack of special method . . . my success lay in my attitude toward the job. By nature I am a sociable person. I like people; I can make friends with most people. Moreover, I like to be kind to people. Not only is my circle of friends wide, I am on intimate terms with most of them. My sources of information have been these friends.

"I have never looked for specific information . . . I have formed my own opinion on the subject in hand, formulating in my own mind a comprehensive picture of a general trend on the basis of various reports and rumors. I never ask specific leading questions.

". . . In these days of political unrest, individual news items have little intrinsic value, however important or secret they may be. This is because even important decisions are apt to be changed suddenly. For instance, the government or the army may wish to be stubborn, but external circumstances beyond their control often force a change of heart. Therefore, the important thing is to ascertain the general trend rather than to know exactly what has been said or what has been decided. The only information of importance which I was confident I might obtain in advance was the exact timing of a possible attack on Russia by Japan."

It was Miyagi Yotoku, rather than Ozaki, who devoted himself consistently to the small details, such as activation of divisions, new weapons, troop movements, reports on casualties, and the like. A great deal of this information was easy for a Japanese to pick up from gossip in bars, talk in a doctor's office, in a ladies' sewing circle, or in a military barracks. While the Red Army was primarily interested in the big picture which Ozaki was painting for them, they did not share his lack of interest in specific bits of secret information, and Miyagi kept supplying it through his autonomous intelligence net. Despite his disclaimers at his trial, however, Ozaki, too, supplied such information, as for example, a complete division roster in 1941.

Ozaki on World Affairs

Ozaki's study of world events had convinced him as early as 1937 that the China Incident would develop into a second world war. He believed that this second world war would end not in a redistribution of colonies, as in the case of the first world war, but in a fundamental social change throughout the world. The Communist revolution, he believed, which had started in Russia would reach a decisive stage, even though it could not be expected to reach its final completion so soon.

As for Japan, Ozaki considered the country's economic structure unsound because of feudalistic tradition, poverty of natural resources, and the preponderance of military expenditures. Japan would be the first to undergo a fundamental social upheaval, he thought. In the end, Japan was destined to clash with England and America. She would be victorious during the first stages of the war, but the victory would be short-lived because of Japan's economic weakness and because of her exhaustion from the prolonged China Affair. This prediction was made by Ozaki during interrogation of March 3, 1942, in the midst of the Japan's military successes. In the final stage, the ruling classes would be powerless to change the course of the country or to effect its reconstruction. The proletariat alone could save the nation, he believed. He thought that Japan's only proper course was to join with the Soviet Union and with Soviet help change and reconstruct her social and economic system. When Japan had become a socialist state and when Communist hegemony had been established in China, Japan and China with the Soviet Union could form the nucleus of a "New Order in East Asia."

His political opinions were camouflaged in various ways to preserve a cloak of legality, but his real aim was always to reorganize Japan into a state which could co-operate with Soviet Russia and Communist China. He hoped to create a new order in East Asia as a step toward a new world order, and knowing that he enjoyed the confidence of the Russian leaders and the Chinese Communists, he dreamed of becoming the head of a reorganized pro-Communist Japan.

His idea of a "New Order in East Asia," as it appears in the interrogation records, seems particularly significant in the light of the postwar Pan-Asiatic trends:

"I have already told you that the present world capitalist society will inevitably transform itself into a world Communist society, even though, historically speaking, such a transformation cannot take place overnight, as witnessed by the fact that the Soviet Union has been the only full-fledged Communist state in the world since 1917, and that the Chinese Soviet government, which enjoys regional autonomy, is the only other example of a Communist society.

"Judging from the situation in Europe and the conflicts of interests between the imperialist powers in China, I came to the conclusion about 1935 that a second world war was at hand, and my opinion was fortified by the outbreak of the China Incident. It was my belief that the defeated and war-torn powers in World War II would experience socialist revolutions, exactly as Russia did in World War I, and that these revolutions, giving birth to socialist states, would complete the world revolution.

"I believed that the process leading to world revolution would be as follows:

"1. The Soviet Union ought to and would maintain a policy of peace, remaining aloof from all conflicts between imperialist powers.

"2. The conflict of Japan, Germany, and Italy with England and America, which could be interpreted as a struggle between a group of modified imperialist states and a group of true imperialist states, would degenerate into a protracted war of attrition ending in common ruin. The war would result in victory for one side and social revolution for the other.

"3. Even the victorious states would be so exhausted that they might very probably be obliged to transform themselves into socialist states, especially in the face of the comparative increase in Russia's strength. In this connection, and particularly in view of Japan's position in the China Incident and the Far East in general, I concluded that it was more than likely that we would experience a socialist revolution in this country caused by complete internal exhaustion and that this development would occur regardless of whether Japan attacked Russia, whether she co-operated with England and America, or whether she maintained her southern policy, fought England and America, and won a temporary victory. The first stage of the revolution would be marked by a transformation of the nation's internal structure which would begin, at the earliest, during the second half of the same year. I made this prediction to Sorge about July, 1941.

"I was aware that the revolutionary forces in Japan would be very weak during the period of transition, and that a complete transformation could not be accomplished and stabilized by a domestic reorganization alone, particularly in view of the fact that the nation was in the midst of a struggle against British and American imperialism. This consideration led me to realize the necessity of close co-operation by the Soviet Union and a Communist China with a Japan which had liberated itself from the capitalist structure of society. What I have called the 'New Order in East Asia' is a league of the peoples of the Far East headed by the U.S.S.R., China, and Japan.

"The creation of such a co-operative body would not necessarily entail the communization of every component nation. In the transitional period, China, for instance, could have a political structure conforming to the so-called New Democracy, which is a thoroughgoing application of the principles of Sun Yat-sen, and Japan could be a socialistic national unit, preserving all the distinctive qualities of the Japanese. The important thing is that all the nations of the Far East be united in close co-operation with Russia, China, and Japan. India, Burma, Siam, the Dutch Indies, French Indo-China, and the Philippines, liberated from England, America, France, and the Netherlands, should form national units and enter into political, economic, and cultural co-operation with the Japanese-Russian-Chinese coalition. For the time being, these national units need not be Communist states but may adopt political structures conducive to their independence and mutual assistance. In addition, we must also consider, as possible components of the New Order in East Asia, Mongolian, Mohammedan, Korean, and Manchurian national units. Whether the Korean people should form a separate state or be made part of the Japanese national unit must be decided in consideration of conditions in the Far East as a whole, public opinion in Korea, and the extent of Korea's economic self-sufficiency. I would like to see the replacement of Manchukuo by a co-operative, multi-racial Communist society.

"Such is the outline of what I planned under the name of 'New Order in East Asia.' It goes without saying that the new order was to form a link in the chain of world revolution, and it was my belief from the outset that the China Incident had made it a prerequisite to the total collapse of world capitalism. I was confident of enlisting Russian aid and co-operation because I had been closely connected for more than ten years with the leaders of the Comintern and the Soviet Union through my work with Sorge. I also had no doubts concerning China's co-operation."

Ozaki's single allegiance was to the Communist cause. He recognized no proper boundaries between the various countries or between the various Communist organizations throughout the world. The earth was one world centered in the Third International, which happened to be in Russia. The benefits which the U.S.S.R. might derive from the spread of communism were merited by the assumption of leadership of world communism by the Russian Communist Party and by the Soviet government. In March, 1942, Ozaki declared to the prosecutor:

"In my long intercourse with Sorge in Japan, I was often requested to give information which had a direct bearing upon the plans for the defense of the Soviet Union. Hence I suspected that the data which I submitted was being used directly by the U.S.S.R. However, this did not disturb my peace of mind because the defense of the U.S.S.R. was one of the duties of members of the International Communist Party. In brief, our group belonged to the Comintern. The Comintern today is almost completely in the hands of the Russian Communist Party. The Russian Communist Party is the central force in the Soviet government. Thus, in a sense, all three organizations can be considered as one."

It will be remembered that Sorge was an agent of the Red Army, not the Comintern. This was a minor detail as far as Ozaki was concerned. His loyalty was to the Comintern; his channel was Sorge.

Ozaki supplied Sorge with crucial information during the decisive months of 1941. The information was interrelated but for convenience may be classified as relating to: (1) Russo-Japanese relations, (2) Possibility of war between Germany and Russia, and (3) Japanese-American negotiations.

Sound Estimates by Ozaki

Ozaki's accounts of his reports on these three subjects can be summarized as follows: After the signature of the Soviet-German nonagression pact in 1939, the possibility of a Soviet-Japanese war became more remote. When the German Wehrmacht invaded Russia in June, 1941, however, the danger again became great. Ozaki then concentrated his efforts on learning the details of Japanese mobilization, industrial strength, and actual war plans. He paid much attention to troop movements during the general mobilization of July, 1941. When the German Army was stuck at Smolensk, however, and the relations between the United States and Japan steadily worsened he learned that some who earlier had agreed to the general mobilization in expectation of an early Soviet collapse had become hesitant about attacking the U.S.S.R. Later about the middle of August he discovered that the Japanese government had decided against war with Russia. He transmitted this vital information to Dr. Sorge.

Ozaki's close relationship with Prince Konoye's advisers gave him unsurpassed opportunities to learn the exact nature and progress of Japanese-American negotiations during the summer and early fall of 1941. He reached the conclusions that despite numerous Japanese-American common interests great disparity between the positions of the two powers was such that compromise was impossible. Although the upper strata of the Japanese political and financial circles were anxious to avoid war, the Japanese people, as a result of violent military propaganda since 1937, were confident that they could successfully win their "holy war" and were opposed to compromise with the United States and Great Britain. Although the economic situation in Japan as a whole was extremely bad, the fighting services, especially the navy, had never been so well equipped. By the beginning of October, Ozaki was able to give his considered opinion that Japan would embark upon a major military campaign to the South, which would include the capture of Singapore. He only erred in his timing, for he believed that Japan would not attack Russia in 1941, but before the year was out would attack southward against the United States and Great Britain. Retrospectively, it is clear that Ozaki made a completely

sound estimate of the situation, and the government of the
U.S.S.R. was fully informed on Japanese intentions.

DISCOVERY, IMPRISONMENT, DEATH

Ito Ritsu—Unwitting Judas

Dr. Richard Sorge and his group were exposed through
no errors of their own. Their operations were faultless; no
one ever suspected them. Paradoxically it was a Communist,
Ito Ritsu, one of the four or five most influential leaders
in the postwar Japanese Communist Party, who betrayed
them out of malice and jealousy. Even he had no conception
of what he was doing. Although under suspicion of Communist sympathies Ito Ritsu worked in the investigation department of the Tokyo branch of the South Manchurian
Railway, the same organization which Ozaki was serving as
special adviser. Then aged twenty-nine, he was arrested in
June, 1941 on suspicion of secret Communist activities. Under guidance of officers of the Tokyo Metropolitan Police
Board, Ito made full confession, claimed to have erred by
his Communist faith, and then began to implicate others.
Among those on whom he informed was a woman, Kitabayashi Tomo, whom he had known as a former member
of the American Communist Party. He had noted that since
her return to Japan, she had refused to have any intercourse
with Communists, and appeared to have become an apostate.
But she continually asked questions on all sorts of matters.
Possibly hoping to enlist the aid of his enemy, the police, for
the punishment of a party traitor, Ito named this woman as
a Communist and a probable spy. It does not seem that Ito
Ritsu had any real grounds to think of her as a spy, and
certainly he never imagined that she was a member of the
most successful ring of spies ever to operate in Japan on
behalf of his spiritual fatherland.

The police at once began hunting for Kitabayashi Tomo,
and upon finding her, put her on the watch list to develop
her contacts. They did not arrest her until September 28,
1941, at Konagawa-machi, Wakayama Prefecture, when they
pulled her in along with her innocent husband. Mrs. Kitabayashi does not seem to have been a very strong character.
She soon confessed, and named Miyagi as her mentor. Miyagi
was arrested on October 10. From his attempted suicide
and from evidence found in his house, the police realized
that he was a member of an important spy ring. Much
information was picked up from continuous interrogation of

Miyagi, a frail, consumptive man who certainly was not treated gently. He talked freely. Much more was gathered by using his empty house as bait and picking up all callers. Ozaki was soon uncovered, and by October 14, he, too, was behind bars. Since these men had not established an emergency warning system, and only met by prearrangement, none of them was able to warn any of the others.

Days of Anxiety

Max Klausen went to Sorge's home on October 15, 1941 to discuss a projected transmission to the U.S.S.R. Sorge was disturbed. Miyagi had arranged to meet him on the 13th, but for the first time he had missed an appointment. Ozaki was supposed to come to the meeting on the 15th but he too had not appeared and both Klausen and Sorge were worried. Sorge showed Klausen the draft of a dispatch on the Japanese Army's advance in Indo-China, followed by a request for new instructions based on his belief there was no further reason for the group to continue operations in Japan. Klausen thought this message was premature, and returned it to Sorge unsent.

Two days later Klausen again went to Sorge's house, where he found de Voukelitch who also was much disturbed by the silence of Miyagi and Ozaki. On his way home, Klausen met an officer of the Special Higher Section of the Metropolitan Police (*Tokkora*), named Aoyama. This meeting upset him greatly. He wondered if it were more than accidental, and debated in his own mind whether to burn the documents then in his possession and bury his transmitter in the garden. Finally, he decided to do nothing and went to bed.

The next morning, October 18, while Max was still in bed, Aoyama and another police officer walked in and arrested him. Anna was not arrested until November 19. While Aoyama was telling Max to get dressed and come along, other officers were giving similar instructions to Dr. Richard Sorge and Branko de Voukelitch. By October 18, 1941, all the principals of the Sorge ring were in jail and what probably was the most successful and most unusual organization of Red Army Intelligence anywhere in the world was completely broken.

Sorge's Uneasy German Friends

Sorge's arrest was a great shock to his close friends, Ambassador Ott and the Gestapo chief, Colonel Joseph Meisinger. They could only believe that the Japanese had committed another of the blunders for which they were famous, and they worked hard to get their friend out of jail. There also was a disturbing question: If by some remote chance, good Nazi Sorge actually was a Soviet spy, where did that leave two highly placed Nazi officials who had trusted and confided in him for so long? But the obstinate Japanese police were adamant. They insisted that they had the principals of the most dangerous spy ring ever discovered in Japan.

Ott and Meisinger reported the arrest to Berlin, but tried to minimize their relations with Sorge, so that if by some weird chance the Japanese police were right, their reputations would not be hurt too badly. After the turn of the year an agent of the German counterintelligence, Abwehr, in Harbin, heard a somewhat garbled account of the Sorge affair from his Tokyo contact and reported on it to his principals in Berlin. It was not till then that the German government became really disturbed. Von Ribbentrop sharply demanded an explanation from Ott. Ultimately, he replaced him with Dr. Heinrich Stahmer, so that the unhappy Ott sat out the war in Peiping, since he couldn't very well get back to Germany. Meanwhile, in reply to Meisinger's inquiry, Gestapo headquarters in Berlin turned up a complete dossier on Sorge from his earlier days in Germany, indicating his Soviet connections. Meisinger turned this over to the Japanese, and in some manner managed to save his own political skin. He was still German Gestapo representative in Japan when Eisenhower accepted the German surrender in 1945. He was flown to Poland in the autumn of 1945, and charged with commission of atrocities at Warsaw, where he was hanged.

The Japanese Police Records

The Japanese police records show that the following persons were arrested in connection with the Sorge case:

Name	Age	Occupation	Date of Arrest
Kitabayashi, Tomo	57	Dressmaker	Sept. 28, 1941
Miyagi, Yotoku	40	Artist	Oct. 10, 1941
Akiyama, Koji	53	None	Oct. 13, 1941
Kuzumi, Fusako	53	Company employee	Oct. 13, 1941
Ozaki, Hozumi	42	R.R. Consultant	Oct. 15, 1941
Mizuno, Shige	33	Editor	Oct. 17, 1941
Sorge, Richard	48	Journalist	Oct. 18, 1941
Klausen, Max Gottfried	44	Manufacturer	Oct. 18, 1941
De Voukelitch, Branko	38	Journalist	Oct. 18, 1941
Kawai, Teikichi	42	Company employee	Oct. 22, 1941
Taguchi, Ugenda	40	Broker	Oct. 29, 1941
Klausen, Anna	43	None	Nov. 19, 1941
Yamana, Masazane	41	Company employee	Dec. 15, 1941

Kitabayashi, Yoshisaburo	61	None	Sept. 28, 1941
Okai, Yasumasa	26	Student	Oct. 11, 1941
Haga, Yu	44	Research Consultant	Oct. 12, 1941
Suzuki, Kamenosuke	50	Broker	Oct. 13, 1941
Matsumoto, Itsuo	21	China Research Inst.	Oct. 18, 1941
Takahashi, Yu	32	S.M.R.R. employee	Oct. 22, 1941
Akemine, Miye	32	Government Consultant	Oct. 25, 1941
Shinozuka, Torao	41	Factory owner	Nov. 14, 1941
Takeda, Takeshi	39	Laborer	Nov. 24, 1941
Takeda, Toshiko	31	None	Nov. 24, 1941
Funakoshi, Hisao	41	China Research Inst.	Jan. 4, 1942
Kawamura, Yoshio	33	Manshu Nichi-Nichi	Mar. 31, 1942
Koshiro, Yoshinobu	34	Company employee	Apr. 11, 1942
Yasuda, Tokutaro	45	Doctor	Jun. 8, 1942
Tanaka, Shinjiro	43	None	Mar. 15, 1942
Kikuchi, Hachiro	31	War Correspondent	Mar. 16, 1942
Saionji, Kinkazu	37	Former Consultant Foreign Ministry	1942
Inukai, Ken	47	House of Representatives	Apr. 4, 1942
Kaieda, Hisataka	35	R.R. employee	Apr. 11, 1942
Goto, Noriaki	44	R.R. employee	1942
Miyanishi, Yoshio	33	S.M.R. Research Dept.	Apr. 13, 1942
Isono, Kiyoshi	36	War Correspondent	Apr. 28, 1942

The police proceeded unhurriedly with the investigation, although Premier Tojo Hideki kept urging speed. So many of their prisoners talked freely that they had no problem in getting a full picture of the whole case and in separating the guilty from the innocent. Having proved their case, they became concerned with the deeper implications of the spy ring. They wanted to know more than the mere facts of how the spies had operated and what they had found out. They wanted to know what had motivated them, especially the Japanese traitors. Although Sorge attempted to maintain silence, and was most contemptuous of Klausen's turning informant, before five months had passed, even he came to talk freely and, seemingly, willingly.

The police discovered that Klausen's prosperity had dulled his enthusiasm for the Soviet cause. His growing disillusionment, as well as a heart ailment which had kept him in bed from April to August, 1940, made him reluctant to send the radio traffic which Sorge was preparing for him in increasing volume. Until the autumn of 1940, however, he had sent every message. From then on he had begun to cut down and during 1941 transmitted only about a third of the messages. Not being suspicious, neither Vladivostok nor Sorge could check on what was not sent. Klausen did receive complaints from "Wiesbaden," but he replied that atmospheric conditions interfered with his work. Subsequently, in July, 1941, when Sorge gave him the call signal and wave length of a new radio station with which he was to communicate in addition to the old one, Klausen failed to use it.

Klausen's diary substantiated this testimony. It shows that in 1939 he sent 23,139 word groups; in 1940, 29,179 word groups; but in 1941, the most critical year, only 13,103 word groups. Since Sorge himself sent 40,000 word groups in 1941, however, Klausen's sabotage had not interfered materially with the success of the mission.

Because of the evidence of Klausen's change of heart, and because of his free confession, the Japanese court only gave him life imprisonment. To Anna, upon whom they looked as a woman who had worked against her will they gave three years. She was out waiting for Max when he was released from the Akita prison on October 9, 1945 by order of the U.S. Army.

Ozaki had never really feared the consequences of his treason. He had always believed that if he were discovered all he need do was die. Actually he found this not so simple. Questions of affection for his family, who never suspected his treason, and of loyalty to the innocent friends whom he had involved weighed heavily upon him. His confessions were filled with the testimony of a conscience weighted by the guilt of having wronged good friends.

After a full and unhurried investigation the various members of the Sorge ring were brought to trial, separately, *in camera*. Only the briefest mention of the case was released to the press in May, 1942. In this release the Japanese Intelligence deliberately connected the accused with the Comintern net, although they had established that the ring worked for the Red Army. There was no point in telling the Russians all they knew.

Sentences were handed down by the Tokyo District Court in September, 1943. Both Sorge and Ozaki appealed to the Supreme Court. Oddly, Sorge and Ozaki both claimed that they had not done anything illegal. Their theory of defense was that they had not used force to acquire their secrets and they they had passed to Moscow only information available to any intelligent man. Sorge summed up his defense thus:

Sorge's Defense

"Japanese laws are subject to interpretation, either broadly or according to the strict letter of the text. Although leakages of information may, strictly speaking, be punishable by law in practice the Japanese social system is not amenable to the keeping of secrets. . . . I consider that in the drawing up of the indictment insufficient consideration was given to our activity and to the nature of the information which we obtained. Data which de Voukelitch supplied was neither secret nor important; he brought in only news which was well known to every press correspondent. The same may be said of Miyagi who was in no position to obtain state secrets. What may be termed political information was procured by Ozaki and by me.

"I obtained my information from the German Embassy, but here again I consider that little if any of it could be termed 'state secret.' It was given to me voluntarily. To obtain it I resorted to no strategy for which I should be punished. I never used deceit or force. Ambassador Ott and Commander Scholl asked me to help them write reports, especially Scholl, who put much confidence in me and asked me to read all of his own reports before he sent them to Germany. As for me, I placed much trust in this information because it was compiled and evaluated by competent military and naval attachés for the use of the German General Staff. I believe that the Japanese government, in giving data to the German Embassy expected some of it to leak out.

"Ozaki obtained much of his news from the Breakfast Group. But the Breakfast Group was not an official organization. Such information as was exchanged within the group must have been discussed by other similar cliques, of which there were many in Tokyo in those days. Even such data as Ozaki considered important and secret was actually no longer so, because he had procured it indirectly after it had left its secret source."

The Supreme Court was not impressed by this logic. Sorge's appeal was dismissed in January, and Ozaki's in April, 1944.

It is an interesting and perhaps surprising commentary on the quality of Japanese civil justice to note that in the midst of a bitter war, the most dangerous spies ever captured were given the benefit of every protection offered by Japanese law. It also seems surprising that of the nearly twenty guilty men and women only two were sentenced to death, although under Japanese law every one of them had incurred the death penalty.

The following is a list of the convicted prisoners, as well as their sentences and ultimate fates:

Name	Sentence	Fate	Date
Sorge, Richard	Death	Hanged	Nov. 7, 1944
Ozaki, Hozumi	Death	Hanged	Nov. 7, 1944
Voukelitch, Branko de	Life	Died	Jan. 13, 1945
Miyagi, Yotoko	No Sentence	Died	Aug. 2, 1945
Klausen, Max	Life	Released	Oct. 9, 1945
Koshiro, Yoshinobu	15 years	Released	Oct. 8, 1945
Taguchi, Ugenda	13 years	Released	Oct. 6, 1945
Mizuno, Shigo	13 years	Died	Mar. 22, 1945
Yamana, Masazane	12 years	Released	Oct. 7, 1945
Funakoshi, Hisao	10 years	Died	Feb. 27, 1945
Kawai, Teikichi	10 years	Released	Oct. 10, 1945
Kawamura, Yoshio	No Sentence	Died	Dec. 15, 1945

Kuzumi, Fusako	8 years	Released	Oct. 8, 1945
Kitabayashi, Tomo	5 years	Released Unknown Date	
Akiyama, Koji	7 years	Released	Oct. 10, 1945
Klausen, Anna	3 years	Released	Oct., 1945
Yasunda, Tokutaro	2 years with 5 years suspension.		

In addition Saionji was found guilty of passing secret information to an unauthorized person, Ozaki, and was given a sentence of three years' imprisonment with stay of execution. The court and prosecutors recognized that Saionji's guilt had been too great a trust in a friend, and not a conscious act of treason. This was an obvious "whitewash"; it is understandable in the light of this man's family connection; he was the adopted son of Prince Saionji, last remaining *genro* revered by the nation.

Although the Supreme Court had denied their appeals in January and April, 1944, neither Ozaki nor Sorge was informed definitely of the time set for his execution. During the intervening months they were questioned from time to time, chiefly on the wider implications of their conspiracy. While Ozaki was more loquacious than Sorge both talked quite freely. Both men bore themselves well during these last hopeless days. Sorge had boasted that Stalin thought highly of his work and that if Japan and the U.S.S.R. should reach an understanding Stalin would secure his release. Ozaki filled part of his dreary days writing many letters to his wife, part of which have since appeared as a best-selling book, *Love Was Like a Falling Star* (*Aije wa Hoshi no Furu Goteku*).

Ozaki Is Hanged

Finally the last day came. Early on the morning of November 7, 1944, Ozaki had just finished a postcard to his wife full of solicitude for her aged father. He had no reason to suspect that this day would end any differently from any other. When the governor of Sugamo Prison entered his cell, however, he knew at once that his time had come. He changed his clothing for a set of clean garments which he had been saving for this day, and composed himself for his final grim minutes.

The prison governor, Ichijima, formally asked the name, age, and domicile of the condemned man. Having officially ascertained that this was the man for whom death had been decreed, he stated that by order of the Minister of Justice, Ozaki's execution would take place that day. He added that if Ozaki wished to leave behind a will he should entrust it to the Chief Chaplain, a Buddhist priest. Ozaki listened with outward calmness and courtesy and bowed formally in the Japanese manner.

Led by the governor and other officials, Ozaki Hozumi then walked down from death row, across the prison courtyard to the place where stands the small concrete execution chamber hidden by high walls. When the condemned man walked through the only door of this awesome building, he found himself standing in a small anteroom facing a large, beautiful, taper-lit altar to Amidha Buddha. The Chief Chaplain offered Ozaki tea and cake and inquired who should be notified of his death and how he wished to dispose of his possessions. After hearing Ozaki's explanation about his written will and giving Ozaki time to compose himself to listen, the chaplain said:

"Life and death are one and the same thing to one who has attained impersonal beatitude. Impersonal beatitude can be attained by entrusting everything to the mercy of the Buddha."

Then with Ozaki kneeling before the image of the Buddha the chaplain recited the Three Promises of the Great Sutra of Constant Life (*Dai Muryoju Kyo*). Ozaki listened quietly, burned incense, closed his eyes, and bowed. Then he thanked all the officials present for their courtesy and indicated that he was ready.

Ozaki was led around the side of the altar and found himself in a gloomy, windowless, bare room, with a gallows standing in the center. He was led across the room and placed beneath the gallows, while a noose was affixed around his neck. There were no stairs to climb, no platform to stand on. The trap was in the floor immediately beneath his feet.

Ozaki began to recite the simple Buddhist ritual of comfort, "*Namu Amida Butsu.*" When he had recited the phrase twice the trap was sprung. This was at 0933. At 0951 Ozaki Hozumi was pronounced dead.

The same day his attorney was notified of his death, and when his wife presented herself at the prison all that remained of Ozaki Hozumi, Japanese subject, Communist fanatic and Soviet spy, was delivered to her.

Sorge Follows Ozaki

Ozaki's body had scarcely been removed from the execution chamber befor the prison governor, Ichijima, was making his final, solemn call on Dr. Richard Sorge in Sugamo's death row. As custom required, he ascertained the name and age of the man before formally telling him that according to an order of the Minister of Justice he was to be executed that day and was expected to die calmly. The governor asked Sorge whether he wished to add anything to the will which he had written previously concerning the disposal of his body and his few possessions. Sorge replied calmly, "My will is as I have written it." The governor then asked, "Have you anything else to say?" "No," said Sorge, "nothing else." After this brief exchange Richard Sorge turned to the prison chaplain and other prison officials and said, "I thank you for all your kindnesses." These were the last recorded words of Dr. Richard Sorge.

Having said them, Sorge started on the long walk from death row down to the wide prison courtyard through the somber gray wall around the death house, and so through its single fatal door. Unlike Ozaki, who had preceded him on that long walk he did not stop before the golden altar. Sorge was led directly into the execution chamber. He stood firmly on the trap door, the noose was slipped quickly over his head and without a word or any sign of agitation he met his end. The trap was sprung at 1020 and he was pronounced dead at 1036.

Conclusions and Deductions

The Sorge case is much more than an interesting spy story. Like the Canadian espionage case it presents detailed information on methods of Soviet espionage. These methods as shown in the Sorge case can be summarized as follows:

1. Communist parties and known Communist workers are not used for high level, highly sensitive Soviet espionage. That is not to say that such parties and persons do not indulge in espionage for the Soviet Union but when they do so, they are not included in the important network. They are too vulnerable.

2. Communists or Communist sympathizers, on the other hand, are the persons recruited for basic espionage. They have loyalty and devotion to the Soviet Union, through their devotion to the abstract cause of communism which is essential and which is beyond price.

3. Study groups of economic, social, and Marxian subjects are common sources both of recruits for the Communist party and for Soviet espionage. Among others, Miyagi, Ozaki, Kawai, Mizuno, and Kitabayashi Tomo were recruited in this fashion. While such study groups normally do not bear a Communist label they are partially identified by their names such as: Proletarian Arts Society, Dawn Society, and the like.

4. A very useful cover consists of a research institute devoted to a particular problem of general interest: The

China Research Institute, for example, in which Kawai and Nakanishi Ko, the latter a member of the House of Councilors and lately editor of the *Tokyo Mimpo,* were active.

5. Persons not members of the Communist party, merely sympathetic to it through reading and participating in study groups on Marxism and social problems show an extraordinary willingness to work for the Soviet Union. They are ready to betray their country through espionage with very little urging.

6. Persons of such sympathies, recruited in this manner, do not seem to care what the channel of their command and of their information may be, so long as it relates to Communist activity in general. As an example, not until after his arrest did Ozaki Hozumi know definitely that he was working for the 4th Bureau of the Red Army General Staff. Whether he worked for them, or for the Comintern as he had vaguely surmised, was a matter of indifference to him. It was all for the same Cause.

7. There is a very sharp dividing line between Soviet intelligence agencies, and there is little if any intercourse between the members of different agencies. For example, after Ozaki started working for Sorge in Japan he was forbidden to have further communications with Agnes Smedley who was running a Soviet intelligence agency in Peiping. Yet previously, the three had worked closely together in Shanghai. As another example, after Guenther Stein left Japan in 1938, Sorge was forbidden to communicate with him, and did not look him up when they were both in Hong Kong in 1939.

8. Soviet Russians are rarely used as field agents; they are too likely to be under suspicion. In the Sorge case there were Japanese, Germans, a White Russian (wife of Klausen), a Dane, and a Yugoslav, but no Soviet Russian agents. Only after necessity drove him to it, did Sorge deal with representatives of the Soviet Embassy, and he can scarcely be numbered as a member of the ring.

9. An absolute minimum of communication with the local Soviet Embassy is maintained. Every effort is made to keep away both from Russians and from local Communists in order that no suspicion shall be directed to the members of the ring.

10. As much as possible direct communication with the Soviet Union is maintained and the channel through the local Soviet Embassy is used as little as possible. Both in China and in Japan the Sorge ring had their own radios and their own couriers.

11. Every member of the net shall have a logical cover,

and his conduct and inquiries shall always be related to his cover. For example, Klausen, the businessman, didn't go around asking general questions, while de Voukelitch, the journalist, did. Because it is their business to ask questions and gather information on every subject, journalists are especially useful both in their own right and as covers.

12. The best agent is a man who not only has cover but is a recognized expert on a general subject, preferably related to the target. Both Ozaki and Sorge were recognized as experts. Ozaki on China by the Japanese, and Sorge on Japan by the Germans.

13. Within an espionage network contact between members is kept down to a minimum for efficiency, and subordinate members deal only with specified persons within the hierarchy. For example, while Sorge did meet some of the lesser Japanese, most of them did not know him. They dealt either with Miyagi or Ozaki. Unfortunately for Sorge, this precaution did not protect him or his net, since his lieutenants talked as soon as their subordinates had implicated them. The principle, however, remains.

14. It is likely that a Soviet agent who is not a Soviet citizen has left a trail somewhere in his career. A file check on Sorge or Klausen in Berlin any time after they came to Tokyo would have exposed them. Similarly, the records of Miyagi or Mrs. Kitabayashi or Mrs. Kuzumi or Kawai, to name a few, would have betrayed them if any energetic attempt had been made to check their past histories. Similarly a check into de Voukelitch's record in Yugoslavia would have raised reasonable doubt. Naturally in this case the Japanese would have needed the assistance of foreign police departments which would not have been impossible. Had the German Embassy, however, instituted a routine check on Sorge before confirming him as press attaché in 1939, he would have been exposed. Naturally, American police files on subversive activities are less complete than those of totalitarian countries, but a great deal can be found in a four-way check. The Sorge case underlines the urgency of making a check of a man's whole life history, not just a decade, every time he is considered for a post of trust and confidence under the government.

15. A Communist or Communist sympathizer must be considered *ipso facto* a traitor who will use his position to betray his country. The pressure to employ experts with leftist leanings in government departments in times of crisis must be avoided no matter what their technical skill or how hard pressed the government agency may be for expert assistance. The employment of Communists and Communist

sympathizers by the research department of the South Manchurian Railway illustrates this point. Although Ozaki was not under suspicion, and so does not fit this evidence, Nakanin Ko and many others had considerable records of Communist front activity and Communist sympathy. Nevertheless, these men were hired and advanced in the service of this important agency. They in turn used their positions and information in the service of the Soviets. Japanese authorities, like some of their American counterparts, confused liberalism with communism. The fact that in relation to the Japan-China War, American sympathies were with the Chinese should not obscure the issues for American understanding.

What has happened to the surviving conspirators? Apparently Edith de Voukelitch went to Australia. After the war Taguchi Ugenda and Yamana Masazana lived in Hokkaido, but their occupations were unknown. Former Corporal Koshiro Yoshinobu and Kawai Teikichi were reported living in Tokyo.

Dr. Yasuda Tokutaro moved back to Tokyo in July, 1947 from Gifu where he had sought refuge during the war. He talked garrulously of the great days when he was helping that most successful of Soviet spies, Dr. Richard Sorge. Kuzumi Fusako was an old woman, but probably she was still propagandizing for the Cause in the small town where she lived in Okayama Prefecture. Akiyama (Frank) Koji, the only mercenary in the ring dropped out of sight after his release from prison in October, 1945.

Max Klausen was in Akita Prison and Anna Klausen in Tochigi Prison when the war ended. Under the American order for the release of political prisoners both were let out of jail early in October, 1945 and under the care of American officers were reunited in Tokyo. Few knew anything about Sorge at that time, and in any case American-Soviet relations were friendly. The unhappy thought that a Soviet spy who had worked against the Japanese might later work against the United States had not yet occurred to many Americans.

Max was ill and very weak from beriberi and much in need of medical care. Soon after he reached Tokyo, he called at the Soviet Embassy where he was welcomed and given money. What he told them of his apostasy and free confession, or what they told him in praise and admiration for his highly successful work can only be imagined. For a time Max and Anna lived in the country, in Saitama Prefecture not far from Tokyo. In December 1945 Max received permission to go to Karuizawa for treatment by his prewar German physician. He made two calls on this doctor, and then returned to Tokyo with Anna, where they lived in a small apartment. No American has seen him officially since early January, 1946.

In late February, 1946, the Japanese man who had shared quarters with Klausen in Saitama Prefecture received a letter from Max saying that he intended to return to the country when the weather became warmer. Apparently Max was referring to the cold of the Siberian winter, however, for by early March the word got around that Max and Anna "had gone to another country." How warm their welcome in the homeland of all Communists was can only be guessed. Sorge's contemptuous remark should be recalled that even though Klausen escaped the noose in Japan, if he ever got back to the U.S.S.R. he would be taken care of. If Max and Anna are living securely in the Soviet Union today, they must be under a constant strain to maintain an agreed-upon story explaining why Max got life while Dr. Sorge was hanged. Perhaps to prove his zeal and loyalty Max has left for some other country and some other post where his skill and experience in secret telegraphy will be useful to the Soviets.

Those men whose only guilt was that they trusted a friend too well are seared for the remainder of their lives by their innocent contact with the members of the Sorge ring. Even though they were proved wholly innocent, men like Inukai Ken will never escape periodical suspicions.

There are other Japanese who were not a part of the ring, but who were a part of other rings, like Nakanishi Ko, or who simply are Communists who glory in the Sorge case, who try to develop a legend of Ozaki the patriot, murdered by militarists and Fascists. Since no factual account of the Sorge case has yet been published in Japan it is easy for such men to perpetuate a fanciful tale.

The oddest postwar item related to the Sorge case was the man who betrayed them all, Ito Ritsu, a member of the Central Committee of the Japanese Communist Party and a leader of the Youth Action Corps (*Totsugekitai*), admired, respected, and followed by thousands of the faithful.

PART TWO

RICHARD SORGE'S OWN STORY AND KLAUSEN'S TESTIMONY

I consider it most important to present, for the first time an exclusive English translation of Sorge's "own story" representing the typed original pages, rescued by Mr. Yoshikawa, from the holocaust of bombed Tokyo. Here is a rare glimpse into the mind and soul of a professional Communist, tracing the psychological evolution, that turned a young patriotic German soldier into a mechanistic tool of the Kremlin, into a mercenary espionage agent. A fitting introduction to this story is a voluntary contribution received from Germany:

Bad Konig i.O. (16)
6 Leipsig 2nd of July 1951.

To General Willoughby,
Dear Sir:

Having read in the papers that you are writing a case study in international espionage in the Far East, and that this study concerns Dr. R. Sorge I am writing to you, as I was an old friend of "Ika" Sorge and a witness of his change and development. Richard Sorge was born in Baku in Caucasus, a son of a German Engineer and a Russian mother. His father died when he was only a few years old and his mother (not a Communist but a quiet, decent woman) lived with her children in Berlin. Richard Sorge did not know any Russian then; they spoke only German in his family.

I am in possession of a number of photos of Richard Sorge, and willing to present you with them; one of them which I like best I enclose (however I would be thankful if you would return just this photo after having made use of it). Richard Sorge fought and was wounded at Ypern and Langemark as a volunteer. We all like Ika (Richard), he was good-natured and straightforward. We could not share the ideas he developed later, but always were on friendly terms with him. He was not a Communist in his youth, but studying in Kiel after the war, came entirely under the influence of a Communist professor whose wife later went with him to Moscow. He never made a secret with us of his Communist ideas, and later of his mission in the Russian service. He was a fanatic idealist. At the beginning he worked about a year in a Ruhr mine to study labor conditions there, as a simple Communist.

He paid us a brief last visit, before he went to Japan, at our former estate in Thuringen. The last news from him was a letter from Colombo; after that I did not hear of him again till the news of his tragic death reached us.

Somewhere I have a poem written by him which begins: ". . . eternally a stranger who condemns himself —never to know real peace . . ." which shows that he suffered occasionally. Fuller particulars and photos I am ready to supply in case you desire.

FRAU DOROTHEA VON DURING.

RICHARD SORGE'S OWN STORY: PARTIAL MEMOIRS "MY PAST HISTORY AS A GERMAN COMMUNIST"

(a) My Childhood and School Years

World War I from 1914 to 1918 exerted a profound influence upon my whole life. Had I been swayed by no other considerations, it alone would have made me a Communist. When it broke out, I was only eighteen and a half years old, a high school student in the Richterfelder district in Berlin.

Until the war, my boyhood was passed amid the comparative calm common to the wealthy bourgeois class of Germany. Economic worries had no place in our home. What made my life a little different from the average was a strong awareness of the fact that I had been born in the southern Caucasus and that we had moved to Berlin when I was very small. Our home also differed immensely in many respects from that of the average bourgeois family in Berlin. The peculiarities of the Sorge family endowed my early childhood with certain distinguishing features, and, like all my brothers and sisters, I was slightly different from the average school child. I was a bad pupil, defied the school's regulations, was obstinate and willful and rarely opened my mouth. In history, literature, philosophy, political science, and, of course, athletics, I was far above the rest of the class, but I was below average in my other studies. At the early age of 15, I developed an avid interest in Goethe, Schiller, Lessing, Klopstock, Dante, and other difficult authors and, in addition struggled in vain with history of philosophy and Kant. My favorite periods of history were the French Revolution, the Napoleonic Wars, and the time of Bismarck. I knew Germany's current problems better than the average grownup. For many years, I studied political developments carefully. At school I was known as "Prime Minister." I knew what my grandfather had done for the labor movement and I also knew that my father's ideas were diametrically opposed to his. Father was unmistakably a nationalist and imperialist, and throughout his life he was unable to shake off the impression made upon his youth by the building of the German Empire during the War of 1870-71. He was strongly conscious of the property he had amassed and the social position he had achieved abroad. My elder brother became an extreme leftist; I recall that he had strong anarchist leanings rooted in Nietzsche and Stirner. I was a member of a workers' athletic association for many years which meant that I had constant contacts with the workers, but I had no clear political stand as a student. I was interested only in collecting political knowledge; I neither desired nor was able to adopt a definite attitude of my own.

(b) World War I, Impact of Defeat

One summer vacation I visited Sweden and returned to Germany by the last boat available. World War I had broken out. I volunteered for service immediately, joining the army without reporting to my school or taking my final graduation examination. I was impelled to make this decision by a strong urge to seek new experiences, a desire to liberate myself from school studies and what I considered the whole meaningless and purposeless pattern of living of an 18-year-old, and by the general outburst of excitement created by the war. I did not consult my superiors, my mother, or the other members of my family (my father had died in 1911). After a completely inadequate six-week training course at a drill ground in the outskirts of Berlin immediately after the outbreak of the war, I was shipped out to Belgium to take part in a great battle on the banks of the Yser. This period may be described as "from the classroom to the battlefield" or "from the school chair to the slaughter block."

After this fierce and sanguinary conflict had stirred up the first and most serious psychological unrest in the hearts of my comrades and myself, and after our thirst for battle and adventure had been glutted, several months of silent and pensive emptiness began.

I mused over my knowledge of history and realized that, on this several-hundred-year-old—nay, several-thousand-year-old battlefield—I was fighting in one of Europe's innumerable wars. How meaningless these oft-repeated wars were becoming! How many times before me German soldiers had fought in Belgium to invade France and the armies of France and other nations had poised here ready to overrun Germany! Was the significance of these past campaigns ever remembered?

My political curiosity led me to wonder what motives underlay this new war of aggression. Who cared about this region, or that new mine or industry? Whose desire was it to capture this objective at the sacrifice of life? None of my simple soldier friends ever desired annexation or occupation. None of them even understood the meaning of our efforts. Nobody knew the real purpose of the war, not to speak of its deep-seated significance. Most of the soldiers were middle-aged men, workers, and handicraftsmen by trade. Almost all of them belonged to industrial unions, and many were Social Democrats. There was one real leftist, an old stonemason from Hamburg, who refused to talk to anybody about his political beliefs. We became close friends, and he told me of his life in Hamburg and of the persecution and unemployment he had gone through. He was the first pacifist I had ever come across. He died in action in the early days of 1915, just before I was wounded for the first time.

At the outset of the war, my attention was arrested by the fact that we common soldiers were living a life completely apart. There was very little off-duty contact with officers. They kept to themselves, and I was never able to feel a great affection for them.

Shortly after I returned to Germany to nurse my wound, I learned for the first time how difficult it was to maintain a normal standard of living. I found that there were two true standards for weighing this [Original translator's note: Inequalities and the existence of the black market.] Money could buy anything on the black market. The poor were irate. The initial excitement and spirit of sacrifice apparently no longer existed. Wartime profiteering and surreptitious buying and selling were beginning to appear, and the lofty ideals underlying the war were receding farther and farther into the background. In contrast, the material objectives of the struggle were gaining increasing prominence, and a thoroughly imperialistic goal, the elimination of war in Europe through the establishment of German hegemony, was being publicized.

I utilized my period of convalescence to prepare for my graduation examinations, in which connection I entered the Medical Department of Berlin University and attended two or three of its lectures. I was not very happy in Germany and at a loss as to what to do. The political works and trends which I had been studying so diligently had been deprived of real significance by the war. I volunteered for service again before my convalescence time was up, finding very few of my old comrades when I returned.

I was sent to the Eastern Front. The great offensive and our gains there alleviated the general weariness to some extent, but all the men dreamed of peace in their spare moments. The fact that, although we had already pierced deep into the heart of Russia, there was still no end in sight, made some of them begin to fear that the war would go on forever.

The situation at home was critical when I returned in the beginning of 1916 after being wounded a second time and making a hard and long trip across the occupied zone of Russia. I knew people of almost every class (that is, the families of my comrades); simple working families, my middle class bourgeois relatives and my wealthy friends and acquaintances, and I was able to make a fairly complete observation of the economic situations of a number of classes and social strata. The bourgeoisie, steadily slipping to the level of the proletariat, was endeavoring to escape its fate by sedulously bolstering the myth of German spiritual superiority. I abhorred the efforts of these ignorant and supercilious representatives of the so-called "German spirit." A few political leaders were already beginning to feel uneasy over the war, with the result that domestic and foreign policy became cruel and brutal. In other words, reaction and imperialism were on the upswing. I became convinced that Germany was unable to provide the world with either new ideas or new contributions in other forms, and that Britain and France were similarly incapable of assisting Germany and the rest of the world. No long-winded dissertations on spirituality and lofty ideals could move this conviction of mine, which has been responsible for the fact that ever since that time, and regardless of the race of people involved, I have looked askance at claims of spirituality and idealism trumpeted forth by a nation at war.

Still more discontented than after my first convalescence,

I lost no time in volunteering for front-line duty again. I felt that I would be better off fighting in a foreign land than sinking deeper into the mud at home.

The general atmosphere I found in my unit was even gloomier than before, but more of the men were showing an interest in political problems and in the issues involved in the termination of the war. The notion was slowly growing among them that a violent political change was the only way of extricating ourselves from this quagmire. I met two soldiers who were in contact with radical political groups in Germany, one of whom frequently talked of Rosa Luxembourg and Karl Liebknecht. In my discussions with these men and my own reflections, the termination of the war did not figure prominently. Far more important was the question of how to eliminate the causes of all this meaningless self-destruction and endless repetition of war here in Europe. This issue seemed to us a great deal more basic than the ending of the current war. We were not so cowardly as to fear its continuation or to exhaust all available means in a desire to see it end. We knew too well that a mere laying down of arms would simply offer Germany's enemies a free hand for their imperialistic designs. What was important to us was a broad solution, a permanent answer on an international scale, but we were still at a loss as to how to achieve it. We were too far removed from the leftist movement in Germany and other countries.

Our discussions were spurred on by the vigorous propaganda of nationalistic and imperialistic political bodies, which were sending large numbers of propaganda leaflets to the front. They tried to raise the morale of the men by explaining in detail every one of the demands that Germany had to make on other countries to establish a lasting supremacy and by defining our broad war objectives, but the actual results were far from what they had expected; as far as the leftist radicals at the front and within Germany were concerned, their efforts were like pouring gasoline on a fire. As was my habit, I merely listened to these discussions and asked questions; I still had no convictions, knowledge, or resolution. The time was ripe, however, for me to pass from my long period of fence-sitting to the final stage of decision. Just at this time, I incurred my third injury, a very serious one. I was struck by numerous shell fragments, two of which smashed bones.

At the field hospital, where I required serious attention for several months, I met a very cultured and intelligent nurse and her father, who was a doctor. A little later, I learned that both of them had close relations with the radical Social Democratic faction. They gave me my first detailed account of the state of the revolutionary movement in Germany, of the various parties, factions, and groups that had been established, and of international phenomena in the revolutionary movement. For the first time I heard of Lenin and of his activities in Switzerland. I was now able to feel that, if I were to probe deeper into the basic questions concerning imperialistic wars which had come up at the front, I could find an answer to them, and I became firmly resolved to discover that answer, or rather that set of answers, as soon as I recovered. Already, I regarded myself as an apostle of the revolutionary labor movement.

My convalescence at the field hospital was useful to me in other ways as well. I undertook a study of philosophy, learning Kant and Schopenhauer thoroughly, grappled with history and the history of the fine arts, and became interested in economic problems. The nurse and her father gave me adequate literature in any field I cared to explore. Despite the seriousness of my injuries and the excruciating pain involved in their treatment, I was happy for the first time in many years. My strong will to study, which emerges from time to time even today, was developed in those days.

When partially recovered, I resumed my studies at the university, although I was still a soldier, and visited the field hospital for treatment, I abandoned medicine, deciding to concentrate on the study of government and economics to answer my growing interest in the social, economic, and political changes affecting Germany and Europe.

At this time, that is, during the summer and winter of 1917, I realized most thoroughly the meaninglessness and the devastating efforts of the Great War. Already several millions had perished on each side, and who could predict how many more millions would go the same way? The highly vaunted German economic machine had crumbled in ruins; I myself, like countless other members of the proletariat, felt the collapse through hunger and constant food shortages. Capitalism had disintegrated into its component parts: anarchism and unscrupulous merchants. I saw the downfall of the German Empire, whose political machinery had been termed indestructible. The members of Germany's ruling class, shaking their heads in helpless despair over these developments, split morally and politically. Culturally and ideologically, the nation fell back on empty talk of the heritage of the past or turned to anti-Semitism or Roman Catholicism. The militaristic and feudalistic ruling class and the bourgeoisie were unable to produce a single idea capable of charting a new course for the nation and saving it from total ruin. Germany's foes fared no better. Their political demands already augured further solution through arms in the future. The only fresh and effective ideology was supported and fought for by the revolutionary labor movement. This most difficult, daring, and noble ideology strove to eliminate the causes, economic and political, of this war and any future ones by means of internal revolution.

I spent my time at the University of Berlin in a detailed study of this ideology, with particular reference to its theoretical basis. I read the ancient Greek philosophers and Hegel for his influence on Marxism. I read Engels and then Marx, studying every book to which I had access. I also studied the enemies of Marx and Engels, the men who had challenged them on their theoretical, philosophical, and economic tenets, and delved into the whole history of the labor movement in Germany and the rest of the world. In these several months, I acquired a basic knowledge of Marx and the rudiments of a practical way of thinking.

The outbreak of the revolution in Russia indicated to me the course which the international labor movement should adopt. I decided not only to support the movement theoretically and ideologically but to become an actual part of it. All of the solutions to my personal and material problems at which I have arrived since have perforce stemmed from that decision. World War II, now approaching its third year, and particularly the German-Soviet War, have strengthened my conviction that my decision of some 25 years ago was correct. I am able to say this with due consideration for all that has happened to me in the past 25 years and, especially, during the last year, as a result.

(c) The German Revolutionary Labor Movement, 1918-1924

After my release from all further military service in January, 1918, I enrolled in Kiel University. Needless to say, I little thought that a German revolution would start there within a year. At Kiel, I joined a revolutionary organization, the Independent Social Democratic Party. I did not join the Spartacus Group for the simple reason that I could not find any way of getting in touch with it in Kiel. My first work with the party was in connection with a socialist student organization. I established it, with two or three other students, and later became its leader. For the party organization itself, I acted as the head of a training group in the district where I lived, teaching the history of the labor movement, the difference between revolutionary and counter-revolutionary movements, etc. Of course, I recruited new party members from among my student friends and attended to minor details.

I contributed to the revolution, touched off by insurgent sailors at the Kiel naval port, by delivering secret lectures on socialism before groups of sailors and harbor and dock workers. One of these lectures I can recall even today. I was called for early one morning, secretly led away to an unknown destination, which proved to be a sailors' underground barracks and there asked to conduct a secret meeting behind closed doors.

Immediately after the revolution, my work for the party consisted in handling the countless membership applications which were pouring in and in propaganda and teaching activities. I also had plenty to do in connection with the socialist student organization, which was now very strong.

At the end of the year, two or three of my comrades and I went to Berlin on official party business to work at the party headquarters there. Fierce fighting had broken out in Berlin between the faction led by Noske and the revolutionary movement under the leadership of Scheidemann; the army had sided with Noske against the revolution. The party needed assistance, but it was already too late to do anything when I arrived in Berlin. The Spartacus rising was suppressed later after much bloodshed. We were forced to halt at the station and searched for arms but fortunately my weapon was not discovered. Any person who carried a weapon and refused to turn it over was shot. After being detained for several days inside the station, my comrades and I were sent back to Kiel. One could hardly call it a triumphant return. Early in 1919 I went to Hamburg to prepare for my doctor's examination.

In Hamburg I organized another socialist student group, serving as its secretary, and performed general duties for the party in the district where I lived. At the end of that year, I was appointed training chief of the party's Hamburg area organization guidance department. Shortly afterward, our party, like the Spartacus Group and other revolutionary bodies, was automatically merged with the German Communist Party. Throughout 1920 I served the local organization in Hamburg in the capacity of training chief. At the same time, I was an adviser for the Hamburg Communist newspaper. One day I received a visit from the famous socialist Scheidemann. He asked me if, as Adolf Sorge's descendant, I would be interested in joining his movement, but of course I gave him a flat refusal.

I next secured a teaching position in a higher school in Aachen and prepared to move inland, but before doing so,

I was ordered to appear before the central committee in Berlin, where, after I had delivered a report on conditions in Hamburg, I was asked to carry on various positive activities in the Aachen area for the party. The area was dominated by the workers, and the Catholic labor organizations were extremely powerful. Shortly after my arrival in Aachen, I was made a member of the city guidance department of the party organization and put to work handling training problems. At the same time, I engaged in active propaganda work among the miners. Soon I established contact with the Rhineland regional guidance department at Cologne. I was frequently invited to their meetings, and I was asked to help the Communist newspaper there as I had done in Hamburg. Once, during a school vacation, I edited a Communist newspaper for two months while its editor was in prison. I also attended some of the central committee's expansion and guidance conferences as the representative of the Rhineland region.

Needless to say, it was impossible for me to contniue my political activities for the party in Aachen and retain my assistant professorship at the higher school. Toward the close of 1922, I was expelled from the school for engaging in a heated political controversy.

After consulting with the party, I decided to intensify my activities among the mine workers and to work with them in the Aachen coal mining region to cover my living expenses. I was able to find employment in a mine near Aachen as an inexperienced worker without being detected. It was a hard life, and my work suffered immensely because of the serious injuries I had received at the front, but I never regretted the decision. The experiences that I went through as a miner were just as valuable to me as those I gained on the battlefield, and my new vocation was equally significant to the party.

Within a short time, my work among the miners had produced a number of beneficial results. I organized a Communist group in the first mine at which I was employed, saw it develop soundly, and moved on to another mine near Aachen. During the same year, I changed mines again.

An effort to do similar work for the party in the coal mining district of Holland failed. I was discovered immediately, expelled from the mine, and deported from the country.

In the meantime, I had become known in the Aachen mines, with the result that I was no longer able to find work. The authorities threatened to turn me over to the Allied Military government (the war had just ended and the Rhineland was under the military occupation and political administration of the victorious Allies), so I was forced to leave Aachen and the occupied area.

I then went to Berlin to discuss my future party activities with the central committee. They offered me a salaried position with the party guidance department, but I refused because I wished to gain more practical experience and to complete my academic training. My friends suggested that I take a position as assistant in the social science department at the University of Frankfurt, and at the same time double as a private lecturer, and the guidance department approved the idea, requesting me to engage in positive activities with the party organization in Frankfurt.

At Frankfurt, I was appointed a member of the city guidance department and, as in the past, handled training matters and served as adviser to the Communist newspaper. Shortly after that, the party was outlawed in Germany. My name was not very well known to the authorities in Frankfurt, which meant that I was able to render valuable assistance to the party. I handled all the secret liaison between the central committee in Berlin and the organization in Frankfurt. The party funds and propaganda material were sent to me. I hid most of the party's property in my study room at the university or in the social science library, concealing large bundles in the coal bin in the classroom. There were two or three party members working there, so there was no need to fear discovery. Concealment of these materials permitted the guidance department to utilize them constantly, with the result that, despite the ban on the Communist party, there was no appreciable slackening of its activities in Frankfurt. Meanwhile, over in Saxony, an armed rebellion had set up a workers' republic, with which, by party orders, we were in constant secret communication. I visited Saxony frequently on special missions to deliver essential political and organizational reports and directives which it was possible for the party to route through us in Frankfurt.

As I was engaged in secret liaison for the party, it was not surprising that, at the Communist convention held at Frankfurt am Main in 1924, I was selected by the guidance department to protect delegates from the Soviet Communist Party who had entered the country illegally to represent the Comintern. Throughout the session, I looked after the security of these important delegates, saw to their quarters, and decided upon the activities in which they might safely engage. As the German Communist Party was facing serious political hardships, the Comintern had sent us four of its leading figures, Pyatnitsky, Manuilsky, Kuusinen, and Lozovsky. In addition to discharging my responsibilities as a delegate to the convention, I fulfilled this far from simple mission to the satisfaction of all concerned. Of course, my relations with the Comintern delegates were very intimate, and we grew more friendly every day. At the close of the session, they asked me to come to Comintern headquarters in Moscow that year to work for them. I could not go at once because I had to attend several organizational and intelligence councils immediately after the Frankfurt convention, but the proposal of the Comintern delegation, which was to have me set up an intelligence bureau for the Comintern, was approved by the party leaders in Berlin, and I left for Moscow at the end of 1924 to begin work in January 1925. At the same time Pyatnitsky switched my name from the German Communist Party to the Soviet Communist Party.

Before closing, I would like to mention my meeting in 1923 with a delegation from the Moscow Marx-Engels Research Institute, led by the illustrious scholar Ryazanov, who, while touring Germany to collect material for this great new research center, asked me for information on the posthumous political papers of Adolf Sorge, who had served as secretary for the First International during Marx's lifetime. Ryazanov invited me to join the Institute in Moscow, but the German party leaders would not release me.

Finally, I must add that my career as a writer was not confined to Communist journalism. In 1922, I wrote a pamphlet called *The Accumulation of Capital and Rosa Luxembourg,* which was a critical and theoretical study of the theories of Rosa Luxembourg. I am convinced that my handling of this difficult topic was clumsy and immature, and I hope that the Nazis burned every last copy. While in Moscow, I published *The Economic Provisions of the Versailles Peace Treaty and the International Labor Class,* and in 1927, I published *German Imperialism.* I believe that these were competent pieces of work. Both were read widely in Germany and translated into Russian.

My activities for the German Communist Party ceased with my removal to Moscow in 1924-25 and my transfer to the Soviet Communist Party. My relations with the German Communist Party were confined to the period 1918-24.

GENERAL NATURE OF SORGE'S GROUPS IN JAPAN AND CHINA

(a) Comintern Intelligence Division From 1925-1929

The Comintern Intelligence Division, one of three major departments which laid the groundwork for the concrete organizational and political decisions by means of which leadership was exerted over the International Communist Party, was already in existence in early 1925, and the passing of time brought the need for expansion on the largest possible scale. I assisted actively in that expansion.

The Intelligence Division's duties were to prepare regular reports of various nature concerning the International Communist Party, to handle special party problems, to report on national labor movements and political and economic conditions in different countries and, on occasion, to compile special reports on exceptional problems of international import. The basic data used in these reports were derived from material sent to the Comintern by party representatives, newspapers, magazines, and books from the various countries and occasional reports brought in by travelers and representatives.

Only a party comrade with years of international experience, as, for example, Kuusinen and others who held the position for a time, could rise to the position of chief of the Intelligence Division. Under the chief, there was a secretariat headed by a chief secretary, under which the affairs of the various countries were controlled and grouped in the following manner: Europe, British Empire, North America, South America, and East Asia, including all the nations and parties in the Southwest Pacific. These major classifications were further subdivided, the Europe group, for example, being broken down into German-speaking nations and parties, Romance language nations and parties (France, Italy, Spain), Scandinavian parties, and Balkan nations. East Asia was divided into China, Japan, Korea, the Netherlands East Indies, and a single office lumping together all the other parties in the area. When a group had a single joint reporter, he handled its business. Large parties were represented by one or more reporters, but in most cases small ones were grouped together by languages under one man. Major international problems were handled by persons who were specially designated from among the ranks of the regular reporters and who worked directly under the head of

the Intelligence Division of the secretariat. All reports were
filed with the secretariat. Before submission to the chief of
the division, important reports were criticized at conferences
of limited scope attended by the reporter, a large number
of other reporters, and members of the secretariat. Top secret and secret reports were given special handling by the
secretariat. Included in the above categories were reports on
insurrectionary movements, big strikes or, for example, partisan battles in China.

On special occasions, representatives of the Soviet Communist Party attended secretariat meetings, and at other
times Red Army men were present to consider military
problems arising in connection with partisan movements. As
time went by, the number of reporters in the Intelligence
Division grew until there were about thirty, a figure which
was further swelled when international conferences or other gatherings of an international nature were held.

(b) Division Espionage Agents

With the passing of time, it grew increasingly necessary
to supplement previously acquired basic data with firsthand
information obtained by special Intelligence Division espionage agents operating in all countries and at all times. It
had long been a practice to send special emissaries from
the Organization Division of Comintern headquarters to assist local parties with organizational problems, and it was
decided that such functions would have to be expanded to
include intelligence work. In accordance with that policy, I
was sent to the Scandinavian countries in 1927 to engage
in intelligence activities concerning their Communist parties,
their economic and political problems, and any important
military issues which might arise. I began operations in Denmark, complying with instructions by assuming a position
of active leadership alongside the other party heads, attending meetings and conferences and visiting the main party organizations in the country. In so far as time permitted, I
also did intelligence work on Denmark's economic and
political problems, discussing my observations and findings
with party representatives and incorporating their opinions
in my reports to Moscow. I then went from Denmark to
Sweden to study problems there in the same manner. In
1928, I participated in the work of the political committee
of the Comintern's second world conference, after which I
went again to Scandinavia, this time primarily because of
the difficult party situation in Norway. I operated in Norway in the same way as in Sweden and Denmark, but party

roblems of various descriptions seriously impeded intelligence work in the fields of economics and politics. Orders came for me to go to England to collect information there rior to my return; *i.e.*, to study the labor movement, the atus of the Communist party and the political and economic conditions in Britain in 1929. My instructions to remain rictly aloof from intraparty disputes accorded perfectly ith my personal inclinations and enabled me to devote more attention to political and economic intelligence work han had been possible in Scandinavia.

Upon my return to Moscow, I presented to the Intelligence Division not only my regular report but also a frank nalysis of what had been wrong with my information-gathering trips and my investigations in the countries visited. In ddition, I submitted the following fundamental propositions: iz., that any basic and comprehensive intelligence program hould be kept apart from the internal quarrels controlling ocal parties; that, when deemed necessary, special envoys ould have to be sent out to settle purely national and imited party problems, but that such men should be able o devote themselves, if not exclusively, at least primarily, o basic intelligence activities concerning problems of economics, domestic administration, and foreign policy and, when necessary, to military problems in the broad sense. This separation, I said, was also imperative because of the requent need of the intelligence operative for secrecy. I urther suggested that, at the Moscow end, such espionage gents in foreign countries would have to be more definitely divorced than in the past from the over-all Comintern organization in order to assure a degree of separation adequate or purposes of secrecy. I cannot tell with certainty to what xtent the above proposals, made at the above juncture, were nfluential in the fundamental transformation in the nature f my duties which subsequently transpired, but it was clear o me that a basic change had been planned in the organization of my next trip, which was to China, and in the scope f my assignment. At the same time, there was a complete hange in my personal contacts and relations with the Comntern.

I followed a simple procedure in effecting liaison with the Organization Division in connection with my intelligence activities in the Scandinavian countries and England, sending orrespondence to Moscow through a local party or hrough the consolidated liaison office in Berlin or, in are cases, transmitting telegrams via the same channels. Most of the time I went to Berlin myself to arrange to have reports sent. In other words, I had absolutely no independent means of communication.

(c) Fundamental Changes in Intelligence Activities Between 1929 and 1941

As my relations with the Comintern had been severed upon my return from Scandinavia and England late in the summer of 1929, I began to conduct my intelligence operations in my hotel room and at houses in various locations. My nonprofessional contacts with other Comintern comrades ceased and I met only two or three key men directly connected with my work. When I conferred with a few Comintern men and representatives of other Communist bodies to arrange my trip to China, which was planned in line with the policy of isolating my intelligence activities and cloaking them in secrecy, this separation was made even more clear-cut than before. Persons present at our meetings included not only representatives of the Soviet Communist Party and its central committee but also men from the Red Army and the 4th Bureau, the Red Army Intelligence arm. Most of the arrangements which I made with them concerned the technical aspects of my future work. Two members of the Peoples Commissariat for Foreign Affairs of the U.S.S.R. also attended one meeting to discuss the political side of my intelligence activities. I subsequently visited the so-called 4th Bureau two or three times to make arrangements concerning technical phases of my operations in China and, later, in Japan. My separation from the Comintern became definite with the change in the nature of the duties assigned me, and I was specifically forbidden to have anything whatever to do with the Communist parties in China and Japan; I could not meet with them at my own discretion or even help them out.

The major objective of my intelligence activities was to evaluate the political situation; the secondary objective, to gather information concerning the nation's economy, with particular emphasis on its wartime economy. Third in line of importance was the collection of military information. News concerning party problems was reported only when of vital significance and when acquired by chance and not through party channels. I occasionally transmitted such news in China, but never in Japan.

I received no explanation concerning my organizational affiliation in Moscow; that is concerning the specific agency to which I was attached, and, naturally, I asked no questions on the subject, with the result that I do not know to this day whether or not I was attached in the line of duty to Comintern headquarters or whether I was an agent of the so-called 4th Bureau or of some other agency, as, for example, the Peoples Commissariat for Foreign Affairs of the U.S.S.R. or the Soviet Communist Party's central committee. The nature of the assignments and instructions given me, however, makes it possible to draw the following definite conclusions.

Although I do not know whether my information went to the central committee of the Russian Communist Party, to the Secretariat, or to some intelligence office especially created by the central committee to handle it, I am sure that it was used by top party circles and thus by top Soviet government circles. I shall attempt to indicate below the nature of the intelligence activities in which I was engaged.

Technically and organizationally speaking, my reports were sent to the specialized agency known as the 4th Bureau, which furnished all the technical aids (wireless contacts, radio men, etc.) and other assistance required to carry on my work. The bureau occasionally assigned me a few duties of a military nature, but the major emphasis was always on political information for the party leadership. Accordingly, my relationship with the Moscow authorities must be described in the following terms. All reports were sent to the 4th Bureau, whence they were forwarded to the leaders of the Soviet Communist Party and, in so far as they contained intelligence value to it, to the Comintern. They might also be made available to such other agencies as the Russian Army and the Peoples Commissariat for Foreign Affairs. In short, I was connected with Russian Communist Party headquarters from a subject-matter standpoint and with the 4th Bureau from a procedural standpoint.

The reasons for the change in the nature of my intelligence activities after 1929 were as follows:

1. The changing international situation caused a general shift in center of gravity from the Comintern to the Russian Communist Party and the U.S.S.R. itself.

2. My own talents were suited not so much to intelligence work designed merely for the handling of party political problems as to activity in the broader fields of economic, political and, to some extent, military intelligence.

In short, I was better able to meet the urgent need of the Russian Communist Party leadership for comprehensive economic, political, and military intelligence than to satisfy Comintern demands for information concerning local parties and labor movements.

These considerations, plus the fact that I had been a member of the Russian Communist Party since 1925, were responsible for the orders which I received directing me to engage in the broad intelligence activities outlined above.

I have expressed my opinion concerning the nature of my Japan group in the general summary. I have already intimated that I have no direct evidence to support that opinion, but it is based upon personal experience and I am convinced of its accuracy. If we leave the realm of "belief" and "conviction," we must limit consideration exclusively to the facts with which I dealt. Only the following can then be definitely stated: from November, 1929 on, my espionage groups and I were technically and organizationally a direct part of Red Army Intelligence; *i.e.,* of the so-called 4th Bureau. If final conclusions are to be based upon that narrow viewpoint; if they are to be drawn solely on the basis of incontrovertible fact, my groups in China and Japan must be regarded as special branches of the 4th Bureau.

THE COMINTERN AND THE SOVIET COMMUNIST PARTY

(a) Relationship of Party to Comintern

The espionage group which I operated in Japan was a special arm of the U.S.S.R. Communist Party, and all of its members have frankly confessed that they were working to advance the cause of communism and not for money or personal gain. This circumstance renders the relationship between the U.S.S.R. Communist Party and the Comintern, and the role of both in the world Communist movement, of immense significance in the present incident.

The Comintern is not a party but a world organization of national Communist parties. It consists of many sections representing individual parties, one of which is the U.S.S.R. Communist Party Section. Its program as a world organization is to work for world communism, for the incorporation of the whole world into a single Communist society. That is, it seeks to organize a world-wide Soviet union—to do away with private ownership of the means of production, with class exploitation and oppression, and with racial tyranny, and to unite all nations in accordance with a single master plan. This unified and consolidated plan, which indicates the roles to be played by various countries and races in the steady march toward world communism, makes the global policy of the Comintern far more than a mere summing up of the different programs of the various sections.

Without such a synthesis by the Comintern leadership, the sections would produce at the most nothing more than a variegated and ill-proportioned socialistic racial mosaic. There would be no international planning; no decisive equalizing factor.

It should be noted in this connection that the Comintern's program is not rigidly fixed but is subject to a process of development comparable to the constant and never-ending evolution of the Communist structure of society itself. Thus, the nature of the Comintern may be expected to change after a period of major development. As the revolution proceeds, for example, we shall doubtless witness an increasingly apparent shift from today's organization for class struggle to organization for the establishment of socialism on a national basis. The Comintern will some day become an economic general staff headquarters for the socialist nations of the world and subsequently a general staff headquarters for the creation of Communist societies.

At the present stage of the movement, the Comintern's immediate major objective is to furnish positive guidance to the sections in their struggle for the acquisition of political power in their respective countries. In form and theory, the Comintern is the brains—the general staff—directing the activities of the sections as they endeavor to achieve the goal for this stage in the development of world communism. Its actual work consists in preparing analyses of world economic and political conditions and objectively prevailing upon individual sections to adopt necessary and feasible aims based thereon. For example, it will judge the prospects for a general strike movement in a given country on the basis of the international economic health of world capitalism. Similarly, it will discourage rebellion when objective conditions do not favor violent revolution but will vigorously encourage revolt when world capitalism exhibits symptoms of acute crisis. It will also assist individual parties by consolidating national political and economic struggles and by furnishing national movements with propaganda materials, financial resources and, when necessary, political, propaganda, and organization advisers. Such aid has clearly been important and effective, particularly when trained men with ample experience in other parties have been chosen to perform advisory functions. Finally, the Comintern has helped individual sections by establishing special schools and training institutes in Moscow for middle and lower echelon party leaders.

Formally speaking, the Communist Party of the U.S.S.R. is a section of the Comintern like any other section. Like any other Communist party, it bows to the Comintern's will. The parties have no direct contact with one another, a rule which applies equally in the case of the Russian Communist Party. All communication between sections is through the international organization: *i.e.*, through the Comintern leadership organs, which means that the Soviet Communist Party cannot render direct assistance to any other party in the world. All aid and support come through the Comintern, which may, however, call upon individual parties, including the Russian, to furnish indirect assistance when such action has been unanimously decided upon by the party representatives. Such assistance can in no circumstances be rendered by recourse to means other than those available to the party as a party; the Red Army or other armed forces, which are not party instruments, could never be employed. The Red Army and other military forces belong to a country, *i.e.*, to the U.S.S.R. and not to the Soviet Communist Party. The party may, upon the Comintern's request, send food, money, or party members especially trained or especially qualified by experience to serve as advisers or assistants to sections in need of the Comintern's help, but the Red Army will never become seriously involved in the struggles of the sections for national power in their respective countries. Setting aside the fundamental principle of communism that the laboring class alone is capable of achieving a Communist revolution in any given state, the fact remains that the Comintern organization is incapable of rendering direct military assistance, because while it is a global organization of parties, it is not a global organization of nations and their armed forces. Of course, theoretically speaking, there have been exceptional cases, such as the White Russian counter-revolution against Siberia, when Outer Mongolia became a base of operations, but Trotskyite demands for armed intervention by the Soviet Union in the revolutions of other countries are entirely inconsistent with the principles and the actual setup of the Comintern.

In summary, it may be said that theoretically the Soviet Communist Party is, like any other, subject to the leadership of the Comintern, that it maintains no direct or special relations with other sections of the Comintern and that it can render assistance to other parties only through the Comintern. Worthy of special note here is the strong stand of the Soviet Communist Party with regard to aid to the Chinese Communists, to whom it has sent special military advisers. In other countries, such as Germany, Poland, and the Baltic nations, only a few Soviet Communists, far outnumbered by the regular party members, have gone to assist the local parties.

(b) Working Structure of Relationship

In recent years, there has been increasing disparity between the theory governing the relationship of the Comintern to the Soviet Communist Party and the practical application of that theory, until today the leadership of the party may be said to far outweigh that of the Comintern in importance. That leadership, in other words the Central Committee of the Soviet Communist Party, is a decisive factor in the international Communist movement as well as in the government of the Soviet Union. Its ascendency to power, which became clearly perceptible around 1928 and 1929, is attributable to the following causes.

Location of the Comintern in Moscow, which facilitates intimate relations between the party's leadership and the Comintern. This intimacy is particularly understandable when one considers the difficulties involved in liaison with other national parties in widely scattered areas.

As by far the most prominent and largest Communist party in the world and the dominant political party in Russia, the Russian Communist Party possesses very considerable financial resources and its monentary contributions to the Comintern have been immeasurably greater than those of any other party. Supported by the mighty Soviet Union, it provides the Comintern with all its technical, organic, administrative, and political needs. Moreover, the Soviet Communist Party is able to operate freely within the Soviet Union without interference from any armed organization.

Of all the Communist parties of the world, the Soviet Party, which includes people of over 150 nationalities and races, is best suited to maintain actual contact with a heterogeneous group of nations and races. It follows, therefore, that as long as they continue to be associated with the Comintern, the Russians, with their variegated racial background, will participate very actively in its functions.

Owing to its long history, the Soviet Communist Party has the most capable and experienced leaders. The fact that they are veterans of the international labor movement with experience dating as far back as prerevolutionary Russia, coupled with their records of distinguished service during the revolution and the founding of the Soviet Union, adds to their value. The stand taken by these leaders at international conferences and assemblies has far greater moral weight than the attitudes and declarations of the delegates of other parties. I myself vividly recall how non-Russian delegates were impressed by the mere presence of old Leninists like Stalin at these conferences.

From the early years of the Comintern on, these factors have influenced the standing of the Soviet Communists in the organization to such an extent that whenever controversies have arisen over vital issues, the opinions of the Soviet Communist Party have been accepted as final, particularly when expressed by such men as Lenin and Stalin. Such factors have become increasingly powerful in the last ten to fifteen years, during which radical reshufflings of key personnel in other parties due to intra-party disputes and persecution have brought about violent fluctuations and frequent deterioration in the quality and experience of national leaders, with the result that top men in the U.S.S.R. Communist Party have been forced to concern themselves more and more actively with questions of Comintern policy.

The dominant influence of the Soviet Communist Party in the Comintern today can be further ascribed to two specific major reasons; first, the fact that, despite reactionary influences and difficulties of all descriptions, the effort to establish a socialist system in the Soviet Union has been immensely successful; i.e., that the Soviet Communist Party has successfully carried out its major assignment from the Comintern, the formation of a socialist state; and, second, the fact that the center of emphasis in the developing international situation has executed a fundamental shift from the political national revolutionary labor movement to the policies adopted by the U.S.S.R. in her role as a socialist state in the society of nations. Unaided, the Soviet Union has attained the status of a world power; one to be reckoned with by all others. These two objective factors are of immeasurable significance to any general evaluation of the Comintern or appraisal of the position of the Soviet Communist Party leadership in the Comintern.

(c) Establishment of Socialism in the U.S.S.R.

The Soviet Communist Party was the only section of the Comintern charged with the special mission of actually establishing state socialism in a country as a step towards a Communistic social order. The current Soviet-German war has enabled us for the first time fully to evaluate the party's achievements with respect to this assignment, particularly in the economic realm. Even the German leaders have been forced to admit that they had underestimated Russia's economical potential. The theoretical controversy between Leninists and Trotskyites over the feasibility of attempting state socialism in a single country has been resolved in recent years through practical experimentation. The job of building done in the Soviet Union has not only proved that the U.S.S.R. Communist Party has accomplished its task brilliantly but has also been of overwhelming importance to the international Communist movement. Through these accomplishments, the Soviet Communist leadership has so signally increased its influence in the international labor movement as to overshadow the Comintern. The workers of the world are now more familiar with its key men than with those of the Comintern.

(d) Shift in the International Center of Gravity

The second major objective factor involved is the shift in international center of emphasis from the Comintern leadership to the leadership exercised by the U.S.S.R. in its role as a socialist state. As early as 1928—1929, it was obvious that the wave of radical revolution was receding. The tide of swift and mammoth revolution was going out temporarily, and with it was going the Chinese Communists' great struggle against Chiang Kai-shek, the Nanking government, and the imperialistic world powers in China. The international revolutionary movement was forced to give increasing thought to problems of defense against counter-revolutionary forces, particularly fascism, national socialism, and ultra-nationalism; the labor movement was driven back on the defensive; and an early revolutionary offensive by the laborers and the oppressed races became out of the question. Moreover, there was an ever-increasing danger that war would break out between the world powers, or that they would converge on Russia in an imperialistic attack. For all these reasons, it became critically important for the labor movement to set up a suitable defense.

In the meantime, the part played by the U.S.S.R. in international issues as a nation and a world force was gaining in importance, her increasing political and economic strength compelling the leading nations of the world to reckon with this socialist state in the realm of international politics. This point was brought out clearly when the U.S.S.R. and the Comintern adopted opposition to fascism and national socialism as the cornerstone of their foreign policy and strove to implement their decisions in their policy toward France and Spain. It was for this reason that the revolutionary labor movement willingly accepted Soviet Russia as the mainstay of its struggle for self-protection and survival. At the same time, objective developments in the world situation caused the Soviet leadership to move further to the fore of the international labor movement, enhanced the significance of the role played by the key men in the U.S.S.R. Communist Party, and increased the importance attaching to the establishment of Socialism in Russia as a foundation for the international military and political position of the U.S.S.R. The workers had realized that Russian advances in the struggle against the forces of fascism and national socialism would invariably increase the threat of an anti-Soviet offensive by the said forces. Whether or not the Fascists and National Socialists would attack Soviet Russia would depend upon the extent of the economic results obtained by the Russians in their socialist state, for which reason these results become a practical problem of overwhelming urgency for the U.S.S.R. and the revolutionary labor movement; more than ever before, the building up of the Soviet Union came to be regarded as the vital mission of the international labor movement. Trotskyism, forgotten for all practical purposes, was relegated to the status of an empty topic of debate for the intellectuals, and there was increasingly wide acceptance of the fact that only through accelerated construction of a socialist structure of society in the U.S.S.R. could the security of the international labor movement be guaranteed. At the same time, the need for defense against every attack aimed at Russia was recognized. The idea of possible participation by the Red Army in proletarian revolutions in other countries became nothing more than an unfounded fear in the minds of persons unfamiliar with actual conditions in the international labor movement. In the eyes of the movement itself, the paramount mission of the Russian Communist Party was not to send the Red Army out of the country, but to establish with all possible speed a socialist economy capable of protecting the U.S.S.R., labor's most concrete asset, from the imperialist aggression which was already making itself felt.

(e) Summary

Thus the Soviet Communist Party, far overshadowing the Comintern, functions today as the actual leader of the Communist labor movement, a fact clearly apparent in the working relationship between Soviet and Comintern leaders. In the past, the Comintern was extremely independent, consulting the party only with respect to occasional individual problems, but with the passing of time it has turned more frequently to Russian leadership for advice, and today such consultation may be considered routine. Comintern leadership can no longer map out a set course for the international labor movement in defiance of the Soviet Communist Party as it could in the past when, for example, Zinoviev was at the helm. The unification of Comintern leadership and Soviet Communist Party leadership was consummated through recognition of the latter's supremacy, a fact further reflected in the increasing alignment of the foreign policy and slogans of the revolutionary movement with those of the U.S.S.R. We may recall in this connection the common slogans aimed at fascism, imperialist war, and domestic reaction in Spain, Germany, and Italy. Likewise, I know many men who, like myself, were transferred from posts in the Comintern or similar bodies to agencies of the Soviet government or to work on some phase of the Soviet economy. Finally, we may cite the large number of workers, foreign refugees, who have recently begun to work to build up the Russian economy. In the past, such persons emphatically preferred work connected with the Comintern and related government work to activities managed by the Soviet Union. It is my impression—although it cannot be corroborated here—that a new political fallacy may be prevalent among a small minority of Communists, who, because of the tremendous achievements of Soviet socialism, seem to underestimate the value of the Comintern and its activities and to regard it as obsolete. This political fallacy with respect to the Communist point of view is clearly indicative of the profound significance of the actual progress made in Soviet construction and, indirectly, of the predominant importance of Soviet Communist leadership in the international labor movement.

The extraordinary part now being played by the Soviet Communist Party is, of course, neither permanent nor constant, for another shift in the center of emphasis may result should one or more Communist parties seize national political power and embark upon a program of socialist construction. Hence, the present Soviet Communist Party domination must be regarded as temporary, though under existing conditions its supremacy will not be challenged within the next ten years. At any rate, its progress, as well as that of Soviet socialist construction, exerted a tremendous influence on the operations of my ring, and any appraisal of the ring's activities must be made within the framework of the foregoing shift in leadership.

(f) Shift in Writer's Orientation and Activities

The aforementioned shift in the center of emphasis of the revolutionary labor movement from Comintern leadership to Soviet Communist Party leadership was clearly reflected in my activities, my transfer from the Comintern organization to the Soviet Communist Party being but an inkling thereof. This shift, however did not mean that we (the writer and members of the ring) abandoned our revolutionary activities on behalf of communism; we merely shifted the direction of our Communist activities from the field of party activities under the Communist International to another equally important field, namely, activities to promote the welfare of the U.S.S.R. The latter included economic and political construction in the Soviet Union, the demands of Soviet foreign policy, and defense against political and military aggression from the outside. To be more specific, the shift in my activities meant a transfer to new work designed to further Soviet foreign policy and bolster Soviet defenses against external attack. Such activities are as important and universal an expression of Communist ideals as are Comintern activities on behalf of individual Communist parties.

When questioned during the early phase of the interrogation with regard to the agency which delegated authority and issued orders to me, I deliberately employed a general and ambiguous term, the "Moscow authorities." For reasons of my own, I did not elaborate on the question of whether that term referred to an organ within the Comintern or to a key agency situated in Moscow. At the time, it was impossible to explain to the police officer through an interpreter all the complexities surrounding the change in my field of operations and the shift in Communist leadership which I have endeavored to describe in the preceding paragraphs. During the minute interrogation conducted by Procurator Yoshikawa, I barely managed to cover the complicated details concerning the changes which occurred in my direct superiors in Moscow. I have related herein in detail that prior to 1929 the Comintern organization was my "Moscow authorities" and that after 1929 my chain of command underwent a basic change corresponding to the change in the general world political situation. Had I attempted to cover all this complicated material in the early interrogation conducted by the police, it would certainly have caused delay and confusion.

The fact that I continued to meet with such leading members of the Comintern as Pyatnitsky, Manuilsky, and Kuusinen after transferring from the Comintern to another organ in Moscow may be explained as follows: these Comintern leaders are old associates of mine and personal friends of long standing. They were my teachers in the movement, they vouched for my character and my new undertaking to the central committee of the Soviet Communist Party, and they became my sponsors when I joined the party. Possessing wide and international experience in the revolutionary movement, they continued to advise me on various matters after my departure from the Comintern (they were the only persons I saw after I left). Moreover, they were not only leading members of the Comintern but also members of the central committee of the Soviet Communist Party. It must be remembered here that my far-flung spy activities in China and Japan, which were something completely new, were regarded with special interest by these three old friends. This was particularly true of my activities in Japan, where I was the first and only person to succeed in carrying out such an extended mission. To my knowledge my experiment was the first to succeed. Orders and requests invariably came through the 4th Bureau of the Red Army; this organ alone had authority over me. Such being the case, my meetings with members of the Comintern and others were purely unofficial—what I received from them was friendly advice, not directives or orders.

As has been mentioned previously, the operations of the writer and the direct members of his ring in Japan exemplify the shift in center of gravity which occurred in the Communistic movement. Through our work, we contributed directly to the future welfare of the Soviet Union—to what extent we need not attempt to determine here—and indirectly to the cause of world revolution. Or at any rate, so we believed. Within the limits indicated, we worked not only for the U.S.S.R. but also for the Communist world revolution.

"MY CONTACTS WITH MOSCOW AUTHORITIES"

I have already described in another section the manner in which I effected business contacts with the Moscow authorities from Japan. I relied upon courier service and radio communication with the 4th Bureau of the Red Army; no other type of contact with other agencies of Moscow was ever made from China or Japan.

Prior to the winter of 1929, my only business contacts while I was in Moscow were with Comintern agencies and the only contacts I had as a party member were through cells in such agencies.

(a) Direct Associations in the Winter of 1929

My withdrawal from the Comintern in the winter of 1929 marked the end of my business relations with it. At the same time, my contacts as a party member with party cells ceased. All further business contacts were made through the 4th Bureau of the Red Army. I became a member of the Secret Department of the Soviet Communist Party Central Executive Committee which controlled my party membership card and my relations with the party. As a party member, I am still responsible to the department and under obligation to report to it each time I return to Moscow. Once a person joins the party through this department, he must report to it for travel abroad. My subsequent business contacts were restricted to the 4th Bureau. My relations with it consisted chiefly of fairly frequent meetings with the department chief, General Beldin, and his substitute, Major General Davinov. Beldin agreed with my views on comprehensive political intelligence work, which he had heard from Pyatnitsky, so our talks on that subject progressed smoothly. At the same time, he stressed the fact that I would have to supply military intelligence urgently needed by the 4th Bureau. We decided that a military expert would accompany me to China to ensure the accuracy of my reporting. I had already made up my mind to go to Asia rather than to return to Europe, and as China had already been a center of interest in 1929, it was decided that I should be sent there.

I was briefed for the military aspects of my trip to China directly by officials of the Eastern Section of the 4th Bureau. General Beldin consulted other quarters on the details of my political and economic mission. He told me that he had seen the highest heads of the military and central committee. Beldin was intimate with all the leaders, whom he had known for years through the party movement, and I knew that he kept in touch by telephone with the military heads and the key men in the central committee. All chiefs of the 4th Bureau had to be party members, and it is clear that they had close personal ties with party leaders. Without this personal intimacy, the bureau could not have functioned, and the fact that such ties existed explained why it operated so smoothly as the link between me and top party circles, particularly after I began to forward information and reports from foreign countries. Thanks to the nature of the personnel in the 4th Bureau and the intimate relations between the bureau chief and top officials, my most important reports were quickly and smoothly transmitted to key Soviet leaders.

Before leaving for China, I visited the Eastern Section, the Political Section and the Code Section of the 4th Bureau for last-minute discussions. I knew there was a radio school, but I did not call there because I was scheduled to meet my future radio engineer, who was to accompany me to China, in Berlin. He was Seber Weingarten. I was not responsible to the 4th Bureau for routine work during that stay in Moscow or at any later date. I was not a permanent member of the 4th Bureau. My official contacts and my contacts as a party member were confined to special individuals in the bureau and the party central committee. My meeting with Pyatnitsky, Manuilsky, and Kuusinen on the eve of my departure was purely personal and friendly.

(b) My Trip to Moscow in 1933

As soon as I returned from China, I contacted Beldin, the chief of the 4th Bureau, and his new deputy, who gave me an enthusiastic welcome. I was told that my work in China had been most satisfactory and was asked to see the two of them for details about my future activities and mission, I was not given a desk at the department or assigned any work. I was occasionally called in to discuss some matter, but most of the time Beldin or his deputy called at my hotel or invited me to his home.

As I was a member of the party, I reported my arrival immediately to the party central committee, where I again met Smoliansky (alias), who had handled my affairs back in 1929. Here, too, I was praised for my work after I had reported before a small committee and completed the processing required by the party. Smoliansky said that I had a very high standing in the party. He called on me two or three times during my stay and helped me prepare for my new mission. He was highly enthusiastic about my coming trip to Japan and commented on its significance. He did not have the authority to give me orders, but we discussed general pending Soviet-Japanese problems since the Manchurian Incident. Like most party members, he feared a Japanese attack on the U.S.S.R. These talks with Smoliansky had nothing to do with my official duties.

After I had reported on my activities in China to Beldin, I was told that my request to remain in Moscow indefinitely had been rejected and was asked to resume my activities abroad. Half jokingly, I said I might be able to do something in Japan. This suggestion received no immediate answer, but several weeks later Beldin alluded to it with sudden enthusiasm. He gave me to understand that the leaders of the party central committee were equally interested in my work and urged me to make preparations immediately. The Eastern Section apparently had determined my military mission again after discussion with army leaders. Beldin consulted top party leaders and gave me the general picture of the political mission. The plan was for me to observe conditions in Japan thoroughly, explore at first hand the possibilities of operating there, and, if necessary, return to Moscow for final discussions of my future work. Such a preparatory stage was considered necessary by the Moscow authorities, who regarded activities in Japan as most difficult and important.

With Beldin's approval, Radek of the central committee helped me make preparations. About this time, I met an old friend, Alex, at the committee. Radek, Alex, and I engaged in lengthy discussions of general political and economic problems involving Japan and East Asia. Radek exhibited a deep interest in my trip. As I had been in China and he was a recognized expert on Chinese politics, our talks were extremely valuable and interesting. Neither Radek nor Alex was in a position to give me orders, but both offered many suggestions. I got in touch with two members of the Foreign Commissariat who had been in Tokyo and from them obtained a detailed account of life there. I do not know their names or what type of work they were doing. Our talks were purely to exchange general information.

With Beldin's approval, I also saw my old friends Pyatnitsky, Manuilsky, and Kuusinen, who had heard about my activities in China from Beldin and were quite proud of their protégé. Our talks, although they touched on political problems of a general nature, were purely personal and friendly. Pyatnitsky, who had been told about my Japan plans by Beldin, was extremely worried about the hardships I would face but delighted by my enterprising spirit.

(c) My Trip to Moscow in 1935

This trip was brief, lasting only about fourteen days. I saw Ulitsky, the new chief of the 4th Bureau, and Alex, who was working under him. I reported on my experiences in Japan and the bright prospects I foresaw there. I requested a new radio engineer, preferably Seber or Klausen, whom I had known since my China days, asked for absolute freedom to establish any relations I deemed necessary with the German Embassy, where I wanted to do most of my work, and told Ulitsky of my desire to have the central authorities recognize Ozaki as a direct member of our group.

Ulitsky approved these and all of the other important suggestions I made. He warned me to be most cautious at all times and not to rush things. I gained the impression that Ulitsky like Beldin, consulted the party leaders before arranging for my return to Japan. Certainly he must have studied me, my material, and my papers carefully. He was deeply sensible of the difficulties of my position and extended me every kindness. The only people I met at the 4th Bureau were Jim and Klausen at the radio school and representatives of the Code and Eastern Sections. I was strictly forbidden to attend the international convention of the Comintern, which had just started. Manuilsky gave me a flat refusal over the telephone. Kuusinen visited my quarters once. Pyatnitsky was sick and away. It was my personal desire to attend the convention, but security considerations prevented me from doing so.

I called at the central committee once to make a report. This turned out to be my farewell visit, a brief encounter during which my party problems were straightened out and my report was approved. Smoliansky, who had left his old position with the central committee, paid me one friendly call. My social life was very restricted, but I saw Klausen frequently to discuss our joint work in Japan. I left Moscow by plane.

Generally speaking, then, all my business contacts were with the 4th Bureau which acted as my liaison with other offices. I had nothing to do with any other office after 1929. There is no doubt, of course, that the bureau conferred with top leaders of the Red Army and members of the Politburo of the Party Central Committee with respect to the general political and military problems involved in my work abroad. (I do not know whether or not there was any liaison with the Foreign Commissariat.) Similarly, I am certain that the 4th Bureau distributed the information and material I sent to its chief from Japan. The new chief, like his predecessor, Beldin, was on intimate terms with party leaders. He was a party veteran who boasted a long-standing friendship with Lenin, Stalin, and Voroshilov.

(d) My Assignment to the 4th Red Army Bureau

This question of why I was assigned to the 4th Bureau naturally arises after a reading of my earlier notes and what I have just said. Another question also suggests itself: namely, why was I not placed directly under the Soviet Communist Party Central Committee?

The answer to the second question is very simple. The

central committee of the Soviet Communist Party has no international information bureau but only a domestic news office. It relies entirely upon information collected by other branches of the Soviet government and has no thought of duplicating their work; in fact, it has never entertained the idea of establishing an international information department of its own. It has emphasized a wide variety of information collected from various government offices and from various standpoints.

Within the Soviet Union, there are five government agencies engaged in the collection of political, economic, and military information of an international character over a comparatively wide range. These are the Tass News Agency, the Comintern, the Foreign Commissariat, the GPU, and the 4th Bureau of the Red Army. Of course, there are any number of other organizations engaged in the same type of work, but they specialize in particular fields or professions. They are not comprehensive or political, nor do they collect the secret material and information to which the highest Soviet leaders must attach primary importance.

The above-mentioned five government intelligence agencies are somewhat one-sided, and, therefore, unable to meet the growing demand of the top leadership for comprehensive information.

Tass, which handles only legitimate information for the press, is controlled to too great an extent by the censorship regulations of other countries, which must be observed by Tass employees engaged in legitimate work.

I have already described in detail the intelligence work of the Comintern, the primary objectives of which are social problems, the international labor movement, and the Communist party movement. The Comintern does not attempt to collect comprehensive foreign and domestic political reports or secret information.

The reports received by the Foreign Commissariat from Soviet embassies overseas are also defective in that they present only the diplomatic angle; they are one-sided both with regard to the problems handled and with regard to their source (embassy information offices). In most cases, isolated Soviet embassies have been unable to keep up with the mounting demand for comprehensive secret information.

The intelligence activities of the GPU are likewise very one-sided. This agency collects secrets information, but is concerned chiefly with counterespionage, anti-Soviet organizations, and observation of ideological tendencies in foreign countries. It has almost no important information sources of use in the formation of vital foreign policy.

The 4th Bureau cannot be considered a narrow specialized organization whose activities are restricted to military espionage, nor can it be equated with the defense agencies of Germany. To cite a single example, it does not engage in counterespionage like the German National Defense Bureau. It is an intelligence organization which covers a relatively wide field, recruits excellent personnel, and has high technical standards. Pure military espionage is only one of its many activities. It engages in the collection of intelligence in the spheres of military affairs in general, military administration, and economics. Reports accumulate there from military attachés serving with embassies overseas, military committees, wartime economic committees, secret intelligence groups, and spy rings. It also handles and studies a great deal of legitimate and semi-legitimate material on the military governments, purely military problems, and wartime economies of other nations. Finally, there is a political section within the bureau where incoming information is fashioned into highly competent reports or summarized for top army and party leaders.

It was only natural, therefore, that the Soviet high command should turn to the 4th Bureau when the need for secret intelligence became urgent. To cope with the growing demand for information, it was necessary merely to staff the agency with the best personnel available. From the standpoint of technical level and seriousness of purpose, this agency was probably without an equal.

The party leaders and the Red Army have co-operated closely since the founding of the Soviet Union. Most of the old party members joined the army after the revolution. The Red Army has been relatively free from the frequent changes of personnel which have taken place in other branches and offices of the Soviet government and the party, and the so-called purges have not hit the inner core of the old party members as they have in other agencies. The close personal ties uniting the army leaders and Lenin, Stalin, and Molotov have proved lasting and long-standing. It is now easy to understand why the political leaders of the Soviet Union picked the 4th Bureau of the Red Army to answer the growing need for secret political intelligence, although, of course, one cannot deny the fact that other large intelligence agencies were striving to improve the caliber of their own work.

Finally, I must mention the following reasons as partly responsible for my transfer to the 4th Bureau. General Beldin, then chief of the 4th Bureau and a close friend of Pyatnitsky, had known about me since before my days with the Comintern. When, after my return from England, I discussed my past activities for the Comintern with Pyatnitsky and told him that I wanted to enlarge the scope of my work, but that I could not do so as long as I remained with the Comintern, he went to see Beldin about my problem. Beldin was of the opinion that my ambition could be fulfilled satisfactorily at the 4th Bureau and he called me in a few days later for a detailed discussion of comprehensive intelligence activities in Asia. In addition, I had already known various members of the 4th Bureau personally back in Germany. They had visited me in the Rhineland and Frankfurt to converse on political, economic, and military problems and had attempted to interest me in joining the bureau. In other words, Beldin knew about me not only through Pyatnitsky and my activities with the Comintern but also through the reports of two or three of his co-workers during my German days.

I believe I have now covered all the reasons for my transfer to the 4th Bureau in the winter of 1929.

(e) Communications with the 4th Bureau

As this topic has already been discussed in detail in another section, I shall mention here only the different signatures employed by the 4th Bureau on its orders to me. These orders bore the signature "Director," "Dal," and "Organizer." Their significance was as follows. Orders issued personally by the chief of the 4th Bureau were signed Director. Such orders were major directives dealing with political and organizational matters of vital importance to my work. Anniversary greetings always bore the same signature to emphasize the personal touch.

A special indirect style was employed in communications sent to us by important persons. It was possible to guess accurately that radios of gratitude sent to us invariably originated with leading Soviet figures because the chief of the 4th Bureau would express satisfaction to us only when he had been informed that such and such report or material was of value or importance. We received a large number of such messages of congratulations and gratitude from 1936 on, all of which it should be stressed were signed by the director as the originating authority. The above-mentioned three signatures were the only ones that appeared on radiograms or letters. Otherwise all promises would have been broken and our peace of mind would have been destroyed.

I believe that, in addition to the messages of gratitude, a number of orders were sent to us by the director in accordance with instructions from Soviet leaders. The following are only two or three examples.

In reply to a detailed report from me on the secret negotiations for an anti-Comintern pact (which I have described elsewhere), I received a radiogram exhorting me to put more effort into future reports. This incident indicated that the highest political leaders were deeply interested in the problem and in my report. My written report and my lengthy expression of opinion on the diplomatic situation were rewarded with the statement that my views were always welcomed with deep interest in top political circles. In other words, I was told to offer opinions and recommendations on foreign affairs freely. At the same time, I was cleared on the score of having handled a problem which, strictly speaking, I had had no business to touch in Japan.

When, at the time of the Nomonhan Incident, I complained about the inefficiency of Soviet propaganda, I received a reply which expressly stated that my complaint was being sent on to a higher authority and which indicated that appropriate steps would be taken to remedy the situation. The same was true of my reports on the Soviet Union. I was informed that all of them created intense interest among the highest army command. Leaders of the party thanked me, and asked for more news.

During the first several years, comparatively unimportant reports were signed Dal, the Russian equivalent for Far East. Afterward, that is, around the beginning of 1940 or a little later, this was superseded by Organizer. Its appearance on orders meant that they had originated with the Eastern Section of the 4th Bureau and not with the director, although the latter doubtless knew about them. I addressed telegrams or reports that I thought particularly important to the director. This was true of messages pertaining to organizational problems especially important to our local activities, as well as of the more important political and military reports. At times, I appended the word "Confidential" to the address to emphasize the importance of the message still further. This identified the contents as very important, and the message was treated accordingly by the director.

Transitional Notes

Other changes occurred along with the change in the nature of my work; that is, along with the shift from operations on behalf of the Comintern to my present comprehensive espionage activities for the Russian Communist Party and the 4th Bureau of the Red Army. When asked in Moscow whether I would prefer to return to Europe to work for new people who needed my services, to utilize in Europe the experience I had amassed there or, if circumstances warranted, to go to the Far East, I chose the Far East as my new theater of operations. Moscow was very pleased with my decision.

Briefly, my choice and the approval it evoked were based on the following considerations. Before the 1920's, the only theaters of operation in which the revolutionary labor movement and Soviet policy were interested were Europe and a portion of America. Very little attention was paid to the Far East. With the outbreak of the Chinese Revolution, the Comintern and the Soviet Union gradually turned their eyes toward this new area, but the experienced and able men were all more or less interested in European and American affairs. Only a few political observers realized that the Chinese Revolution and, later, the Japanese demarche in Manchuria, were events of far-reaching and worldwide significance. Moreover very few indeed were able to decide to adapt themselves unreservedly to developments in the Far East. I resolved to engage in this work partly because it was congenial to one of my temperament and partly because I was attracted by the new and extremely complicated state of affairs in the Orient. With a small group of others, I believed that a transformation of tremendous consequence in the revolutionary labor movement and in Soviet foreign policy could be anticipated in this new field of the Far East; that the security problem faced by the Soviet Union with respect to external friction and probable attack would have to be reviewed and changed in line with the new role to be played by the Far East; and, finally, that events in the Far East would of necessity cause momentous reverberations in the great powers of Europe and the United States and might bring about a fundamental change in the existing balance of power. That this belief was correct has been demonstrated clearly during the past few months. At the time, it was merely a general idea on my part—a conjecture—but I considered it sufficiently valid to constitute ample grounds on which to transfer my sphere of activity to East Asia. Thus, I made two changes at once, the transfer from Comintern activities to activities on behalf of the Soviet Union, which was tremendously important to me personally (and which, incidentally, showed the shift in emphasis in the Communist movement), and the major shift from Europe to the Far East. Entrusted with a certain mission, I went to China in January or February, 1929 and there embarked upon new and comprehensive espionage activities.

"MY ESPIONAGE GROUP IN CHINA, 1930-1932"

(a) Organization of the China Group

I came to China with two foreign co-workers who had been dispatched on orders from the 4th Bureau of the Red Army. The only person in China upon whom I knew that I could depend was Agnes Smedley, of whom I had first heard in Europe. I solicited her aid in establishing my group in Shanghai and particularly in selecting Chinese co-workers. I met as many as possible of her young Chinese friends, making special efforts to become acquainted with those who volunteered to co-operate and work with foreigners for left-ist causes. I discovered one who was very competent, decided to use him as my interpreter and gradually became so well acquainted with him that I was able to talk to him without reservations. After associating with him for two or three months, I spoke to him briefly of my aims and asked him to work with me. I also asked him to introduce me to suitable persons among his relatives and friends. I called this Chinese "Wang" and added his wife as a second member of my group. Wang gave me the names of his friends in Canton when I went there to spend two or three months, and among them I found a woman, a native Cantonese, who fitted into our work extremely well. She was on close terms with Smedley and I gradually became very friendly with her, succeeding in enlisting her as an associate. Later, her husband, who was a serious tuberculosis case, joined our group. A Chinese whom I used to call Chiang, and whom I met through this Cantonese woman, also became my associate in Canton. The Cantonese woman took care of liaison between me and him. After my return to Shanghai, I increased the number of my associates greatly by selecting suitable people from among the friends of Wang and Chui, the Cantonese woman. Thus, the Chinese members of my group in China were recruited. All of them were sympathizers with the people's revolutionary movement and some had had contacts with the Chinese Communist Party, but none had been party members. In compliance with orders from headquarters, I had been deliberately avoiding any direct connections with the Chinese Communist Party.

I used the same method in obtaining foreign co-workers for my espionage group. At first I selected people from among Smedley's friends, approaching them by asking Smedley to introduce me to them and then waiting until I could negotiate with them directly. I kept the number of foreign co-workers obtained in this manner down to three. They were not actual members of my group, but rather helpers or supporters. The first friend I made in Shanghai was Ozaki, through whom I established connections with other Japanese. I cannot say definitely now, but I seem to remember that I met Ozaki for the first time through Smedley; I am sure that before I met him I asked Smedley repeatedly to introduce a suitable Japanese to me. There is no doubt that Smedley conferred with her Chinese acquaintances concerning my request and that it was relayed to suitable Chinese and Japanese in Shanghai. It was in that way that I met Ozaki, and I think Smedley was the one who introduced us. After that Smedley and I met Ozaki frequently at Smedley's home. As I have stated previously, all of these things happened so long ago that my memory is not very accurate, but I believe that my first meeting with Ozaki was exactly as I have stated above. I do not remember whether I met him for the first time in a restaurant or whether it was at Smedley's house. At any rate, I cannot recall that Kito requested that I meet Ozaki. I cannot recall being at all intimate with Kito. By meeting Ozaki, I was able to realize my desire to become acquainted with a suitable Japanese.

(b) Chinese Members Collect Information

As before, I would like to limit my discussion to a minimum number of Chinese with whom I dealt directly. I worked chiefly with Wang in Shanghai; only in exceptional cases did I work with other members. Wang brought in data and information from various sources and we discussed them. When the information and data submitted were of such a nature as to require more accurate explanations or reports, he and I talked to the persons who had brought them in. I transmitted orders and requests pertaining to the collection of data and information to others through him. I avoided meeting agents individually to explain my orders in other than exceptional cases. However, in the presence of Wang, I usually met agents who came from places other than Shanghai. With the passing of time, it became apparent that individual agents possessed special interests and skills with respect to certain of the subjects on which information and data were being gathered, and we began to divide the work in Shanghai roughly according to individual specialties. Agents in Peiping, Hankow, Canton, etc., had to handle all kinds of problems. We met late at night most of the time, using crowded streets when the weather permitted. Meetings were also held in private homes, for instance, at Wang's home or, more convenient, at foreigners' homes which I could visit easily. Since frequent meetings at one place would attract attention, I took care to change the location from time to time. I avoided using my own home as a meeting place as much as possible. Working in this manner made it necessary for me to meet Wang frequently before a project was undertaken, but in the Shanghai of those days not much risk was involved and it was not at all impossible to do so.

(c) Methods of Contacting Japanese Members

My meetings with Japanese members took place at restaurants, cafés, or Smedley's home. Since it was dangerous for Japanese to walk around the streets of Shanghai at the time of the first Shanghai Incident, for safety's sake I waited for the Japanese member at the Garden Bridge at the boundary of a Japanese Concession and put him in an automobile or escorted him myself to the meeting place. In order to avoid detection by the Japanese police, I hardly ever visited Japanese in the Japanese Concession. There were exceptions, however; I met Ozaki once or twice at a café in Hankow. I felt most at ease when we met at Smedley's home and I took Ozaki and Kawai there on many occasions. We went back and forth to the meetings by automobile, since they were usually held late at night. I avoided unduly frequent meetings. As far as possible, I tried to separate them by intervals of at least two weeks. After Ozaki was replaced by other Japanese, I changed the rendezvous to main streets in the International Settlement. We usually met in cafés or in the restaurants of large hotels on Nanking Road. We had to avoid going to Chinese restaurants as much as possible because the Chinese were antagonistic toward the Japanese. Meeting dates, fixed beforehand, were strictly observed to obviate the necessity of utilizing the telephone and the mails. There were times when we were at a loss as to what to do when something important happened suddenly, but we decided to stick to this policy. Whenever I met Japanese I did so alone; I did not allow my foreign national assistants to accompany me. The first time I introduced a Japanese to Paul was when I made liaison arrangements in connection with my departure from Shanghai. We very seldomed exchanged written materials when we met; we transmitted information orally. Kawai's reports were exceptions.

For the most part, I met foreign members at their homes. My own home was also often used. Meetings were held very frequently, with arrangements usually being made by telephone. Later, we also met at the homes of members' friends. At times, we had supper at restaurants or went to the Japanese Concession. We hid the materials we collected and the documents we compiled in our homes. I destroyed or returned the materials after sending my reports to Moscow, but, even so, we always had a great many documents in our possession. Unlike Japan, Shanghai at that time was comparatively safe for persons engaged in activities such as ours. We left very important documents with friends for safekeeping. Our friends did not know the nature of the things that were left in their custody. We merely said that they were confidential documents when we asked them to hold them for us.

(d) Personal Collection of Information

The information brought in by the members was not enough to satisfy me, so I personally went out and collected all the facts and materials that I possibly could. There was no embassy in Shanghai, but I immediately gained an entree into German social circles and there gathered information of various descriptions. In these circles, which revolved around the German Consulate General, I became very well known and much sought after by people who wanted favors done. I associated with German merchants, military instructors, and scholars, among whom the most important were the military advisers to the Nanking government. I selected and associated with the ones who were active not only in military but in political affairs at Nanking, as, for example, Colonel van Glieber, then senior military adviser and later consul general. The military advisers frequently invited me to Nanking and came to Shanghai to visit me. I also traveled with them to Chiahsing and Hangchow. I received a great deal of information from them as to the inner workings of the Nanking government, plans for subjugation of the war lords and economic and political policies and, at the time of the Shanghai Incident in 1932, they provided me with accurate facts concerning the methods of warfare and actual strength of the Japanese. By becoming friendly with the Eurasia German fliers, I was able to learn about conditions in remote Chinese districts. Moreover, I made several trips into the interior to study various aspects of the Chinese scene. By constantly broadening my knowledge and reading books about China, I was able to become enough of an authority to submit information and make timely judgments on subjects of many descriptions.

(e) The Writer's Duties in China

I shall now endeavor to explain my two types of espionage activity: *i.e.*, the duties assigned to me by Moscow and the study projects which I selected myself.

Duties assigned by Moscow:

1. *Social and political analysis of Nanking government.* Among the main things which we attempted to ascertain through our espionage activity in this connection were the classes of people actively supporting the Nanking government and the true nature of the change taking place in the government's social foundation. At that time the attitude of the Chinese masses—the laborers and farmers—toward the Nanking government was either passive or antagonistic, while the Shanghai bankers, the Chekiang financial clique, the large landowners, the gangs, the opium smugglers, and other big business interests were gradually beginning to regard it with favor. The attitudes of the intellectuals varied, but with the expansion of the government's bureaucratic structure some of them had become government officials. I had to study and report to Moscow the attitudes of the important classes of the people toward the Nanking government and the manner in which those attitudes were changing. I gathered pertinent information mostly through conversation with members of my group, association with people in various walks of life, and other types of personal research. I sent voluminous reports to Moscow twice, once during the latter part of 1930 and once around June or July, 1932, and smaller supplementary reports on several occasions.

Investigation of the military strength of the Nanking government called for the constant collection of all sorts of information about the various divisions maintained by the government and the reorganizations effected by the German military advisers. Moreover, we had to keep on the lookout for changes in the military high command, in the armament of fortresses and military units and in military training. We gradually compiled complete information concerning the so-called Chiang Kai-shek divisions, which were equipped with the latest weapons; the divisions loyal to the Nanking government; and the divisions of dubious reliability; and, in addition, were able to ascertain in a general way the situation of major units with respect to modern weapons and reorganization. Since conditions were always changing, however, it was next to impossible to know exactly how things stood at all times. I gathered facts of this type chiefly through the

Chinese members of my group, but I had to obtain important information personally from German military advisers and businessmen engaged in importing weapons.

2. *Six Groups and Factions Opposing Nanking Government.* My main objects of study were the Canton, Kwangsi, Feng Yuhsiang as well as other factions, among which the first two I was able to investigate with particular thoroughness. The important point here, too, was to clarify the nature of the basic social elements of which these groups and factions were composed. Although foreign banks were also involved, the Canton bankers and wealthy Kwangsi men, who were exclusively Chinese, were playing an important role behind the scenes. I personally gathered most of the material which the group obtained with regard to this problem, but after I left South China my associates sent me supplementary reports more or less regularly.

3. *Nanking's Social and Foreign Policies.* The investigation of these problems called for an examination of the theoretical bases and actual operation of the various laws promulgated by the Nanking government for the benefit of the laborers and farmers, but, as the government was not very interested in such matters, I had very little to report. My Chinese associates collected the materials. I cannot recall any details concerning the reports which I made.

I had been ordered to gather information continuously concerning the Nanking government's foreign policy. I was most concerned with the attitudes adopted toward the Soviet Union, Japan, England, and the United States. It was clear that the government's policy was one of dependence on England and the United States and that, from a practical standpoint, the policy was paying off. Nanking believed that this foreign policy of dependence on England and the United States would enable it to take a strong stand against the Soviet Union and, later, against Japan. I gathered material concerning the problem from my Chinese members and from the German and American consulates. During the Shanghai Incident of 1932, this policy of reliance on British and American support was most interesting to observe. England and the United States made desperate efforts to help the Nanking government resist Japan.

4. *British and American China Policies.* I have already dealt with this problem. It was also my duty to investigate the situation with regard to Anglo-American and Japanese dealings with anti-Chiang factions. England was using Hong Kong as a base for maneuvers aimed at a *rapprochement* with the Canton and Kwangsi factions and Japan was doing everything possible to win over influential elements in North

China, but had not as yet attempted to branch out in other directions.

We had to keep a close watch on foreign garrison forces and fleets in China, with special reference to changes. As soon as the Shanghai Incident broke out, the various powers increased their military strength greatly, with the result that my work in this field became extremely important, and I had to make more minute observations of the various powers' dispositions of military strength than in the past. I collected most of the material myself from German military instructors.

This issue of extraterritoriality played an extremely important role in foreign policy at the time. To the Nanking government it was an internal problem involving considerations of prestige and frequent conferences with the representatives of the various powers were held concerning it. When the so-called Fessenden Mission was sent out to draw up a compromise proposal with respect to the Shanghai concessions, the problem reached the explosive state. The mission came up with a proposal, the contents of which I learned far in advance of the official announcement from German and American sources. The United States, which was very favorably disposed toward the Nanking government, was then endeavoring to settle the extraterritoriality problem and England appeared to be reluctantly following the American lead. The Soviet Union was interested in the problem only in so far as it exerted a very real effect upon relations between the Nanking government and the various powers enjoying extraterritorial rights.

5. *Chinese Agriculture and Industry.* The Nanking government was engaged in a number of projects to overcome the agricultural crisis and it was my duty to observe the results. The government's agricultural policies were designed primarily for the benefit of the wealthy farmers and great landowners and none of them was successful.

I was also supposed to observe industrial developments, with particular reference to any attempt to foster the munitions industry. My investigations disclosed that the textile industry had grown tremendously, that two or three new arsenals had been built, that old arsenals had been renovated, and similar facts. I was able to determine the exact productive capacity of the Nanking and Hankow arsenals, obtaining official diagrams, statistical reports, and other accurate documents. Chinese members of my group and Germans furnished the data. I also had to investigate Chinese air routes, methods of training fliers, etc., in which connection I was able to contact and gather important information from German fliers.

I continued to study the problem of Chinese agriculture, which I had personally selected as a subject of investigation, over a long period of time. The fact that I was particularly interested in it resulted in my accumulating an enormous amount of pertinent data.

Subjects which I personally chose for study as a result of events which occurred after I assumed my duties in China:

1. *Activities of Germans and German Military Advisers.* I was so forcibly struck after assuming my duties in China by the increasing tempo of German activities that I resolved to undertake a detailed study of the subject. The Moscow authorities approved my investigation of German economic activities and encouraged me to become friendly with the German military advisers. The Germans were attempting to increase their political prestige in China, which was then negligible, by virtue of their strong economic foundation at home and of their influence over the military policy of the Nanking government. Germany paid little attention to Japan at the time, most German diplomats believing that Germany would be able to secure a place in the Far East through a vigorous China policy. Such thinking still predominated in the early stages of the China Incident and there was very little support for the pro-Japanese policy advocated by a handful of Nazi leaders. Even today, most Germans favor China over Japan. German economic circles, in particular, see a brighter future in China than in Japan. In other words, not only has Germany traditionally maintained a sympathetic attitude toward China, but she looks to her for the satisfaction of her economic needs. For these reasons, many Germans have not abandoned hope of a Sino-German accord. Germany's economic and military activities in China at the time in question were designed to establish a starting point for such a pact. It cannot be said Germany's desires have been permanently frustrated by Japan's recent China policy, but their realization has certainly become impossible for the time being. The objective of Germany's activities at the time was to gain control of the reorganization of the Chinese Army. She planned to supply war materials to the army and ultimately establish a network of munitions plants and indirect national defense enterprises. At the same time, China was to become the proving ground for the German aeronautical industry. Such were the common objectives of the German military advisers, businessmen, diplomats, etc. in China. Needless to say, these German policies with respect to China became matters of grave concern to the Soviet Union, both economically and politically. The Soviet Union

knew Chiang Kai-shek well enough to be sure that China and Germany could not act in concert against her in Mongolia and Turkestan, but it was still necessary to watch relations between the two very closely. I voluntarily assumed the duty of observing and collecting information on this subject and I believe I did so most successfully. At all times, I was able to collect accurate information from Germans because I associated with a great many and was on friendly terms with the most influential advisers.

2. *New American Activity in China.* American activities in China, which consisted chiefly of large investments in Shanghai and investments in radio broadcasting and aviation enterprises, were being directed systematically by American businessmen and commercial attachés at the Shanghai consulate. The United States had also become active diplomatically in connection with the problems of extraterritorial rights and the cessation of hostilities in Shanghai. The United States will take the place of Great Britain as the dominant power in the Far East, a future development of which signs had appeared at that time; British activities in the Far East were already receding. Thus, the U.S.S.R. was placed in a position where she had to give more consideration to diplomatic relations with the United States.

I received material on this complex problem mainly from Smedley and a young member of the American Consulate, but Smedley's contributions were sporadic in nature.

The Manchurian Incident which occurred in the fall of 1931 changed the position of Japan in the Far East completely. After seizing control of Manchuria, Japan had an incentive to play an extremely active role in East Asia. Furthermore, it was easy to see that the conquest had bolstered her determination to make that role a dominant and exclusive one. The direct effort of the Manchurian Incident on the Soviet Union was to bring her face to face with Japan in a vast border region hitherto more or less neglected from the standpoint of national defense. In other words, a new situation of very far-reaching significance for the Soviet Union had developed. I had no duties with respect to Manchuria, which was the responsibility of the Harbin group, but I was nevertheless forced to watch this new situation in East Asia very closely.

3. *Shanghai Incident.* The outbreak of the battle of Shanghai in 1932 indicated a new trend in Japanese diplomatic policy, although, of course, we did not know definitely at the time whether it was simply a single unexpected skirmish or whether it represented a Japanese effort to conquer China following the acquisition of Manchuria. It was likewise im-

possible to tell whether Japan would push northward toward Siberia or southward into China. Such being the situation, my work became much more important during the Shanghai Incident. I had to try to discover Japan's true purpose and to study in detail the fighting methods of the Japanese Army in the battle of Shanghai.

The Manchurian Incident and the Shanghai Incident presented new Sino-Japanese problems. Relations between the two countries not only exhibited an inevitable deterioration, but they changed completely in nature. China, like the Soviet Union, viewed the new Japanese activity with new eyes and, perforce, with new apprehension. It goes without saying that I devoted the closest attention to these new problems.

Although I investigated all these matters separately, I found myself compelled to deal with the problem of Japan as a whole and I decided to do so in a general way while still in China. As a start, I embarked on a course of study by which I sought to become thoroughly familiar with Japanese history and diplomatic policies.

(f) Other Groups in China

1. *"Jim" or "Lehman" group.* The first group to work in Shanghai was the Jim group, also known as the Lehman group. I had never heard of it until I arrived in Shanghai. Jim had been sent out from the 4th Bureau of the Red Army, arriving in Shanghai slightly before Alex and me. His chief duty was to establish radio communication between Shanghai and other parts of China and Moscow. In short, his duties were primarily technical, preparatory, and experimental in character. When I arrived in Shanghai he had already succeeded in establishing radio communication between Shanghai and Moscow and was trying to establish contacts with other districts in a similar manner. However, it seems that he was unsuccessful in the case of Canton. Jim employed Klausen as his subordinate. Further, he employed a White Russian called Mischa or Mishin in Shanghai. Later, he gave Alex and me the wireless station that he had established in Shanghai and made preparations to leave for Moscow. I do not know when he left Shanghai. I know only that after he returned to Moscow he became principal of the radio school. I met him in Moscow when he was principal of the school. I took care of Mischa until he died. He worked for me in Canton and later in Shanghai. Klausen was with my group for a short time. In 1931, I sent him to the Harbin group on orders from Moscow. Thus, the Jim-Lehman group died a natural death.

2. *Harbin group.* The next group with which I came into contact in the course of my work was the Harbin group, which had also been sent out by the 4th Bureau of the Red Army. Its duty was to gather military information in Manchuria. As a sideline, it gathered political intelligence as well. The Harbin group acted as a letter box for me; I forwarded letters and documents for Moscow to it and it sent them on. Money sent to me by Moscow also came through this channel. Liaison with the Harbin group was established in the following way. To begin with, somebody from the group came to Shanghai to confer on the technique of the "letter-box communication" system, and thereafter members of my group and members of the Harbin group took turns at serving as mail carriers and traveling between Harbin and Shanghai. Klausen acted as contact man for me on numerous occasions. I believe it was in the spring of 1932 that I myself carried mail to Harbin.

I met Ott-Gloemberg, chief of the Harbin group, for the first time in Shanghai. I called on him at Harbin to turn over the mail to him at Harbin. I also met Frolich, sometimes called Theo, who had formerly worked in Shanghai. I do not believe I met the radio technician, Artur, at Harbin, although I had heard about him. Theo and Ott-Gloemberg left Harbin in 1932. I happened to meet them by chance and not in connection with my work in Russia in January, 1933. My relationship with the Harbin group was strictly a letter-box affair. There was no administrative relationship at all.

3. *Frolich-Feldmann group in Shanghai.* The Frolich-Feldmann group was also operating in Shanghai in 1931. Like the others, it had been sent out by the 4th Bureau of the Red Army. Its duty was to make connections with the Chinese Red Army and to gather intelligence concerning it. It had its own radio connection with Moscow and therefore did not use our station. The chief of the group was Frolich, also known as Theo, who held the rank of major general in the Red Army. Feldmann was a radio technician and held the rank of lieutenant colonel. There was another man in the group, but I do not know who he was. Unable to fulfill their mission, these people left Shanghai during 1931. I had no working relationship with them and met them only by chance. Shanghai is such a small city that it was difficult to avoid such chance encounters. I did not receive instructions from Moscow to contact them. They had their own mission to perform and there was no formal connection between us.

4. *Comintern group in Shanghai.* I met the Comintern

group in Shanghai by chance in 1931. It consisted of a political branch of an organization branch, the latter comprised of Noulens, who became famous after his arrest, and one or two assistants. Karl Lease later came to Shanghai to assume the post left vacant by Noulens. The organization branch had various duties to perform, but it was primarily concerned with the maintenance of liaison between the Comintern, the Chinese Communist party, and the political branch of the Shanghai Comintern group. Liaison duty was of three different types: (a) personnel work, *i.e.*, the movement of personnel between Moscow and the Chinese Communist Party, (b) the transmittal of documents and letters, and (c) radio communication. The organization branch also assumed the duty of financial liaison between Moscow, the Chinese Communist Party, and the political branch; assisted in finding meeting places and houses for the organization branch and the Chinese Communist Party; rendered all kinds of technical and organizational assistance to illegal activities in China; took an active part in the exchange of secret materials between Moscow and China; and assumed responsibility for the safety of members of the political branch. In this last connection, it had the authority to issue orders to political branch members, restrict their movements, etc.

The political branch consisted of Gerhardt, whom I had known in Germany and worked with in my Comintern days, and one or two assistants. I did not meet the assistants. I chanced to meet Gerhardt in Shanghai and renewed our old acquaintance, but our work was absolutely unrelated. Gerhardt's duty, or rather that of the political branch, was to act as a spokesman for the political policy with respect to the Chinese Communist Party decided upon by the Comintern general conference. It also acted as an intermediary for the exchange of information between the Chinese Communist Party and the Comintern and submitted reports concerning all the social problems involved in the labor movement in China. The reports were forwarded to Moscow through the organization branch. I must state here that these reports were never sent through my radio facilities or my other liaison channels. With the arrest of Noulens, Gerhardt's status in Shanghai became precarious, and he decided to return to Moscow in 1931. All in all, I met Gerhardt only three times.

(g) The Noulens Incident

I first learned that Noulens was secretly operating in Shanghai when he was arrested. The arrest caused a great sensation among the foreigners in Shanghai. The Shanghai settlement police arrested him at the request of the Nanking government and remanded him into the government's custody. The government had arrested the leaders of the Chinese Communist Party and learned from their confessions of Noulens' existence and activities. It had even discovered the rendezvous where Noulens and the party met. Noulens and his family were arrested at their home, where extremely damaging secret documents were uncovered and seized as prima-facie evidence. Noulens insisted that he was Swiss, but the Swiss authorities vehemently denied it. He was sentenced to a long prison term, but soon afterward the Soviet Union intervened and he was deported.

"ESPIONAGE OF MY GROUP IN JAPAN, 1933-1941"

(a) The Techniques Employed in Espionage

The membership of my espionage group automatically determined to some extent the manner in which the work of collecting information and intelligence was divided. Klausen was unable to take part in the actual collection of intelligence and information, because his purely technical duties kept him fully occupied. Ozaki obtained information chiefly about political and economic affairs, Miyagi gathered economic and military data and took charge of the translation of all documents written in Japanese, and Voukelitch collected news primarily from foreign correspondents and French acquaintances and handled such technical work as photography. I myself gathered and collected information from foreigners, principally Germans.

Generally speaking, the group members knew only what I told them of the functions entrusted to us and the parts specifically assigned to them. At the same time, it was stipulated that when one of them met with me we would discuss all problems in which he was interested or which he thought important, which meant that not only Ozaki but also Miyagi and Voukelitch had to bring in as much political and economic information as they were able to obtain, and that Ozaki brought in whatever military information he could gather. The division of work was intentionally kept flexible so as to obtain information from the widest range possible. For example, it was my duty to see that Miyagi did not become so engrossed in economic and political questions as to neglect military information. I reserved the right to revise when necessary the principle that each member should concentrate on his primary intelligence function. I spared no effort to avoid subjecting members to such revisions, but nevertheless I occasionally made changes.

On special occasions, I had all the members concentrate on a single particular problem regardless of their individual functions. I will cite several instances in which this was done. During the February 26, 1936 Incident, I asked them to devote their full attention to gathering detailed information of every description, from which I then made what sense I could. Again, in 1937, I directed all of them to concentrate for the first few weeks after the outbreak of the China Incident on the preparations for the first mobilization of the Japanese Army. When the Nomonhan battle began, I asked everyone to concern himself exclusively with discovering what reinforcements Japan would send to the Mongolian border in order that I might be able to judge the potential extent of the conflict. When Germany attacked the U.S.S.R., all members collected all manner of detailed information on Japan's political attitude toward the war, and I observed in great detail the scope and direction (north or south) of the great mobilization begun in Japan at the time. After I was convinced that there would be no war between Japan and the Soviet Union, I asked that attention be directed to the American-Japanese conversations, which were taking place under the strained relations then existing between the countries, and to their future progress.

From the wealth of information collected by my agents and myself I sometimes selected and called to the attention of my colleagues questions which I personally felt were worthy of special note. At other times, I told them that such and such a problem was of no interest as far as our work was concerned, or brought to their attention the fact that much contradictory information was being reported and urged them to submit accurate reports on matters in hand, to discover the true causes of events, etc.

I decided what portion of the information brought me and the information I myself collected should be reported to Moscow by radio, what should be reserved for later delivery by courier in more detailed written form and what should not be sent at all.

As a general rule, I did not reveal to my collaborators the manner in which I used information and intelligence.

Only Klausen, who handled the code message, knew what reports I sent to Moscow and how I revised the information I obtained. (Of course, I sometimes consulted Ozaki for increased accuracy in the evaluation and interpretation of news and important political developments.) I kept secret all my documentary reports, no matter what their nature; when it was necessary to round out a report, I would ask someone, usually Miyagi, for additional or supplementary information, but I tried not to go beyond that. I often asked Ozaki and Miyagi to prepare certain military or other information in written form for my next report, doing so whenever I felt that some special problem would be of particular interest to Moscow or that it required immediate attention.

I not only selected the information to be used in our reports to Moscow, but I also decided how to use it. In other words, I did not pass on information obtained from my collaborators exactly as I received it. I used information of every type as a basis for my wireless and other reports, relating it to other information and evaluating it for worth and accuracy. This was why my wireless messages and reports did not necessarily repeat the actual wording of reports from my collaborators. Of course, I do not mean to say that I acted in an arbitrary fashion; I used the information I received very conscientiously and after careful deliberation.

I very seldom told all my co-workers about information and data which I personally acquired or about reports brought me by group members; I did so only when I thought it necessary in order to indicate a definite direction for their efforts or to avoid the collection of false information. There were times, however, when, for general political reasons, I felt that it was necessary to inform my co-workers of information I had obtained personally or from the members of the group.

To sum up, I personally handled the division of work, the selection of information, and the preparation of reports for Moscow.

(b) International Liaison of Espionage Group

Our international liaison activities consisted almost exclusively of the transmittal of mail to and from Moscow. In other words, we maintained technical liaison with the central authorities by courier; but we had no personal contacts with other activity groups or organizations, either in Japan or abroad. There were hardly any instances in which courier liaison from here or from Moscow was not of a purely technical nature. At a prearranged meeting, a courier from my group would deliver a carefully wrapped packet to a Moscow courier and receive in return a packet from Moscow. That concluded their business; nothing more was said, except for a few general questions and answers, and no reports were exchanged. Conversation on secret matters regarding the work was sanctioned only when Moscow had been consulted beforehand. It was permissable, however, to ask the courier if he had been to Moscow lately and, if he had, to inquire about conditions there and about old friends. If we had met the same courier several times before, we asked general questions about the Soviet Union and our friends. As previously noted, the work, its nature, and the organization were referred to only under very special and unusual circumstances.

The couriers from Moscow were not authorized to give us orders. With one exception, they were all strangers to us, and we knew neither their names nor their positions in Moscow or abroad. We had the impression that most of those whom we met over a long period of time were "professional" couriers; that is to say, that they were entrusted with carrying the Soviet Union's official courier mail and the so-called unofficial mail (*i.e.*, such as that for my espionage group).

In most cases, we did not know whether their main headquarters was in Moscow or in some one of the official or unofficial organizations maintained by the Soviet Union abroad. Most of the ones we met were fairly young men, whose general level of training, political and otherwise, seemed quite ordinary. Meetings with them were arranged with Moscow in advance. The place of the meeting, the time and the formal technical conditions were agreed upon by radio. If the couriers were unknown to one another, special distinguishing signs, passwords and series of recognition phrases were decided by radio. For example, the following arrangement was once made for a meeting with a courier in a certain restaurant in Hong Kong. The Moscow courier was to enter the restaurant a few minutes past three o'clock, take from his pocket a big long black Manila cigar, and hold it in his hand without lighting it. When the courier from here (on that occasion it was I) saw the signal, he was to approach the restaurant counter, take a conspicuous pipe from his pocket, and fail to light it. When the Moscow courier saw him do so, he was to light his cigar, after which I was to light my pipe. The Moscow courier would then leave the restaurant, I too would leave and follow him slowly to a certain park where we were to hold our conversation. He would begin by saying, "Greetings from Katcha" and I would say "Greetings from Gustav," after which everything was to take place as planned.

For other meetings, for example, the one that took place in a certain coffeeshop in Shanghai, it was arranged to signal with small packages; that is, one person would carry a yellow package and the other a red one.

A third type of rendezvous was planned at a very small Japanese restaurant in Tokyo, a place where other foreigners never came. The courier who was to come in last was to order a very special Japanese dish, and the man I sent was to use this as an opening to begin a conversation with him, asking if the dish were sweet and saying that his friend "Paul" always ordered it too. The courier from Moscow was to answer that he had heard of it from his friend "Jimmy." As all the arranged passwords had then been given, they would begin to discuss delivery of the material.

If the same couriers met frequently, it was agreed that they themselves would arrange their next meeting. Moscow was informed, however, if, in the course of time, some unexpected change became necessary.

Too much time has elapsed between 1933 and 1941 for me to be able to give the exact number and dates of the meetings which occurred between Moscow couriers and representatives of my group, but I will describe the ones I remember.

The first meeting, which had been arranged in Moscow before my departure, took place in Tokyo toward the end of 1933 or the beginning of 1934, when a courier whom I did not know came from Shanghai with my name and the German Embassy as an address to contact. He telephoned the embassy and also informed me by letter that he had arranged to have a doorman wait for me in the lobby of the Imperial Hotel on the morning of a certain day and take me to him. The meeting was carried through as planned. We arranged to go on a sight-seeing visit to Nikko the following day, and we exchanged what we had to deliver there. His package contained chiefly money. He left me the number of a post office box in Shanghai for use in case of need.

Arrangements were made for another meeting around May of 1934 in Shanghai. This courier spoke English so as to give the impression that he was very clever, but I took him for a Scandinavian. I did not know what he did or where, nor did I ask. The passwords to be exchanged at the hotel for the first meeting had been arranged previously in

Moscow. I have now forgotten them, although I remember that they were names of fictional characters.

For the next meeting, which, as I said before, took place in Shanghai, I sent Bernhardt's wife. In accordance with arrangements, she was summoned to the Palace Hotel on the morning of a certain day, and on the following day at about the same time she was visited in her room by a certain woman and the remaining arrangements were made.

Bernhardt himself went to the next meeting, also in Shanghai, which occurred in the autumn of 1934. It had been arranged by radio. As I remember, packages of various colors were used as recognition signals and two personal names as passwords.

Bernhardt's wife went to Shanghai again at the beginning of 1935, at which time arrangements had already been made for the two of them to return to Moscow within the year. Besides serving as a courier, Mrs. Bernhardt also made a number of purchases for us.

I myself carried our next lot of mail direct to Moscow, when, as previously noted, I went to report in 1935. I had originally been forbidden to dispense with the services of a special courier and make a long journey carrying articles to be delivered through many countries, but I made photographs of the documents and brought them safely. In Moscow I wrote out the reports which had hitherto been sent by courier and also made a detailed verbal report.

After my return to Tokyo on September 26, 1935, I sent a courier to Shanghai again for the first time in the spring of 1936. As far as I can recall, I sent Klausen, who had to go to Shanghai anyway to bring back his wife. This meeting was arranged in advance by radio.

I myself went to Peiping in August of 1936 to deliver material. This time it was not an ordinary courier whom I met, but my old Moscow friend "Alex" (not the same man as the Shanghai "Alex" of 1930), who had formerly worked for the Secretariat of the Russian Communist Party in Moscow but was then with the 4th Bureau. At this meeting he was to consult with me about all kinds of problems connected with the work, i.e., about organizational and political problems. It had been arranged beforehand by radio that we were to meet at the Temple of Heaven in Peiping on a definite date and the meeting was held as planned.

Around that time, Guenther Stein and his friend Miss Gantenbein joined our activity group in Japan. Thus, I was able to make use of a number of people as couriers: Klausen, Mrs. Klausen, Guenther Stein, and Stein's woman friend. Between the beginning of 1937 and the summer of 1938, I sent these people to Shanghai by turns to deliver mail. As far as I remember, I sent someone three times in 1937. I sent someone two or three times in 1938 before summer. At the end of 1938, I myself traveled to Manila and Hong Kong as a courier for the German Embassy, at the same time carrying materials to be delivered to Moscow. The other courier appeared to have come by air from Chungking to Hong Kong where we met. The meeting place had been designated by radio; the recognition signals were, as I said before, a cigar and a pipe.

I no longer remember whether it was in 1939 or in 1940 that I stopped sending couriers to Shanghai. I may have sent Mrs. Klausen or Klausen himself to Shanghai once in 1939. At any rate, courier liaison with Shanghai gradually became more difficult as a stricter control came to be exercised over return trips to Japan. I then inquired about the possibility of meeting in Tokyo and, after much trouble on the part of Moscow, a liaison system was established in Tokyo.

The technical side of the matter was entrusted to Klausen. I do not know how many times he met couriers in Tokyo in 1940, but I am certain it was not less than three; it may have been more. Once, when he was ill, I myself met a courier in a small restaurant close to the Shimbashi Station. This meeting was arranged in the manner I have already described. The recognition signal was to order a certain special Japanese dish. Meetings were held frequently in 1941. We delivered material to couriers especially often from the sixth to the eighth week after the outbreak of the Russo-German war. Once I attended a meeting in Klausen's office to see the courier myself.

I believe that two different couriers came to the meetings in Tokyo, a tall strong-looking young man and, later, a still younger, slightly built courier. However, I was unable to identify the picture shown me by the police officer in the last examination as the tall strong man. The man I met did not wear glasses. The picture of the second man shown me bears some resemblance to the man I met in Klausen's office, but I hesitate to swear that it is the same man. The last courier I met was, I thought, in every respect a typical professional courier, traveling from country to country. I used to avoid asking questions about such things. We parted after a brief conversation on the Russo-German war.

The last meeting with a courier before my arrest was probably held in the first part of October. Because it was Klausen who went, I do not remember the date. No photographs were given to the courier at that time, but only some information, collected for the most part by Miyagi, which was handed over in the form in which it had been submitted. As far as I know, the next meeting was to have taken place in November.

Technically speaking, the material which we sent to Moscow by courier consisted of numerous rolls of film taken with a Leica or similar camera. We rolled the film tightly to make it as small as possible. When we had not sent anything for a long period—that is, for four or five months—twenty-five to thirty rolls of film would accumulate. After the European War began, the amount of material which we sent gradually decreased because we began more and more to report the main results of our work by radio. After the outbreak of the Russo-German war, in particular, we cut down on long reports and bulky documents and concentrated on reporting essential facts by radio.

For the most part, the couriers from Moscow brought only money; very rarely did we receive written orders. Such orders as they did bring were always couched in very simple terms. Again, only very rarely did we receive evaluations from Moscow on information which we had sent, or messages indicating that such and such information was of little interest but that such and such information was highly important. Occasionally we were urged to report in more detail on a certain question.

International liaison of this type by specially delegated persons was the only contact we had; other than that, we were completely isolated.

(c) Missions of My Espionage Group in Japan

The duty outlined in 1933 and the more detailed duties assigned by Moscow in 1935 may be summarized as follows:

1. To observe most closely Japan's policy toward the U.S.S.R. following the Manchurian Incident, and, at the same time, to give very careful study to the question of whether or not Japan was planning to attack the U.S.S.R.

This was for many years the most important duty assigned to me and my group; it would not be far wrong to say that it was the sole object of my mission in Japan. In 1935, when Klausen and I bade good-by to General Olitsky of the 4th Bureau, he strongly stressed its significance. Its accomplishment, in the sense that it would enable the U.S.S.R. to avoid fighting a war with Japan, was a matter of extreme concern to all quarters in Moscow. What must be taken into account here is the fact that the U.S.S.R., as it viewed the prominent role played and the attitude taken by the Japanese military in foreign policy after the Manchurian Incident, had come to harbor a deeply implanted suspicion that Japan was planning to attack the Soviet Union, a suspicion so strong that my frequently expressed opinions to the contrary were not always fully appreciated in Moscow, especially during the Nomonhan battle and the large-scale Japanese mobilization which followed in the summer of 1941.

Besides our primary mission of discovering whether or not Japan intended to attack the Soviet Union, we were also naturally expected to observe all other foreign policy issues involving Japan's policy toward the Soviet Union. However, Moscow was more concerned with the Manchuria-Siberia border problem and the Mongolia-Manchuria border problem than with fishing problems or the Sakhalin question.

2. To make an accurate observation of any reorganization and augmentation of Japanese Army and air units which might be directed against the Soviet Union.

This duty, which was related to the first one, entailed the obtaining of very broad military intelligence, because the Japanese military, in order to justify their increased budget demands, were pointing to the Soviet Union as Japan's principal enemy. Accordingly, my espionage mission was not concerned solely with increases in the number of Japanese forces in Manchukuo but covered all measures, particularly army reorganizations, that seemed to indicate that war was being planned against the U.S.S.R. Naturally, a close watch on the mechanization and motorization of the Japanese Army was an important part of our work. To everyone's surprise, the Japanese armed forces had carried through a very large reinforcement program and a wide reorganization, which, it was considered, were aimed not solely at China but at the Soviet Union as well. Troop strength had been tripled and army divisions brought to a fair approximation of their Soviet counterparts, and mechanization had gone forward by leaps and bounds after the Nomonhan Incident. These particular developments, taken together with the open declarations of many military leaders, could be regarded as aimed at the Soviet Union, and I was accordingly greatly interested in them. Of course I could make no more than chance observations with regard to war preparations in Manchuria since it was impossible to keep a constant watch on them from Japan, but, inasmuch as I was unable to decide whether or not some secret organization in Manchukuo was handling the problem directly, I took an interest in it. I had to keep a constant watch on Japan's troop strength in China because it was possible for Japanese forces to be quickly dispatched from occupied areas there to the Soviet border.

3. To study closely German-Japanese relations in the sense that they would inevitably become closer after Hitler came into power.

Of course, in the middle of 1933 and the summer of 1935 it was still too soon to predict how far the slow improvement in relations between Germany and Japan would go, but Moscow was convinced that a *rapprochement* was taking place, and moreover, that it was directed chiefly against the U.S.S.R. The Russians were so prone to suspect that the Japanese and the German foreign policies were aimed against the U.S.S.R. that in 1941, when Japan took the last great turning in her career, Moscow was taken completely by surprise.

This particular duty was assigned to me as one of my major functions because, in view of the manner in which I had operated in China, Moscow rightly thought that I would be able to establish sound connections in high German circles in Japan. Of course, it was assumed that I would get a firm foothold in the German Embassy, which was the sole place where I could study such developments in detail.

4. To obtain constant information on Japan's policy toward China.

This may be thought of as a continuation of the espionage and investigation activities which I had performed in China. At the time the duty was assigned to me, no one foresaw to what a broad sphere it would extend by the summer of 1937. Moscow merely supposed that a knowledge of Japan's China policy would, to a certain degree, reveal Japanese intentions toward the U.S.S.R., and that the course of Japan's relations with other countries easily could be deduced from her China policy.

5. To keep a close watch on Japan's policy toward Britain and America.

This duty ws especially important because, prior to the start of the China Incident, Moscow believed that there was a possibility that Japan would turn upon the U.S.S.R. with the support of Britain and America. Moscow's opinion was that the idea of all the great powers' fighting a war to contain the Soviet Union was not one to be dismissed lightly.

6. To keep a constant watch on the real part played by the Japanese military in deciding the course of Japan's foreign policy: to watch closely all trends within the army likely to affect domestic policy, with particular reference to the young officer group; and, lastly, to follow closely general trends in domestic policy in every political sphere.

This duty was assigned because Moscow was fully cognizant of the leading part the Japanese military played in all of Japan's policies, and especially in her foreign policy. The Russians were well aware after 1931 that the power of the army had increased greatly, and during the next several years they could not help wondering if the influence of the military over Japan's political leaders would continue to grow. This question had a very real significance for Moscow because, for several decades, Japan's military leaders had considered Russia and the U.S.S.R. as Japan's only real hypothetical enemy. Since no one foresaw in 1933 that the Japanese Navy would gradually increase its political influence or that wartime economic needs (petroleum, rubber, and metals) would be sought in the south, it was natural for Moscow to believe that should the army's decisive influence continue to grow, it would be turned against the Soviet Union. This particular duty was, therefore, exceedingly important.

7. To obtain constant information on Japan's heavy industry, with particular reference to the expansion of her war economy.

Since the degree to which Japan was able to solve this problem would largely determine the effectiveness of her army, it was natural for Moscow to be interested, the more so because until 1931 Japan had devoted her energies to developing light industry on a peacetime basis. Since the U.S.S.R. itself had experienced practical difficulty in converting to heavy industry from light industry the manner in which Japan would solve the problem was also of great interest to Moscow.

This particular duty included a general consideration of the economic development of Manchukuo with particular reference to heavy industry but I was able to collect only two or three pieces of information on the subject because of the impossibility of close and constant observation from Tokyo.

(d) Independent Missions in Japan

The most important duties which arose in the course of various political events may be summarized as follows. (I shall discuss them in chronological order.)

1. *The February 26th "Incident" in 1936. Effect on Internal Situation.* The February 26th Incident was of such great significance that first the incident itself and then its internal repercussions had to be considered a special duty. Although for some time prior to February 26th, signs of internal strain had become increasingly evident, the explo-

sion, and particularly the unique course it pursued, came as a complete surprise to foreign countries and foreigners. Nevertheless, the incident had a very typical Japanese character and hence its motivations required particular study. A discerning study of it, and, in particular, a study of the social strains and internal crises it revealed, was of much greater value to an understanding of Japan's internal structure than mere records of troop strength or secret documents. The resolution of the internal crises under the Hirota, Hayashi, and First Konoye Cabinets also offered material for large-scale research. Lastly the fact that the February 26th Incident was completely suppressed by the China Incident provided excellent first-hand information of the type for a understanding of Japan's foreign policy and her internal structure. It is easy to see, therefore, why our espionage group made the incident one of its special duties. There is no doubt that in Moscow, too, it attracted the greatest interest, not from a purely military standpoint but from a broad political and social standpoint as well. Needless to say, attention was also given to the resolution and suppression of the internal crisis that followed it.

2. *The Alliance Between Germany and Japan.* The first conference concerned with the so-called Anti-Comintern Pact made it clear that the German ruling class and the powerful Japanese military leaders wanted not merely a political *rapprochement* between the two countries but as close a political and military alliance as possible. The problem assigned me in Moscow, that is, the study of German-Japanese relations, now appeared in an entirely new light, since no doubt was felt that the chief object which bound the two countries together at that time was the U.S.S.R., or more precisely speaking, their hostility toward the U.S.S.R. The fact that at the outset I had got wind of the secret negotiations in Berlin between Oshima and Ribbentrop made the duty of observing the relations between the two countries one of the most important of my activities—all the more so because, as is well known now, these negotiations were designed not simply to arrange an anti-Comintern pact but to conclude an actual alliance. The negotiations between the two nations at various periods and amidst many changes in the international situation always claimed a major share of my attention during my years in Japan. It is undeniably true that the strength of the anti-Soviet attitude displayed by Germany and Japan during the alliance negotiations was a matter of great concern to Moscow. After the start of the Russo-German war in the summer of 1941, the question of whether Japan would take action con-

sistent with her first attitude, upon which the negotiations to conclude an alliance with Germany had originally been based, was again a matter of grave concern to Moscow. To find the answer to this question was one of the most important duties which arose during my years in Japan, and one which my espionage group accomplished with outstanding success.

3. *The China Incident in and after 1937.* The China Incident was another unforeseen event which imposed an especially important duty upon us. It placed Sino-Japanese relations on an entirely new footing, one giving Japan monopoly rights in China. Having hitherto been regarded as impossible by the other powers, such a basis for relations between Japan and China confronted not only Britain and America but Moscow as well with an entirely new problem.

The Incident was confined to China, its course being such that while it was in progress Japan's expansionist policy could not abruptly or easily be shifted to the North. As Japan advanced into South China, her economic, political and military interest in southern problems gradually came to the fore, a fact which meant that Siberia was not the chief target of Japanese expansion.

The China Incident was very important to us from the economic standpoint as well, inasmuch as plans for Japan's war economy and her conversion to heavy industry were laid during that time. That is to say, it offered an excellent opportunity for the observation of Japan's shift to a war economy, one of the duties assigned me by Moscow.

Lastly, the China Incident afforded an excellent opportunity for a detailed study of Japanese methods of waging war and the strengthening and organization of the Japanese Army. The China Incident provided a proving ground for the expansion of Japan's armaments and the reorganization of her army. To observe the various aspects of these two operations during this period was not at all difficult.

Aside from the above, the Soviet Union's China policy was radically altered by the Incident, as was China's development, with which my work had previously been concerned for a number of years. These were all reasons why the Incident posed a special problem for us.

4. *The collapse of Japan's long-standing relationship with Britain and America.* It was apparent that prosecution of the China Incident on an all-out basis would lead either to a complete surrender to Japan by Britain and America or to a major crisis in relations with those two countries. A change became apparent within a few months after the China Incident, and the only doubtful point was whether

England and America would surrender to Japan's policy or whether a crisis would develop. The tendency of Britain was, as is well known, to appease Japan, or rather to countenance her China policy but her increasing dependence upon the United States which was especially obvious after the outbreak of the European War, obliged her to follow the diplomatic lead of the United States instead of adopting an appeasement policy. When Japan's southward advance was added to the China Incident and the policy of a German-Japanese alliance, the ultimate collapse of relations with Britain and America was the result. England, Japan's former ally, and the United States, which had favored the alliance thus became Japan's enemies.

Since the China Incident embraced both of the above possibilities in its early stages, all attentive diplomatic observers were obliged to follow the progress of relations among the three countries very closely. Later developments justified the work that I undertook in this regard.

5. *Japan's Attitude toward World War II and the Russo-German War.* I believe it is not necessary to explain the nature and significance of the duty to which I assumed in this connection. Its extreme importance is obvious when one recalls the efforts made by Germany to draw Japan into the war during the past two and a half years. Just before the outbreak of the war, Germany tried to conclude an alliance with Japan aimed chiefly at England; in 1940, she succeeded in getting Japan to sign a treaty against England and America; and in 1941 she devised all manner of plans to incite Japan to war against the Soviet Union. Thus Japan's attitude toward World War II was of great concern to Moscow, and, needless to say, her stand following the outbreak of the Russo-German war was also of vital interest. No other issue had had as direct a relation to my most important mission in Japan—that is, to the question of war or peace between Japan and the Soviet Union—as had the attitude of Japan toward the two world political events just mentioned. The above reasons will enable you to understand the interest taken in this particular mission by my espionage group and our intense desire to accomplish it. At any rate, we had to work on it until October, 1941.

6. *The Great Mobilization in the Summer of 1941.* The fact that for several months it was an extremely important mission for my espionage group is reason enough to consider it separately. A correct knowledge of the scope of the mobilization and its direction (north or south) would give the most accurate answer to the question of whether or not Japan wanted war with the Soviet Union. At the outset, the

large-scale nature of the mobilization and the fact that some reinforcements were sent northward gave us cause for anxiety, but it gradually became apparent that it was by no means directed primarily against the Soviet Union. This conclusion enabled us ultimately to answer the question, that is, to assert that Japan was not planning to attack the Soviet Union that summer or autumn, or, to put it differently, that no attack would be forthcoming until the spring of the next year at the earliest.

The problem confronting us after we reached this conclusion was that posed by the decisive crisis in American-Japanese relations. In December the crisis finally resulted in war, but we were able to study only the first phase. We were unfortunately deprived of the opportunity to accomplish this mission.

GENERAL REMARKS ON EFFICIENCY

I must now say something about the execution of the duties I have just outlined.

(e) Information Sources Available to Members in Japan

I do not know all the information sources which were available to the direct members of my group. I know only those which were most important and which had a sustained usefulness, and I know their general character rather than individual names and personalities. That I lack knowledge of the sources employed by the members of my group is not because I was indifferent to their activities and efforts or because I was indolent. Because of the nature of the work I had to perform, most information sources dried up as soon as they were cultivated, and I never accepted one as truly valuable and useful until it had been proved over a long period of time. Therefore, I considered a knowledge of my confederates' sources important only when they had passed the above test. I made it a principle not to attach any weight to the names of the people in question but to be satisfied with knowing their general character. This was intentional on my part so that if I were questioned about them, I would know very little likely to get them into trouble. That is a traditional principle for illegal activity.

1. *Ozaki's Sources*. I believe Ozaki's most important source of information was a group of men around Prince Konoye, a sort of brain trust, to which Kazami, Saionji, Inukai, Goto, and Ozaki himself belonged. Perhaps there

were others, but I remember only that I occasionally heard the above names. When Ozaki and I referred to these men, we usually called them the Konoye group. If I wished to name the source in my reports to Moscow, I called it "circles close to Konoye." I had the impression that if the greater part of Ozaki's information on domestic and foreign affairs did not come from his own rich knowledge and sound judgment it came from this group. Information from the Konoye group concerned the situation regarding the Konoye Cabinet's domestic policy, influences molding domestic and foreign policy, and plans in the making. Sometimes he obtained economic information, and on very rare occasions political and military information. He continued to obtain information from the group when Konoye was no longer premier, but not as frequently, nor were the facts always accurate. I cannot say who among the men in the group gave the most information. That was very difficult to determine. I had the idea that the man most intimate with Ozaki was Kazami, or possibly Inukai, but I must emphasize that that was merely a vague impression and not anything I heard Ozaki say in so many words. I believe Ozaki's personal relations were closest with these two men. Sometimes, however, they seemed to change. Ozaki had too independent a mind always to see eye to eye with them, and for that reason, differences of opinion and tensions may often have clouded his relations with them.

Ozaki sometimes met Prince Konoye directly, whether in private or not, I do not know. The information he obtained from these meetings did not take the form of concrete individual political reports but was concerned with broad political opinion and thinking in general, and sometimes with Prince Konoye's frame of mind. While such information was not concrete, it was extremely important, providing a far deeper insight into the Japanese government's policy than mountains of detailed facts. I remember in particular Ozaki's report on his meeting with Prince Konoye in 1941, which revealed very clearly what great efforts the prince was making to settle the China problem and avoid any conflict on the diplomatic front. It depicted better than the largest array of political documents or anything else the policy of the Third Konoye Cabinet toward the U.S.S.R. and toward Britain and America. However, such personal meetings between Ozaki and Prince Konoye were very rare.

Through his work for the South Manchurian Railway, Ozaki had access to a great deal of political and economic information, a part of which he was able to use for our purpose. At times he also got possession of political and economic documents and sometimes of purely military data. I believe a small part of what little military information I did obtain came from this source.

What I must emphasize is that I never asked about such information sources except in a very general way. On most occasions, it was enough for me just to have Ozaki say that this information was valuable, this was average, or that was not very helpful.

I think Ozaki made monthly economic and political reports for the South Manchurian Railway; at least I believe that some of the economic and political reports he gave me were based on information he got through the company and were prepared as a part of his work for it.

The trips which Ozaki made for the company were also extremely useful. I was very much inconvenienced by his absences, but his travels were most profitable. Owing to his connections with important people and his acute powers of observation, he always brought back information very valuable for our purposes. He went to Manchuria once and to China several times at the request of the South Manchurian Railway, and on each occasion I explicitly asked him to give his attention to certain political and military problems for our work.

2. *Ozaki's Newspaper Connections.* As a very well-known ex-newspaperman himself, Ozaki had many friends among Japanese reporters. I think most of them had been colleagues of his in the days when he worked for the *Asahi Shimbun.* He was able to get a great deal of information from these reporters, most of it political. On two or three occasions, he obtained political information concerned with the military. I believe he also had connections in the government's information office and, earlier, with the Information Bureau of the Foreign Ministry. Information from these sources was concerned chiefly with day-to-day political developments; information on fundamental principles was rare.

Ozaki himself had an excellent education. His wide knowledge and his reliable judgment made him one of the few men who were information sources in themselves. On this score a conversation or a discussion with him was highly rewarding, and I often sent his personal opinion on some issue or on future developments to Moscow as information of great value. I depended on his judgment in connection with many questions which were too difficult or too peculiar to Japan for me to have complete confidence in my own interpretation. On two or three occasions I consulted him before making final major decisions fundamental to my work. Thus Ozaki himself was essential to my work and must be considered a direct source of information. I am very deeply indebted to him.

Ozaki had two or three assistants for his work in my espionage group. One of these was Mizuno, whom I had previously known in China. I myself met Mizuno only once, in a restaurant, on which occasion, as far as I remember, the main subject of conversation was the farm question. Kawai must also be regarded as Ozaki's assistant, although, as I have said before, it would be more apt to say that Ozaki was Kawai's means of support. Lastly, I must mention a certain specialist. This man was an old friend of Ozaki's who was brought into our work soon after I arrived in Japan, but who turned out to be far from what we had expected. Instead of a military expert, as we all had thought in the beginning, he gradually turned into a money expert. Miyagi had some relations with these assistants of Ozaki's.

3. *Miyagi's Sources.* I think Miyagi's oldest connection, whom he apparently met frequently, was a friend of long-standing employed as a confidential secretary to General Ugaki. Most of his information concerned domestic affairs, chiefly developments in Japan's internal policies. Not infrequently there were also reports from this source on Russo-Japanese relations, and Japan's China policy. Naturally, problems of the Ugaki Cabinet predominated, and after Ugaki became Foreign Minister in the Konoye Cabinet, his private secretary was able to provide much information. At the time these events were taking place, he gave us full information on the strong opposition Ugaki encountered when he attempted to form a cabinet. During Ugaki's term as Foreign Minister, he provided full details on the tension that arose between Ugaki and Konoye over the China policy and the establishment of a China Board.

Miyagi had a connection of long-standing with a man from Hokkaido who provided much detailed information on Hokkaido and, sometimes, Sakhalin. The information was chiefly on military matters: mobilization in the Hokkaido garrison area, complete tranquillity, the dispatch of individual units to Sakhalin, and the construction of airfields in Hokkaido and Sakhalin. Occasionally this source supplied economic information on commodity supply difficulties in the north and news concerning the prohibition, for military and political reasons, of travel in the north.

Of Miyagi's sources of purely military information, I knew Koshiro fairly well. Miyagi occasionally mentioned other names, men who had just left the military service or men just about to be conscripted, but I had the impression that they were not constant or regular sources of information. I believe they were temporary acquaintances rather than genuine confederates.

Koshiro was the only person I judged to be a genuine collaborator. After Koshiro returned from Manchuria, Miyagi formed a close relationship with him, for which reason I decided I wanted to know him better and met him once or twice in restaurants. I got the impression that most of our information on the mobilization of the Tokyo and Utsunomiya divisions came from Koshiro, and that he was also responsible for two or three reports on the organization of new combined units from the old Tokyo and Utsunomiya divisions. Koshiro gave Miyagi a variety of data on the living and working conditions of troops on the Siberian border, and I believe that he also furnished several individual pieces of information about the army's new artillery and tanks.

I believe Miyagi picked up other military information on the streets of Tokyo, in restaurants, and in bars. I had the impression that in order to collect such information he made a practice of frequenting all sorts of bars. He often complained to me about the amount he had to drink in order to obtain trivial facts.

Miyagi made frequent trips to Osaka, but I do not know the names of his connections there. He said only that he visited two or three acquaintances. On such trips he sometimes went on to Kobe to learn something about mobilization of divisions there or cancellation of mobilizations.

Lately it seemed that Miyagi was often meeting a former friend from America. It was my impression, however, that he did not want him as a new source of information but rather as a translator and general assistant for much of his other work. He talked about him several times, and whenever I expressed any anxiety about his association with this former friend from America, he declared emphatically that the man was trustworthy.

Miyagi also seemed to have a large number of temporary acquaintances who probably furnished him information from time to time, but they cannot be considered regular or constant sources of information. In recent years he was on close and friendly terms with Ozaki because he translated Ozaki's information and relayed Ozaki's individual reports to me; that is, he brought me partial data consisting of reports and translations of information obtained from Ozaki's sources.

As I have said before, Miyagi also maintained contact with Ozaki's assistants: Kawai, Mizuno, and the "Specialist." For that reason these men too may be considered occasional information sources of Miyagi's. As with Ozaki, I was on close personal terms with Miyagi.

4. *Voukelitch's Sources.* Voukelitch had two duties in the group: he assisted in the technical aspects of our activity and he collected information.

His most important source was the Domei News Agency. He went there every day in the course of his work and therefore could easily find out all manner of information, both published and unpublished. He also was able to grasp the political undercurrents within Domei itself. His information from this source was purely political, some of it indicating the political atmosphere. In principle, important information could not be obtained from it, but such scanty news was important and very interesting as a supplement to the large amount of information my group collected from other sources. I am thinking in particular of Voukelitch's report on the atmosphere within Domei with regard to World War II and the sentiment at the time the Russo-German war broke out. Domei's attitude which was never pro-German, expressed the feeling of a majority of the Japanese people.

Voukelitch was often able to learn news which was well known at Domei but had not been made public due to censorship. This information provided another good indication of political conditions in Japan and the government's attitude. He also obtained several bits of information by talking with the French at Havas. From this source, he learned the general political attitude of his French friends toward Germany after the fall of France, as well as their attitude toward Japan's Indo-China and southern policies. However, this was atmosphere material rather than definite information.

Havas was in contact with the French Embassy, as was Voukelitch himself on occasion, a fact which added interest to the general and background information he obtained there. Voukelitch also talked with the military attaché of the French Embassy a few times, but the information he obtained was of little importance.

As a correspondent for the Havas News Agency, Voukelitch was able to make a trip to Nomonhan authorized by the Japanese military, which, of course, gave him an opportunity to collect information for our work.

Lately he had been obtaining a good deal of information from foreign newspapermen, particularly Americans, some of which was very interesting. It was concerned primarily with diplomatic policy; for example, the most important thing he brought me was the speech made by Ambassador Grew in September, 1941. He seemed recently to have greatly improved his relations with American newspapermen.

5. *Guenther Stein's Sources.* Stein was acquainted with Ambassador Dirksen, whom he had known since Moscow, and who looked upon him as an intelligent and important person. More significant for our work was the connection with the British ambassador which Stein enjoyed by virtue of the fact that he represented a British newspaper. He was especially close to the famous Sir Sanson in the British Embassy. From the British Embassy he was able to obtain information chiefly on general diplomatic policy. At times he had opportunities to talk to the then British ambassador and British naval attaché. As Stein was also on very intimate terms with all foreign newspapermen, especially the British and American reporters, he sometimes learned interesting individual facts from them. Lastly, he had close connections with Domei and hence, like Voukelitch, was able to scent out the general political undercurrent and atmosphere there. He was also valuable as a source of information in that he had studied the Japanese economic situation very conscientiously and had written excellent books about it. His economic studies clarified many facts hitherto little understood. His chief fields of study were Japan's foreign trade and financial problems.

6. *My Own Sources.* German businessmen and engineers: When I first arrived in Japan, I heard much talk of general economic conditions from businessmen and engineers. They never looked at the whole picture, however, and could supply nothing but very general information about the limited fields in which they were engaged. Fearing that their competitors might learn something from me, they said they did not possess any detailed information. Generally speaking, I preferred to talk to the engineers, who were not as timid as the businessmen, and who at least knew their own fields. After 1938 I had no further dealings with businessmen and engineers. I caused the German Embassy to give a good deal more study to individual economic problems, especially those bearing on national defense, than had been customary. After the embassy had assembled pertinent source material, I would assist in compiling reports for the military attaché and for my own purposes. I no longer relied on businessmen and engineers for my information. Before that I was friendly chiefly with an engineer named Mueller of the German Machine Company (D.M.A.G.) I was also friendly with his competitor, the Guden Hoffman Refinery. I also used Mr. Kahlbaun, the head of a chemicals concern. I believe these men left Japan before the outbreak of war in

Europe; at any rate, I have not met them for a long time. From the first two men I heard several things about the state of Japan's steel industry and from the last a little about Japan's chemical industry. I also heard that Japan had purchased from Germany a number of patents for the manufacture of synthetic gasoline, but I was unable to learn the full details. Later, however, I found them in the files of the economic section in the German Embassy. On several occasions, I met the engineers in charge of assembly at the Heinkel Manufacturing Company, who had come to Japan with Mr. Haag I have mentioned previously for dealings with the Japan Airplane Industry Company (*Nippon Hikoki Kogyo Kaisha.*) I heard several items of general information from them on the manufacture of engines for German aircarft in Nagoya. After 1938 I no longer met any of these assembly engineers. Later, in the files of the air attaché at the German Embassy, I discovered additional information on the manufacture of these engines and the purchase of German airplanes by Japanese airplane companies. At the time several German airplanes flew direct to Japan from Germany, I naturally asked the pilots about their flight and their plans in Japan. I flew from Japan to Manchuria and back with one of the pilots, Baron von Gablentz, in the Junker he had flown from Germany to Japan. However, negotiations for the purchase of large Focke-Wulf and Junker planes were later broken off. I afterwards found this information in the files of the German Embassy. I heard from the aforementioned Mueller two or three things concerning the establishment of the Wartz Factory in Manchuria by a German heavy industry company. However, as I said before, information like this began to decrease in 1938, and by the beginning of 1939 it had disappeared completely, with the result that I had to base my reports for the military attaché Makki solely on material available in the German Embassy.

Most of the German businessmen and engineers I met only at the German Club or at embassy receptions, but, as I was a German reporter, I was sometimes invited to meetings at the Tokyo German Chamber of Commerce. Hence, for professional reasons, I had to study the general problems faced by German traders in Japan. Conversation between me and the businessmen or engineers at these meetings naturally centered chiefly around economic problems. I had personal relations with only a very small number of businessmen, and they were all contacts entirely distinct from my espionage activity. That is to say, I met them as family men when women and other guests were present.

In my notes with regard to my personal friendships, the names Mohr and Kaumann appear very frequently. In both their houses—because they were businessmen with whom I was on very close terms—I was made to feel most welcome by their families. Their families were also friends of the German Embassy staff families. These friendships were entirely apart from my espionage activity. They were rather the exact opposite, since they were social contacts I maintained to strengthen my legitimate cover in Tokyo or because I was favorably disposed towards the persons as individuals. When I went to China, especially Shanghai, I of course visited the German diplomatic agencies there. The German minister Fisher and I formed a close friendship and I naturally had various political conversations with him. He got a good deal of detailed information from me about Japan's China policy and German interests in China. In addition, Fisher and I shared an interest in Chinese history and ancient Chinese art.

I was friendly with the German businessmen in China, and when I went to Shanghai I always visited two or three to talk about economic conditions and German trade conditions. I also met Doctor Woidt, whom Klausen has mentioned. He came to Tokyo about once a year, and I saw him there, since all of the German businessmen in China got in touch with me when they came into town. Woidt was not a member of my espionage group, but, as a government official, he knew much of interest, for which reason I was glad to keep in touch with him. I used several things he told me for my espionage activity. In my Moscow wireless reports, I referred to him, as to the rest of the China businessmen, as "Kommersant." The last time I met Woidt was about a year ago. I liked him personally; he was one of the few of his kind toward whom I was favorably disposed. Usually I did not care very much for the German businessmen in China and Japan. They were a pain in the neck to me.

The Nazi Party in Tokyo

Having joined the Nazi Party, I often had contacts with the party and with party members, from whom I used to hear various bits of political information on Germany. For example, I heard about the extensive preparations for war and the fact that, even though Germany had come to terms with Russia, anti-Soviet feeling in the Nazi Party ran high when the world war began. From that time on, I was of the opinion that, despite the existence of the pact, sooner or later a break with the Soviet Union would inevitably occur. The attitude of Nazi Party members toward Japan was divided. One faction did not particularly welcome close co-operation between Germany and Japan. They believed that Germany could not gain any economic benefits from such a partnership, and several of them openly advocated a close union with China. Even Mr. Stahmer, an intimate associate of Ribbentrop's whom I have mentioned before, held much the same opinion after the 1939 negotiations for an alliance between Germany and Japan were broken off. Lately a sort of anxiety that the war will last a long time has made itself felt in the Nazi Party, and the certainty of victory has conspicuously declined. Shortly before the removal of the Soviet General Tukhachevsky—early in 1938, I believe—I got many hints from the Nazis in Tokyo that they were privately counting on an impending internal collapse in the Soviet Union. The names of Tukhachevsky and Putona the military attaché in London, were mentioned in this connection. Nazis returning from Germany were responsible for propagating this opinion, which was widely held by party members. I also heard from them that counter-revolutionists in Germany were in contact with Putona who in turn was in communication with Tukhachevsky.

The Dutch Colony in Tokyo

Although it was broken off early in 1939, my connection with the Dutch colony in Tokyo must be considered the next source of information. The fact that I sent dispatches to the *Amsterdam Handelsblatt* put me in contact with Dutch diplomatic and business circles, from which I obtained several items of information with regard to Dutch resistance to Japanese economic penetration of the Dutch East Indies. I also heard a great deal about Dutch and British, and later American, co-operative efforts to resist Japan's economic invasion of Dutch possessions. I learned a number of individual economic facts about trade between Japan and Holland from Dutch banking circles, and I was also able to find out something about Japan's foreign trade and present financial and economic condition. This information source was cut off in 1938 after Germany's policy in Europe had already put a grave strain on her relations with Britain and France and, to some extent, with Holland. At that time Dutchmen were already definitely turning away from Germany and Germans and toward Britons and Americans.

German Newspapermen in Japan

My professional relations with the other German journalists in Japan were naturally very close. I often met Wiesse and Karow of the DNB, Schurtz of the *Deutsche Allegemeine Zeitung,* Magnus of the German Economic News Agency and Zermeyer of the *Transocean Press,* none of whom had an inkling of my true position or real activity. Of course, we exchanged opinions as newspapermen on all sorts of events and political developments, discussed various problems, and indulged in the newspaperman's habit of sneering at all things political. I was considered well informed by the other reporters, who did not give me any news or information worth mentioning; rather, it was a case of their wanting to get news for me. But I say emphatically that I never passed on the information my Japanese co-workers obtained or the secret intelligence I got at the German Embassy to any newspaperman. I was very strict and scrupulous on that score. The other newspapermen respected me not only as a famous German journalist but as a generous friend ready to help them whenever necessary. For example, when Wiesse was on leave of absence I took his place at the DNB, and, similarly, when anything occurred to warrant sending a wire which the others did not happen to know about, I informed them. We not only met at the office but we ate together and visited each other at home. On the other hand, when they knew I did not want to go to Domei or the Information Bureau of the Japanese Government, they would take care of it for me. I was considered a slightly lazy, high-living reporter. Of course they had no idea that I had a great deal to do beside my newspaper work. For all these reasons, then, my relationship with German newspapermen was one of close fellowship.

Foreign Press Correspondents

As the other foreign correspondents, who were all anti-German, assumed that I was a Nazi reporter, I was estranged from them; our relationship was nothing more than a conventional business one, and even that was largely discontinued in 1939. Prior to 1938 I had a few professional contacts with the Reuters representative Cox and the Americans Morin and Thomas, but with the increasing political tension in Europe, the death of Cox, and the departure of Morin and Thomas, my individual relations with foreign correspondents virtually ceased. There was almost no one among those lately in Tokyo whom I knew personally. I always avoided Redman because I detested him. I know nothing about Cox's alleged espionage activities. I always thought of him as a happy-go-lucky, completely naïve reporter. I was indifferent to the foreign correspondents because Guenther Stein and Voukelitch were already in a position to obtain information from them. I myself did not have to take on that job.

The Domei News Agency and Japanese Journalists

For the same reason, I kept up relations with Domei and the Japanese reporters only after I first arrived in Japan, associating with them no more than was customary. Later, as it was of no interest, I broke off even this relationship, relying on the information obtained by Stein and de Voukelitch, and on the political gossip picked up by Wiesse. The latter was a cynic and very fond of gossip. I use this word humorously and not in a bad sense.

As for other Japanese, excluding those in my espionage group, I saw little as possible of them during the last several years. Before that I had mingled with reporters from the *Asahi, Nichi Nichi,* and Domei along with the German correspondents. In recent years I have invited Murata, Kumasaki, and Mori of the *Japan Advertiser* to lunch, but only on rare occasions and chiefly with other Germans. I invited them as a matter of duty and so as not to give the impression that I had broken off all relations with Japanese. I had no ulterior espionage purpose in mind, for I was well aware that I would get no interesting information from them. It was the same in the case of Murata after he turned businessman. Formerly he had at least given me some information about Naskano and the Tohokai, but later he was interested only in making money.

The War Ministry

I had the same relations I have described above with the press section in the War Ministry and the army officers I met through Major General Ott and Colonel Makki. In recent years my association with these people could almost be called nonexistent.

Through Ott and Makki, I became acquainted with General Oshima and met him frequently, interviewing him for my newspaper after the conclusion of the German-Japanese alliance. I was acquainted with the then Colonel Manaki, Majors Yamagata and Saigo, the present General Muto, and other officers whose names I have forgotten. I had met the then Colonel Saito of the press section of the War Ministry sometime previously and he often extended invitations to me along with the other German reporters. I also extended him several invitations as one of a group of German reporters. I did not have much to do with Kaiyama, his successor in the press section, but I met Colonel Utsunomiya several times and called on him once or twice in Shanghai, the last times in the spring of 1941.

Besides the above men, I once interviewed the then Ambassador Shiratori before his illness and talked with him as long as was possible. I frequently met Nakano, politician and party leader, and I also encountered the then Admiral Kobayashi several times at banquets. The present Foreign Minister Togo granted me an interview once a long time ago, and I later met him once or twice at embassy functions.

I have been present at a number of the interviews which it is customary for new foreign ministers to give to foreign reporters, but these were merely formal press conferences. The last one I attended was the interview Foreign Minister Matsuoka gave after his return from Germany and Russia.

My Study in Japan

At the time of my arrest, the discovery of between 800 and 1,000 books at my home proved a source of considerable annoyance to the police. Most of these works were on Japan. In building up my library, I collected every foreign language edition of an original Japanese work that I could lay my hands on, the best books that foreigners had written on Japan, and the best translations of basic Japanese works. For example, I have English translations of the *Nippon Shoki* (collector's item) and the *Kojiki,* a German translation of the *Manyoshu,* an English version of the *Heike Monogatari,* and a translation of that brilliant masterpiece of world literature, the *Genji Monogatari.* I took particular pains with my study of ancient Japanese history, ancient political history, and ancient social and economic history. I studied the times of the Empress Jingu, the Wako (Japanese pirates who operated along the China coast), and Rideyoshi in closest detail to gather material for a good-sized history of Japan's expansion, from the early days on, which I was compiling. The voluminous and excellent translation on Japan's ancient economy and politics proved invaluable. One did not have to look far for material, since many foreigners were making studies of old Japan. I am sure that I had access to much more material than the average foreigner.

With this as a point of departure, it was a simple matter to grasp contemporary Japanese economic and political problems. I studied the agrarian question very closely, and from there went on to small industry, big industry, and finally heavy industry, although the tight veil of secrecy imposed by the law in recent years made my work unproductive and dangerous. Of course, I also studied the social position of the Japanese farmer, worker, and petty bourgeois. In the early days, it was possible to do so. I utilized purely Japanese sources as much as possible, such as economic magazines and the announcements of government offices. The cereal shortage and the uprising of February 26, 1936 provided me with excellent study materials, as did the innumerable domestic conflicts between the parliamentary group and the extreme rightists. The passing political scene told the observer versed in ancient Japanese history far more than the Alien Police suspected. In the light of ancient Japanese history, it was easy to understand Japan's present foreign policy. Japan's foreign policy problems could be readily evaluated if one had a knowledge of ancient history.

I also interested myself in the development of Japanese culture and art, studying the period embracing the Nara, Kyoto, and Tokugawa eras; the influences of the various Chinese schools; and the recent period of modern effort from the Meiji era on.

In addition to my home library, I utilized the German Embassy library in Tokyo, the personal library of the German ambassador, and the Tokyo East Asia German Society Library, which was rich in scientific reading matter. The society often sponsored academic gatherings and lectures at which ancient Japanese history was the usual topic of discussion. I kept more or less in touch with fellow Germans who were interested in these subjects and exchanged views with them.

Shortly after my arrival in Japan, I had translations made of various Japanese histories. I had a large collection of such manuscripts at my home. I also had excerpt translations made regularly from a number of Japanese magazines. By means of this system, I was able to make a close study of Japanese material on the agrarian problem appearing in books and magazines.

My study of Japan was not based solely on material appearing in books and magazines. First I must mention my meetings with Ozaki and Miyagi, which were not confined to the exchange and simple discussion of information. Frequently some real and immediate problem would bring up an analogous phenomenon in some other country, say China, or turn the topic to Japanese history, or to the social and political situation. My meetings with Ozaki were invaluable in this respect because of his unusually extensive knowledge of Japanese and foreign history and politics. Thanks to these two friends and co-workers, I achieved a clear understanding of the singular position held by the Japanese Army in the control of the state, as well as of the nature of the advisers to the Emperor or Genro (elder statesmen), which defies legal definition. It was also from them that I learned of the dominant role played by the Wako in the Middle Ages and their influence upon the Hideyoshi and Tokugawa periods. Their assistance consisted not so much in supplying individual facts and historical analogies as in enabling me to attain an over-all impression and broad general understanding of the subject in hand. Such was the case with respect to the February 26th Incident and the agrarian problem, both of which I studied with special thoroughness. Their frequent advice and general appraisals and evaluations of these two problems were highly significant. Moreover, I could never have understood Japanese art as I did without Miyagi. Our meetings often took place at exhibitions and museums, and it was nothing unusual for our intelligence and political discussions to be pushed into the background by talk on Japanese and Chinese art.

I did my best to familiarize myself with the vital problems confronting me in Japan and to dig deep into my work. My meetings with Ozaki and Miyagi constituted a vital phase of my research.

My frequent meetings with Ambassador Ott and two or three members of his staff were politically educational. The immediate problems discussed helped me to observe the general political picture and draw conclusions concerning it, and they were also useful for purposes of comparison with past phenomena. Ambassador Ott was a shrewd, able, politically realistic diplomat, and his assistant, Marchtaler, drew upon history and literature for his interpretations of contemporary events. My conversations with them frequently presented me with helpful suggestions for my research. Of late, Minister Kort, with his comprehensive knowledge of European political developments and his excellent background, has added fresh interest to our conversations and general discussions. These talks inspired me to study anew the history of Europe, the United States, and Asia.

Finally, I must mention how significant my innumerable trips proved to be to my study of East Asia. Although police restrictions later made it all but impossible, in the old days, that is, around 1938-39, travel in Japan was comparatively simple, and at first I made frequent trips, not as a mere tourist, but in order to learn to know the more important cities and regions. My travels in Japan proper were made not for espionage purposes but to obtain a better knowledge of the country and its people; to provide a substantial intuitive basis for my study of history and economics. Thus, I planned a tour of the Japan Sea coast, Niigata, and the area to the west, visited Nara and Kyoto frequently, and covered the Kii Peninsula in detail. I passed through Kobe, Osaka, the Inland Sea, Shikoku, and down the Kyushu coast to Kagoshima. On Sundays, I used to hike everywhere from Tokyo to the area west of Atami. My primary interest on these hikes was to inspect the rice crop in all seasons and under varying conditions. My observations came in handy for the legitimate articles I contributed to the *Frankfurter Zeitung* and the *Geopolitik*.

I never traveled with any members of the intelligence group because I considered it too much of a risk. The single exception was when I met Ozaki in Nara for a certain purpose. Our meeting there was of short duration.

Practical Value of My Investigations

It has been my personal desire and delight to learn something about the places in which I have found myself, a fact particularly true with respect to Japan and China. I have never considered such study purely as a means to an end; had I lived under peaceful social conditions and in a peaceful environment of political development, I should perhaps have been a scholar—certainly not an espionage agent. My research was, nevertheless, of very real importance to my main work in China and Japan. I did not intend to function merely as a letter box for information collected by others; on the contrary, I considered it absolutely essential that I obtain the most complete understanding possible of the country's, *i.e.*, Japan's problems. My study made it possible for me to determine whether or not problems and events were important from the standpoint of Soviet diplomacy and from a general political and historical point of view. For example, none of the border disputes between Japan and the U.S.S.R. worried me because I had quickly realized that they were comparatively innocuous, but I regarded the various China incidents and particularly the one in the summer of 1937, as the prelude to a great war which would engulf all China. My study of Japan's history, with special emphasis on the

Meiji and post-Meiji era, saved me from vacillation and confusion.

My research also permitted me to evaluate correctly the reliability of information and rumors, an accomplishment of vital importance to my secret activities since intelligence in the Far East contains far more rumors and conjectures than in Europe. Had I failed to screen the reliable intelligence from the false I should certainly have exposed myself to serious censure.

Similarly, I was able to get a general idea of whether or not a fresh problem was important to the U.S.S.R. I had the full confidence of the Moscow authorities in this respect, and I was never criticized for failure to recognize and study a few phenomena or problems of vital importance. My judgment has been respected by Moscow ever since my China days.

Finally, my research enabled me not only to seek necessary information and transmit it accurately, but, at the same time, to formulate independent judgments on economic, political, and military developments. The greater number of my radio messages and reports contained, in addition to basic material, analyses derived from individual bits of information. I was always outspoken. Whenever I felt that my opinions and political analyses were correct and necessary, I never hesitated to forward them to Moscow, and I was encouraged to do so. Moscow frequently hinted that it placed a high value on my power to judge and appraise the general situation.

It is not correct to think that I indiscriminately transmitted all the data we collected. I took it upon myself to see that our information was screened most carefully and only what I considered essential and absolutely safe from criticism was sent. The process of selection often entailed hours of extra work. The same thing was true of analyses of the political and military situations. This ability to select material and present a general appraisal or picture of a given development is a prerequisite for intelligence activity of genuine value and it can be acquired only through much serious and careful research.

Again, one must not think that our work ended when our reports had been sent out by radio. Such messages constituted only one of many phases of our intelligence activities, and certainly not the chief one. At irregular intervals I sent great quantities of mail to Moscow, which included not only documents and other materials but also reports written by myself. I almost always included reports covering the domestic and international political picture and military affairs during the report period. They summarized and analyzed the most important developments since the last mail: *i.e.,* they represented serious and painstaking efforts to present, on the basis of abundant information and research an accurate and objective long-range picture of new developments and of the general situation during the past several months. Such laborious reports could never have been attempted without comprehensive study and knowledge. Unlike Berlin and Washington, Moscow knew China and Japan too well to be fooled easily. The Soviet level of knowledge of Far Eastern affairs was far above that of the American and German governments, and Moscow demanded that I send in systematic, soundly based and carefully planned reports at intervals of several months. I believe I can say that I succeeded in meeting the relatively high standard demanded by the Moscow authorities, an accomplishment which would have been impossible but for my research.

My studies did not interfere with my development as an expert intelligence agent. When necessary I performed my duties with speed, resolution, courage, and resourcefulness.

I never boasted that I was capable of solving all problems concerning Japan. Many times, I relied upon the judgment of Miyagi or, in particular, that of Ozaki. The same was true for the final wording of my analyses of important developments. Before appraising a given development in Japan or wording such an appraisal I frequently talked to Ozaki or Miyagi, and I encouraged Ozaki to take the liberty of correcting me whenever my judgment erred, particularly when the judgment was vital to Soviet policy. For example, I predicted from the very outset that the China Incident would be an extremely drawn out affair and could not but weaken Japan irreparably: at the time of the Nomonhan Incident, I stood firm on the view that Japan had no intention of waging war against the Soviet Union; and I maintained that the great mobilization of August, 1941 was not directed primarily against the Soviet Union. In each of these cases, I placed an extremely high value on the judgment of Ozaki, and, to a lesser extent, that of Miyagi in deciding upon a responsible and well-studied view for transmission to the Moscow authorities.

My Study of Japan as Legitimate Cover

Aside from its immense practical value to my intelligence activities, my research on Japan was an absolute necessity as a cover. Without it, I could not have won the firm position I commanded at the German Embassy and among German journalists. My position at the embassy was not acquired solely because of my personal friendship with members of the staff; on the contrary, some of the staff even resented my influence. My broad fund of general information, my comprehensive knowledge of China, and my detailed study and knowledge of Japan were the main reasons for my position at the embassy. Without this knowledge, *i.e.* without my detailed research, certainly none of the embassy staff would have cared to discuss things with me or to consult me on confidential matters. Many of them referred problems to me because they knew that I would always contribute something toward their solution. None of them was as well versed on China or Japan as I was after my wide travels and long years of research, and most of them lacked the general political training that I had acquired through my connection with the Communist movement since 1924.

My research was likewise of importance to my position as a journalist, since, without it, I would have found it difficult to rise above the level of the run-of-the-mill German news reporter which was not particularly high. It enabled me to gain recognition in Germany as the best reporter in Japan. The *Frankfurter Zeitung,* for which I worked, often praised me on the ground that my articles elevated its international prestige.

I would like to note that the *Frankfurter Zeitung* represented the highest standards of German journalism, and that it was far ahead of the rest of the field in content value. This view is not mine alone; it was shared by the German Embassy, the German Foreign Office, and Germans of culture.

Naturally, my reputation as a top reporter for a ranking German newspaper was extremely important to my intelligence activities. This general recognition of my abilities worked favorably on my position at the embassy. It was because of my stature as a journalist that the German Foreign Office offered me a high position with the embassy.

My journalistic fame brought me innumerable requests for articles from German periodicals, and the *Frankfurter Zeitung* and the *Geopolitik* pressed me for a book on Japan at the earliest possible date. My plans for the book were shattered with my arrest. I had completed 300 pages of the manuscript. Needless to say, my essays appearing in the *Geopolitik,* which were fairly lengthy articles on various subjects, built up my reputation among the German reading public as a journalist and author.

It is far from my intention to boast about myself. I have simply tried to prove that my research work in Japan was absolutely necessary to my intelligence work for Moscow. Without this research and my general cultural background, my secret mission would have been impossible and I would never have entrenched myself at the embassy and in German journalistic circles. Moreover, I could never have carried on for seven years in Japan unmolested. It was not skill nor the examinations that I had to pass at the Moscow Intelligence School but my basic study and knowledge of Japanese problems that counted most.

(End of Sorge Memoirs)

EXTRACTS FROM KLAUSEN'S INTERROGATION

The following are extracts from Klausen's notes. As his ten-year espionage career was richly varied, his notes shed light on many phases of his work and are an interesting supplement to Sorge's own story.

1. *Impression of the Japanese Police.* I received no instructions in Moscow concerning the Japanese police, but before my departure for Japan, a high-ranking 4th Bureau official advised me to find out from my predecessor Bernhardt what conditions were like. I saw Bernhardt several times, and he told me about the Japanese and Tokyo. I remember particularly that he said, "Unlike Shanghai, Tokyo contains few foreigners, so if you are not careful, you will attract undue attention." Before my departure a short, bald major general, about forty-five or forty-six years old (name unknown) attached to the Far Eastern Section of the 4th Bureau, who claimed he had been in Japan, said, "When you get to Japan, study the language. It will be most necessary for your work."

While in Shanghai, I had visited the dance halls in the International Settlement occasionally, dancing mostly with White Russian girls. They knew exactly which of the Japanese who came to the halls were spies, and as we danced they would quietly point out some suspicious-looking Japanese and say, "He is a spy."

Sorge and Weingart had also warned me that the Japanese police observed aliens closely and sent out spies to keep an eye on their movements.

For all these reasons, I was somewhat worried by the thought of the police at the time of my arrival in Japan.

The following incidents occurred after I joined the secret service in Tokyo.

Around the middle of July, 1936, I was on my way to Shanghai to effect contact with another agent and deliver some film. I had just made myself comfortable in a second-class car (I was traveling from Moji to Nagasaki) when a plain-clothes policeman who had boarded the train at Fukuoka sat down beside me and started to grill me about my nationality, address, name, where I had come from, where I was going, etc. My two suitcases were resting on the rack above and the film was wrapped tightly in a white cloth in my left trouser pocket. Inwardly fearing that the Tokyo police had ordered my arrest but as nonchalantly as possible I showed him my business card (Klausen Co.) and received him cheerfully. He asked me various questions with a grave bearing, but about thirty minutes later he left the train at one of the stations without examining my baggage. I had escaped by the skin of my teeth; after I boarded the boat I was constantly worried lest the roving patrol had been contacted. The film never left my pocket and I was prepared to toss it overboard if necessary.

This happened in May of the same year. The radio that my predecessor Bernhardt had left at Voukelitch's home was so bulky and conspicuous that we thought we had better get rid of it. Voukelitch and I decided to toss it into a nearby lake, and around 0700 o'clock one day we boarded a train at Shinjiku dressed as hikers, each carrying a stick and a rucksack loaded with a receiver, three transmission transformers, and other parts. We were worried about baggage inspection en route, but nothing happened, and at Otsuki station we transferred to an electric car which took us to Yoshia. From there we took a taxi to a hotel on Lake Yamanaka. The hotel employees who tried to help us with our rucksacks were surprised by their weight and asked what was in them. We were taken off guard, but managed to save ourselves further embarrassment by replying without hesitation "We brought along half a dozen bottles of beer." "We have plenty of beer here," they said, hurrying off to our rooms with our packs. We were afraid that if someone should discover what was inside he might notify the police, so we talked things over, rowed out to the middle of the lake in a rented boat and tossed everything away. We returned to Tokyo relieved of a heavy burden indeed.

Later, when I talked to Sorge about it, he commented curtly, "You should have got rid of it in Tokyo instead of going so far away."

The most harrowing experience I had was my loss of a large wallet in the autumn of 1937. I had taken a taxi from my neighborhood as usual to radio some messages to Moscow, and upon my arrival at Voukelitch's home, around 1400 or 1500 hours, I discovered that a large wallet I had put in my left trousers pocket was gone. I darted outside but the taxi had already disappeared. The wallet contained 230 yen in Japanese currency, my driver's license with photo attached, and Sorge's English text of a financial report that we were to send to Moscow. It was to be photographed at Voukelitch's house. The other code messages, fortunately, were safely tucked away in my old black bag. I must have forgotten my wallet in the car because I am certain that I took it out and opened it. Of course, I didn't know the license number of the car. I didn't know what to do, so I told Voukelitch I had lost my wallet and a large sum of money and asked his advice. He was talkative by nature, and I was afraid he would tell Sorge about the financial report, so I kept it secret. The following day, I had the audacity to report my loss to the Lost and Found Department of the Metropolitan Police. I said that I had lost some Japanese currency, my driver's license, and a scrap of paper with English writing on it. The wallet was never recovered. I was in a state of constant anxiety for several days.

Around 2100 hours one night toward the end of 1937, my taxi was stopped by a traffic policeman near Roppongi as I was returning to my home at Shinryudo Cho, Azabu Ku, after visiting Voukelitch. I was asked the usual questions: my name, where I had come from, where I was going, etc. I said, "I am on my way back from the German Club. This may serve as identification," and pulled out my business card (Klausen Co.). I had my radio in the black bag: the policeman stared at it but showed no desire to examine it. He let me pass without further ado, but it was quite a scare.

On May 13, 1938, a Friday, Sorge was testing a motorcycle I had sold him when he rammed into a dirt wall on the road that passes by the American Embassy and seriously injured himself. He was given first-aid treatment by Dr. Stedfeld of Azabu and sent to Saint Luke's Hospital. As soon as I was notified, I dropped everything and rushed to his bedside. Badly shaken up but undaunted, he handed me the English reports and American currency which he had in his pocket and which outsiders could not be permitted to see, and, as if relieved at last, fainted. From the hospital, I went straight to his house to remove all papers relating to our intelligence activities, even taking his diary. A short while later Weiss of the DNB came to the house to seal all his property so that nobody would touch it. I shuddered when I thought of how our secret work would have been exposed had Weiss arrived before I did. I was also worried because it was unnatural for an outsider like myself to appear instead of a representative of the German Embassy or the Japanese police.

Every morning around 0700 or 0800 hours in the spring of 1938, an automobile would be parked on the road running by my house in Ryudo Cho. There were always one or two persons in the car searching everywhere for somebody. My sixth sense warned me that they were plain-clothes policemen. Of course, the Commercial Department of the Soviet Union was located nearby, so I could tell myself that that was what they were watching, but inwardly I was uneasy lest they were watching me too. When I spoke to Sorge about it, he said, "You had better be careful. Probably it's because of the regiment and the Russians living nearby, but if they ever discover what we are doing, we are doomed, so you had better move out immediately." Shortly afterward I moved to my present address at Hiroo Cho. Of course, the police were not on my trail, but one of the main reasons for my moving was to eliminate this threat.

One day around January or February, 1939, I was riding in a taxi from Voukelitch's home to my office in Shimbashi when, just as I got to Hommura Cho, Azabu Ku, I was stopped by a traffic policeman because my driver had not signaled for a turn (mechanical signal). The driver was led away to the police box and examined for about thirty minutes. I waited in the car motionless with the bag in my arms. I had a feeling that the policeman was glancing at me and my black bag and asking the driver questions. Those thirty minutes were extremely trying. I was not questioned at all, but I felt I had barely escaped the jaws of the tiger when I was finally allowed to proceed.

Around 1900 or 2000 hours one December evening in 1940, as I was returning from Voukelitch's home, a policeman came out from a police box on the right side of the road near Iikura Machi, Azabu Ku, and, blocking the road, asked, "Where are you going?" Voukelitch was riding with me and I was driving my own car at the time. Voukelitch was clutching the black bag with the radio set, and my heart jumped at the thought that we had been discovered. For some reason or other, the policeman merely remarked, "Your headlights are out; be careful," and walked away without examining our baggage or searching us. Voukelitch and I exchanged glances as we passed the police box.

I always encoded and decoded at my home in a room used only by myself. Usually I was warned of visitors by the ring of the doorbell so that I could clean up my papers before receiving them. On three occasions, my Japanese employees saw the code but did not seem to pay any attention to it. Once, when I was in bed and encoding a message (employing a special board which enabled me to work in a reclining position), Dr. Wurtz, who was always shown in by the maid, suddenly appeared at my bedside alone. He glanced down at the code chart suspiciously but merely said, "You must not do any writing until you get well," went through a routine checkup, and departed. For several days, I was afraid that he might have informed the police, but nothing came of it.

Aoyama, a representative of the Toriizaka Police Station, which had jurisdiction over the area in which I lived, called frequently around the summer of 1941. Most of the time he seemed to leave after talking to the maid, but once he came while I was away and left the following message, "We smeared ink over the last photograph you submitted; please send another copy to the police station." I had an inward fear that a White Russian who had been connected with secret intelligence in Mukden had tipped off the police and that my picture was to be sent to Mukden for verification, but nothing happened.

Sorge was careful not to give me the reports I was to radio to Moscow at either of our homes. We met at pre-arranged dates and hours, usually at the Fledermaus on the Ginza, exchanged customary greetings, addressing each other as Doctor and Mister (because many people were present), had dinner, and exchanged the reports as we drove back in my car. This procedure was followed for some time. My biggest worry was how I could transmit and receive radio messages without being detected. I hired my boy and maid for day service only, disassembled and concealed the radio in a place where it would not be readily discovered, and conducted my radio operations on the second floor (this was also to minimize the effects of terrestrial magnetism). These are some of the precautions I took to avoid arousing suspicion. The most important part of my conduct was to act cheerful before others, to look stupid, and, especially, to make it known that I was interested in amateur radio.

I had several close escapes. One day while I was sending out a message at Voukelitch's home, a worker from the City Electrical Bureau came and asked us to cut the switch so that he could make some repairs in the neighborhood.

It was too risky to go on, so I quit work. Another time, while transmitting from Edith's house, I had to stop work because a roofer who had started to make some repairs on the roof tried to look into the second floor. Again, at my home at Shinryudo Cho, Tanaka of the Akasaka Kempei Detachment called suddenly while I was transmitting a report. I locked the second floor room and met him in the guest room downstairs. Despite these experiences, I was never discovered, whether fortunately or unfortunately I do not know.

The foregoing experiences were totally unexpected, and I was forced to improvise means of escape on the spur of the moment. I had received no special instructions from the Moscow authorities or advice from my comrades as to what methods I should employ to outwit the police, but, as a glance at my past will indicate, I made a point of appearing to be a law-abiding citizen.

I not only established the Klausen Co., but I obtained a driver's license after submitting my photograph and going to the Metropolitan Police Board for fingerprinting; joined the German Club, and attended the parties at the German Embassy. I was cheerful in the company of my Japanese friends, and whenever the police called I received them warmly and was careful not to hurt their feelings.

While adapting myself to this type of life, I was careful to elude suspecting eyes when visiting my comrades. I took various routes to Sorge's house, taking care to avoid using the same course over and over. On the other hand, I deliberately parked my car in front of the Toriizaka Police Station and visited Sorge openly once.

Usually I drove to Voukelitch's house in my own car or took a taxi. I would drop in at the German Club and take a taxi from there to the house, and, similarly, on the way back, I would abandon my taxi at the club and go home in another one.

When going by taxi to Edith's house, I would not drive up to the house but would get off near the American School. I would leave my black bag at the house and return by streetcar. Edith would always return the bag wrapped in a large blue *furoshiki* (kerchief) which I had left for that purpose. Her call would be arranged beforehand so that I could send the maid out on some errand.

As Stein's house was along a straight road flanked on either side by a police box, I usually took a roundabout course. Sorge, who seemed to be quite careful, walked up to my house, glanced around him, and entered only after ascertaining that everything was safe.

I have already described how we effected contact. Usually, Voukelitch would hand me the film together with some Cherry or Akatsuki cigarettes. Most of the time we met at the Sennari, a restaurant in Shimbashi. We were not afraid of being watched. Our conversation in German ran something like this:

Klausen: "Have you a cigarette?"

Voukelitch: "Certainly."

Lighting a cigarette from the pack that Voukelitch offered me, I would pretend to return the rest. Voukelitch would say, "Keep it; I have more," and I would put the cigarettes away in my pocket.

Six dangerous years passed uneventfully. My conclusion was that the Japanese police were too polite to aliens and, therefore, not as efficient at spy control as European police.

* * *

From the point of view of security, Klausen's report on his operation in Harbin (prior to his assignment to Japan) is suggestive since he claims to have utilized the premises of the American Consul.

2. *Klausen in Harbin.* Nothing in particular happened on the trip to Harbin. The water police merely inspected our passports before we landed in Dairen. Like any other traveler, I bought a second-class ticket, boarded a train for Changchun (the present Hsinking), changed trains at Changchun carrying two suitcases containing spare suits and other necessities, and arrived in Harbin in the evening.

I registered at the Priston Hotel Moderne as directed by Benedict in a letter to Lehmann, met Benedict two days later, and took custody of the transmitter, which had been brought in by the diplomat. Soon thereafter, I moved to a lodginghouse near the broadcasting station.

Benedict introduced me to Gloemberg-Ott, who took me to his home, but, perhaps because his wife was a White Russian, refrained from discussing secret matters. Several days later, I accompanied Ott to a café operated by a White Russian and then, for the first time, he asked me to install the wireless set and gave me several hundred Harbin dollars so that I could buy parts for a receiver and defray incidental expenses.

He told me about Lilliestrom several days later. Lilliestrom, a bachelor who employed a young White Russian as a "boy," was a big fat six-footer about fifty years old. His house was a villa-type, two-story gray tile brick building with a large yard enclosed by a palisade. He went to work at the United States consulate from there.

Soviet-Chinese relations were rather tense at the time, with the result that the Chinese police were busily making secret inquiries into the affairs of White Russians and Russians living in China. Ott realized that the best way of escaping detection was to use the private home of the American Vice-Consul, which was conveniently located, and that, needless to say, the easiest way of getting information was to gain Lilliestrom's confidence. I believe it was for these reasons that he won over Lilliestrom as a sympathizer. When I went to Harbin the second time the wireless set was no longer at Lilliestrom's home but had been returned to Ott's house. Ott told me that Lilliestrom had returned to the United States, so I did not pay any further attention to his house.

After spending the first two weeks idly with Ott and Benedict in conferences and at eating places, I went to inspect Lilliestrom's home and decided to use two rooms (both were vacant; one was about an eight-mat room) on the second floor, one as a wireless operating room and the other as a technician's room. I bought an antenna and parts to transform a receiver into a shortwave set, began installation operations, completed the work in about two weeks, tested the set with Wiesbaden for two days, and delivered it to Ott.

Thereafter, for some unknown reason, I was not allowed to go to Lilliestrom's home. Ott told me, "You can spend your time hereafter taking in the sights of the city; I shall have my technician receive and transmit messages. However, I would like you to stay here until you hear from Lehmann." Therefore, I stayed at my lodginghouse without doing anything. I presumed that his reason for holding me was to have me there in case his technician encountered difficulties while receiving or transmitting messages.

I installed the transmitter on a table near a window. Its capacity was the same as that of the one I used in Tokyo; the tubes were UX210's. The method used in transforming the receiver was the same as the one used in Tokyo. The only difference was that we were able to receive Moscow, Berlin, etc., as well as Wiesbaden.

The call signal and wave length used in testing the set were the same as those we used in Shanghai. Lehmann had told me to use Q code, as specified by the international amateur agreement, and Wiesbaden used the same code in reply. I do not know anything whatsoever about the type of code Ott used. As in Shanghai, the antenna I installed faced the yard.

Needless to say, I was not told anything about the organization and intelligence work of Ott's spy ring, probably because I belonged to a different group. As I did not know General Theo at the time, I thought that the information Ott encoded for transmission by his technician came entirely from Lilliestrom and White Russians, except for news collected by Costia and Benedict.

I met Costia by chance at Ott's house; later, as noted above, we met in bars and drank together.

I did not meet Artur and did not know that he was the radio technician.

Ott told me in October that he had received a letter from Lehmann saying that he was coming to Harbin in a few days and asking Ott to tell me to return to Dairen, where he would meet me. He said that there seemed to be no trouble with the wireless set and that he thought it best that I return to Shanghai. Sometime during the month, therefore, I left Harbin for Dairen, where I met Lehmann at the Yamato Hotel, spent the night with him at an assignation house, and parted from him. He told me to keep working for the spy group in Shanghai and warned me not to tell anyone that I had gone to Harbin to install a wireless set there.

The purpose of Lehmann's trip to Harbin was, of course, to contact Ott, to whom he probably delivered espionage documents (film) for Moscow headquarters in return for funds for his ring. I returned to Shanghai the following day.

[Klausen was certainly in a position to appraise Sorge's character or qualities as a man. It is likely that his views were embittered and reflect the uncertainty of imprisonment.]

3. *Klausen's Opinion of Sorge's Character*. It is difficult [said Klausen] to describe Sorge. He never once revealed his real character. But I may say that he was a true Communist and that nothing could make him give up his belief. He would kill his best friend if it were necessary for communism. From what I know of him to date, however, I think he would probably be a miserable coward if the circumstances were different. The work he did for Communism at the German Embassy was not so difficult for him, inasmuch as his knowledge of politics and economics made it very easy for him to make friends there. It was simple for him to photograph the various documents which they

gave him to read. That is to say, the work he did at the embassy did not require much courage.

He tried to stay out of danger himself whenever possible by collecting his information from the members of his spy ring. I noticed several things in this connection. Sorge was occasionally slightly sick and then I had to stay with him constantly. This was because he was afraid to be by himself. Once I was seriously ill and the doctor told me I must not work, but Sorge demanded that I go on working as usual. I am compelled to say that he was not considerate of others. Another thing I noticed was that he seemed to be penny-pinching even when the money was urgently needed, and yet he spent money like water. Hence, I must say that his character was not of the best.

He was a firm Communist, but, on the other hand, he was a man who could not bear up under certain conditions. I say this since it appears that he told everything after his arrest. If at the time of his arrest he had remained a firm Communist, he would have held his tongue and not told everything.

The above facts and his private affairs, which I shall not go into here, lead me to say that Sorge's character as a man was not of the best.

His manner toward me was not so bad, but he always treated me as a sort of errand boy since he had no one else to help him.

His treatment of Voukelitch was not much different. When Havas increased Voukelitch's salary, Sorge reduced the amount of money he received from the espionage group. At one time, Voukelitch was only getting sixty yen from him, and, as that was unfair, Voukelitch was not satisfied. Just prior to his arrest, he had already got fed up with working for communism. I don't know whether Sorge treated him badly or not nor anything else about their relations.

Neither do I know anything about his treatment of Edith. They didn't see each other often but, since Edith was a woman, she got more money than was necessary.

Sorge treated Guenther Stein very well because Stein possessed a large fund of knowledge on political and economic matters and Sorge could use Stein to much advantage. He learned a lot from Stein and so he treated him well.

I don't know much about his treatment of Ozaki and Miyagi because I didn't meet them very often. However, I think his treatment of them was not too bad, since both of them were very important when it came to collecting information. His treatment of Ozaki was cordial because Ozaki was a very intelligent man. Since Sorge was well-informed about politics and economics, he was strict with Ozaki and Miyagi and they couldn't very well bring in false information. Sorge gave both of them adequate living allowances. This is all I know about their relations with him.

PART THREE

AGNES SMEDLEY AND THE WAR DEPARTMENT

Attempt to Suppress the Sorge Story

The news value of the Sorge story is self-evident; even more so its importance as a pattern of Soviet intelligence operation. In December, 1948, the Secretary of the Army had taken steps to clear the story for release.

The American press was thoroughly interested. In the normal course of events, following the initial release, the papers were waiting for further details, in particular for the release of documentary evidence, the confessions of the principal defendants, participants, and eyewitnesses.

G-2 Tokyo was prepared to furnish this material, but the call never came. Instead, a few days later, a shocked and incredulous Headquarters, in Tokyo, became aware of what amounted to a virtual repudiation of the Sorge Spy Report by the very Washington authorities who had so eagerly negotiated for its release throughout an entire year.

This official reversal was reflected in the staccato language of news service radios of the period:

WASHINGTON, FEB. 20: (INS): THE ARMY'S PUBLIC INFORMATION DIVISION SAID FLATLY SATURDAY THAT IT WAS WRONG AND IN ERROR IN CHARGING THAT AGNES SMEDLEY, AN AMERICAN WRITER, WAS A RUSSIAN SPY.

EYSTER SAID "THE DIVISION HAS NO PROOF TO BACK UP THE SPY CHARGES. THE REPORT WAS BASED ON INFORMATION FROM THE JAPANESE POLICE AND THE REPORT SHOULD HAVE SAID SO.

"WHILE THERE MAY BE EVIDENCE IN EXISTENCE TO SUBSTANTIATE THE ALLEGATIONS, IT IS NOT IN OUR HANDS.

"IT WAS A MISTAKE WITHIN THE DIVISION. THE STAFF FAILED TO HANDLE THE RELEASE PROPERLY. NO NAMES SHOULD HAVE BEEN USED AND NO CHARGES MADE."

WASHINGTON, FEB. 19 (UP) IN NEW YORK, MISS SMEDLEY PROMPTLY CALLED THE CHARGES "DESPICABLE LIES" AND THERE WERE OTHERS WHO CRITICIZED THE ARMY'S METHOD OF BRINGING OUT THIS REPORT.

COLONEL EYSTER, THE DEPARTMENT PUBLIC RELATIONS OFFICER, SAID THE REPORT CERTAINLY "SHOULD NOT HAVE BEEN GIVEN OUT WITH THE PHILOSOPHY IT CONTAINED THAT AMERICANS MIGHT WELL LOOK ASKANCE AT THEIR NEIGHBORS." . . . "IT IS NOT THE ARMY DEPARTMENT POLICY TO ISSUE PAPERS STATING FACTS AS IT DID ABOUT MISS SMEDLEY WHEN THE PROOF IS NOT IN OUR HANDS. IT IS NOT THE GOVERNMENT POLICY TO TAR AND FEATHER PEOPLE UNLESS IT HAS PROOF. IT IS STATED POLICY OF AMERICAN JUSTICE THAT A PERSON IS INNOCENT UNTIL PROVEN GUILTY."

EYSTER SAID THAT THE REPORT WAS PREPARED BY INTELLIGENCE OFFICERS IN TOKYO AND THAT THE "YOUNG FELLOWS THAT DID IT PROCEEDED TO PHILOSOPHIZE AND TO ADD THEIR OPINION OF ITS EFFECT." HE SAID "THE REPORT HAD BEEN REVIEWED FOR ITS SECURITY IMPLICATIONS AND SOME PARTS HAD BEEN REMOVED. BUT IT HAS NOT BEEN PROPERLY EDITED FROM A PUBLIC RELATIONS STANDPOINT."

HE SAID HE KNEW OF NO PLAN TO PUNISH ANYONE FOR MAKING THE ERROR BUT SAID HE CERTAINLY WAS "GOING TO MAKE AWFULLY SURE" SUCH A MISTAKE DOES NOT HAPPEN AGAIN."

From a reading of these Press statements, it becomes obvious that the Eyster quotations contain a number of brazenly delivered, bald-faced contradictions.

Damaging Effect of the Washington Repudiation

The Army Department retraction was certain to cool off the eagerness of the press immediately.

The direct practical effect of this inexplicable step was one to suppress for the time being documentary evidence that normally would have reached the public. *Plain Talk* and *Counterattack* were among the first to recognize the vicious impact of this retraction.

Agnes Smedley significantly got space on the air, hired a well-known attorney, and proceeded to defend her fair name. It was a foregone conclusion that this would be done. The implications of international conspiracy, in the Far East, were too overwhelming. Silence would have been fatal for the cause of Soviet penetration of the Orient, especially as the Chinese Communists were then already at the gates of Nanking.

The psychological counterattack was cleverly managed. It was primarily directed at General MacArthur and its weapon was an insolent threat of suit for libel. The magic of MacArthur's name would automatically insure front space in the press. The fact that the release was a Washington-directed affair was blandly overlooked. Nor was there any point in suing me, though the direct responsibility for the preparation of the report, *i.e.* the substance of accusation, was obviously in my department.

A Fake Suit for Libel: Willoughby Accepts

Agnes Smedley expressed her gratitude and appreciation to the Army for clearing her name and reputation of the outrageous and false charge. She hoped that the statement by Colonel Eyster "marks the end of a policy of smear first—investigate later." She called upon General MacArthur "to waive his immunity and she would sue him for libel." In Detroit, John Rogge, attorney for Smedley asked rhetorically: ". . . First we want to know if MacArthur will accept responsibility for reports coming from his office, and if he will, I suggest he get a New York lawyer because we are going to sue. After we get an answer from MacArthur, then we will decide whether to sue Willoughby. MacArthur is the one Miss Smedley wants to sue. . . ."

In order to relieve Rogge of this theatrical dilemma, I immediately issued a public broadcast, in which I accepted suit with the deliberate intent, of course, of forcing the evidence into the open.

". . . *The Sorge Spy Report, collating and evaluating certain judicial and other official records found in Japan at the start of the Occupation, was made under my sole direction and, as Chief of Military Intelligence Section, Tokyo, I am responsible for its preparation and direct transmission to the Military Intelligence Division in Washington. It was a 'secret' document developed solely for military intelligence*

*purposes and was not written or intended for public release.
The scope of its contents embraced all information procurable here with the comments and deductions therefrom, normal to a security investigative agency. This section would have failed in its duty had it done less. . . .*

"I accept fully any responsibility involved and waive any immunities I may possess, to legal or any other action that may be taken or desired. I would in fact welcome, not only as an Intelligence Officer but even more fundamentally as an American citizen, an opportunity thus to emphasize the lurking dangers which threaten American Civilization in subversive systems, hiding behind and protected by our free institutions. . . ."

The statement above, broadcast on the evening of February 21, is not an ordinary action. It represents the public acceptance of a challenge, despite the fact that the official agencies in Washington, appeared to side with an international espionage agent against a general officer of thirty-five years of continuous honorable military service.

This length of military service obviously involves a certain amount of disciplined resignation. Officers do not lightly enter into a controversy with the War Department. There are only three recent historical cases: General Leonard Wood, who could afford defiance, since he had the powerful protection of the elder Roosevelt; General Mitchell, who was actually tried by a court-martial; and Captain Dreyfus, of the French Army, who was crucified by a corrupt general staff.

Traditional loyalty to superior authority, silent obedience, etc., were all involved in this scandalous incident, when the Sorge Espionage Case, an authenticated intelligence report, was released with considerable fanfare but retracted within seventy-two hours with quasi-apologies that ranged from an admission of editorial mistakes to the much more damaging innuendo that there was neither proof on hand nor any evidence to substantiate the allegations.

As a matter of public safety, as well as government integrity, it is important to know why Smedley received the inferential protection of the Department and of the Secretary of the Army. It should be noted that from the hour of my broadcast, Smedley and her mouthpiece lapsed into complete and cautious silence. Incidentally, John Rogge, Smedley's lawyer, appears to handle a number of "Red" cases. It is suggestive of his intellectual attitude that he demanded an end to the New York Grand Jury investigations into Soviet espionage activities. It is equally significant that

Rogge was the attorney for Anne Louise Strong. She was listed as an American agent for Moscow in the "Fifth Report, Un-American Activities in California 1949," p. 179. Rogge, a member of the Permanent Committee of World Partisans of Peace arrived in Moscow, March 7, 1950, and was greeted by Soviet bigwigs: L. M. Leontov, writer and deputy of the Supreme Soviet; Prof. A. N. Trainin; and representatives of other Moscow organizations. Three months later, June 16, 1950, Rogge became attorney for David Greenglass, arrested by the FBI in connection with the atomic bomb espionage net.

The persuasive Miss Smedley, however, was to receive still more support from highest quarters. On the "Meet the Press" radio program of the Mutual Broadcasting System, on February 27, 1949, no less a personage than the Secretary of the Army Kenneth C. Royall said "the Army should have run for cover," that it had made a mistake and that the spy release was "an inadvertence by some personnel in the Public Information Division in Washington." He added he was not advised in advance that the report would be published and said it "was released in his absence."

A functionary of the government is, of course, at the mercy of his underlings; the danger of high office often lies in the manipulation of file clerks. We will stretch a point in favor of Secretary Royall. It is barely possible that the Secretary was not familiar with the year-long negotiations by his Department, to get its hands on this report.

The Secretary of the Army probably did not grasp fully the ramifications of this case and was certainly ill-advised—especially on the element of libel. He probably became apprehensive of a pseudo-legalistic entanglement with a woman —Agnes Smedley.

This is a human touch, completely understandable to anyone at all familiar with American ways of thinking. American women enjoy a baffling immunity under the law. In the courts, skillful lawyers are known to have exploited successfully the feminine advantage on countless occasions. Miss Smedley appears to have cashed in on this vagary of the American male. In any event, the Secretary must have reached a conclusion that it was less embarrassing to throw an army officer to the wolves than tangle with an international agitator with the resources of the Communist press and fellow-traveling hackwriters, at her disposal.

On August 22, 1951, at a hearing held by the House Un-American Activities Committee, Mr. Velde queried me on the motives of the Secretary of War. With an elapsed time of two years, my initial resentments have subsided. I recollect saying: ". . . there is no point in reviving interdepartmental wrangling. Events have moved irresistibly. The Red menace has grown apace. We must forget our grievances and unite against this common danger. I am prepared to absolve the Secretary, with a pontifical blessing."

Columnists' Attack on Tokyo Intelligence

After Washington had suppressed the proffered documentation, G-2 Tokyo found the going rough; the pack was in full cry; "pink" riffraff of every category, several secondrate columnists on the outer fringes of journalistic respectability, and a few opportunist politicians joined forces. One paper orated: "Infamous report, utterly unprincipled." A politician, catching a whiff of free publicity, urged a full Congressional investigation: "It would be most proper for Congress to look into the Army blunder and perhaps into the whole question of efficiency of our intelligence service."

Harold Icke's column was particularly offensive, inaccurate, and uninformed. In a frantic search for impressive "headlines," Ickes managed to give birth to this ridiculous trio: (1) "Army Tricks Cover General's Mistakes," (2) "Some Brass in Rather Than On Army Heads," and (3) "Old Curmudgeon Thinks MacArthur Should be Sued." Events had a way of answering this obviously rhetorical statement made by the grandiloquent Mr. Ickes:

"No one who knows Miss Smedley would ever suspect that *this courageous and intelligent American citizen* has stooped to be so low as to be a spy for any country—even for her own to which she is deeply attached. . . ."

Two years later, *this courageous and intelligent American citizen* bequeathed her ashes and her residuary estate to one General Chu-Teh, Commander of Red China's Armies, now fighting Americans in Korea. When she died, she was working on a book on the life of this Red General—disciple of Lenin and tool of the Kremlin. Smedley named him heir of U.S. Government bonds and royalties due from her published works and "anything else of value included in her estate." The will ordered her body cremated and directed that her ashes "be shipped to China for General Chu-Teh, Commander in Chief of the People's Liberation Army, and there be laid to rest at any place designated by General Chu-Teh or his heirs."

The sudden demise of Agnes Smedley in London, by a strange coincidence on the eve of being subpoenaed by the House Un-American Activities Committee, removed a major participant in the Sorge Espionage Ring. It should be noted that another protagonist, Guenther Stein, disappeared within forty-eight hours of the same ill-fated Washington release.

The French Embassy in Tokyo, however, advised me that Guenther Stein was arrested in Paris, by the French *Sûreté* on charges of espionage. He was under cover, now almost habitually for the clandestine fraternity, as correspondent for the *Hindustani Times*. Since he was a British citizen, vintage of 1941, he was deported to England.

De mortuis nil nisi bonum. Throughout the world the Communist press, especially the Chinese Communist organs, paid tribute to Miss Smedley. Tributes in her memory took up half the space of the Sunday literature and arts supplement of the Peking *People's Daily*.

Mao Tun, leftist Chinese novelist, wrote: ". . . It was Agnes Smedley who first made known to the world the truth about Red China, at a time when the world was still deceived by the stories told by the reactionaries. Peace-loving people the world over will also deem the death of Agnes Smedley a great loss at a time when the international reactionary bloc, headed by American imperialists, is attempting to provoke a new antipopular war. . . ."

The American China Policy Association reported on May 28, 1951: ". . . clippings from *The Daily Worker* tell quite a story. The ashes of Agnes Smedley, an American, were buried with high honours by Peiping Communist big-wigs on May 6th this year. These were high honours for an American traitor during the war between Communist China and the United States. Miss Smedley played an important part, by her writings and speeches, in bringing about the downfall of our friends in China, and the triumph of our enemies. As a friend and adviser of General Stilwell, Agnes Smedley influenced the General's attitude. The clipping about General Stilwell reveals that he had apparently somehow or other gone all out for the Communists before his death. The General Chu-Teh under whom he wrote he would like to fight, was then and still is, the Supreme Commander of the Chinese Communist Armed Forces. . . ."

World-Wide Communist Press Rallies in Support of Smedley

Communist publications, magazines, and periodicals, the world over, rallied to the cause of Agnes Smedley while she was still alive. Her protest against the Army release of the Sorge Report was featured on March 8, 1949, by a mouthpiece for Chinese communism, the *China Digest,* published in Hong Kong. At a distance of ten thousand miles, another

Communist front, the *Far East Spotlight* featured her story on practically the same date.

This perfect timing, over vast geographical areas, is an impressive example of the first-class general staff work and split-second co-ordination of international communism. The propaganda work of the timid and vacillating democracies cannot match this deadly precision.

Incidentally, the *Far East Spotlight* has been proscribed by the U.S. Attorney General as a Communist-front organization. It was sponsored by the Committee for a Democratic Far Eastern Policy (111 West 42nd St., New York City), a noisy aggregate of fellow travelers, habitually engaged in violent pro-Chinese-Communist agitation. The Attorney General's classification placed these people publicly where they belong. The list of officers and sponsors contained some interesting names, viz., Guenther Stein, heavily implicated in the Sorge Espionage records, in Tokyo and Shanghai; Philip O. Keeney, one-time GHQ Tokyo employee disqualified from Federal employment on action of a Loyalty Board under Presidential Exec. Order 9835, March 21, 1947; Philip Jaffe, implicated in the mysterious "Amerasia" case of wartime theft of secret State Department documents; Mark Gayn, writer and news correspondent, also implicated in the "Amerasia" affair, appears as a contributor; Smedley's articles were naturally featured in this Red-front magazine.

The objectives of the *Spotlight* and the Committee were revealing: "No arms. No loans. No aid to Chiang Kai-shek," an undisguised sustained propaganda drive for the cause of the Chinese Communist Armies and the ultimate inclusion of subjugated China into the orbit of Soviet Russia. The definitive orientation of this group, in which Smedley played an important role, points irresistibly toward Shanghai and the clandestine operations in that focal point of Soviet subversion. It is a far cry from the conspiratorial days in the early thirties, and the complex "apparatus" of the Third International but the anti-Chiang Kai-shek pattern remains relentlessly the same, whether on Suchow Road, Shanghai, in 1931 or at 111 West 42nd Street, New York, in 1948.

The Truth About Agnes Smedley

It came as no surprise that Communists all over the world, as well as Communist-front organizations rallied around a valuable contributor to their Cause. Fundamentally it is more dangerous and more far-reaching that responsible government officers and gullible do-gooders like Ickes were stampeded to take up the cudgels for a woman whose sole aim in life was to undermine the American conception of democracy. Inasmuch as they portrayed Agnes Smedley as the besmeared innocent for the purpose of discrediting a carefully prepared and documented intelligence report, her background, her associations and the chronological record of her life deserve detailed attention.

There is no specific evidence of Smedley's membership in the American Communist Party and she repeatedly denied it; however, her own writings contradict her habitual denials of Communist affiliations, the customary protective screen expected to be used by an experienced political agitator.

Agnes Smedley has dedicated her life to the political and geographical advancement of communism in China. Her intellectual evolution is an interesting case history of the development of a party worker and fellow traveler.

She has been one of the most active workers for the Communist cause in China for some twenty-odd years. In her third book, *China Fights Back*, the dedication is "to my beloved brothers and comrades, the heroic dead and the unconquerable living of the 8th Route Army of China" (The Chinese Red Communist Army). This partisan vein runs through all her Chinese reports, revealing her as definite propagandist for the Chinese Communist party, then with headquarters at Yenan.

Whittaker Chambers testified before the House Un-American Activities Committee about setting up a writers' project as a cover for Soviet espionage in Japan, according to an INS dispatch, June 14, 1950. In secret testimony in December, 1949, Chambers alleged that "J. Peters, Commissar of the Washington Communist underground," introduced him in 1934 to Maxim Lieber, a literary agent in New York. Lieber was subsequently shifted to the underground and attached to Chambers. Originally Lieber was to open a front in London in which Chambers could work as a Soviet agent in England, but, with the abandoning of that project, Chambers shifted Lieber's activities to Japanese espionage. His mission was to act as a front for John Sherman, who was sent to Tokyo in 1936. Lieber and Sherman set up an "American Feature Syndicate," with a New York bank account and an ostensible business of securing material for U.S. feature syndicates and newspapers. Chambers testified that Sherman met Smedley in New York. Sherman's mission in Tokyo apparently was a failure and the apparatus in the U. S. was dismantled. This significant dispatch must be read in conjunction with our disclosure of the Shanghai fraternity, the close, interlocking relationship of writers, pseudo intelligentsia, stooges, and the real puppeteers that manipulated the marionettes.

It is noteworthy that Whittaker Chambers served on the 1932 staff of the International Union of Revolutionary Writers, on which Miss Smedley also served in 1933. The I.U.R.W. was founded in Moscow, is Soviet dominated, and held its second conference in Kharkov, November 15, 1930.

Miss Smedley has also served on the staff of the League of American Writers, an offshoot of the International Union of Revolutionary Writers. This League is classified by the United States Attorney General as Communistic, and is cited in the House record of the Seventy-Ninth Congress. Even the gullible Mr. Ickes had to admit that much.

" 'The League of American Writers' is generally regarded as a Communist subsidiary. Its policies, of course, always parallel those of the Communist Party." (State Department, quoted in a letter from Harold L. Ickes, Secretary of the Interior, to Robert Morse Lovett, dated April 25, 1941.) The character and membership of the International Union of Revolutionary Writers and its American offshoot, the League of American Writers which listed Miss Smedley on the National Council, is indicated by a poem by Langston Hughes published in the monthly organ of the Union.

GOODBYE CHRIST

Listen, Christ,
You did alright in your day, I reckon—
But that day's gone now.
They ghosted you up a swell story too,
Called it Bible—
But it's dead now.
The popes and the preachers've
Made too much money from it.
They've sold you to too many.
Kings, generals, robbers and killers—
Even to the Czar and the Cossacks,
Even to Rockefeller's church,
Even to *The Saturday Evening Post*.
You ain't no good no more.
They've pawned you
Till you've done wore out.
Goodbye.
Christ Jesus Lord God Jehova,
Beat it on away from here now.
Make way for a new guy
With no religion at all—
A real guy named

Marx, Communist Lenin, Peasant Stalin, Worker Me—
I said, me!
Go ahead now,
You're getting in the way of things, Lord.
And please take Saint Ghandi with you when you go,
And Saint Pope Pius,
And Saint Aimie McPherson,
And big black Saint Becton
Of the Consecrated Dime.
And step on the gas, Christ!
Move!
Don't be so slow about movin'!
The world is mine from now on—
And nobody's gonna sell Me
To a king, or a general,
Or a millionaire.

Association with this poisonous outfit is of the utmost significance. Fellow travelers, in highest places, have been absolved or regarded with tolerant amusement, in the past; guilt by association has been frowned on; when one considers the traitorous and corrosive quality of these front organizations, however, one cannot condone association forever; the pace is too hard; the stakes are too high.

There is nothing vindictive in the Sorge Report. Agnes Smedley is merely shown as caught in the web of a stupendous international intrigue, through her own choice or her own indiscretions. She could not complain that her gown was spattered by the mud of her surroundings; she walked in the shadow of dangerous companions, of her own free will.

1894: Born in northern Missouri, eldest of the five children of Charles H. and Sarah (Rallis) Smedley. At an early age she moved to southern Colorado where her father was employed as an unskilled laborer and her mother kept boarders. She did not finish grade school and never attended high school.

1911: Student in the Normal School at Tempe, Arizona, supporting herself by working as a waitress.

1912: Married an engineer, Ernest W. Brundlin, on August 25. Subsequently divorced. In her early twenties she went to New York where she spent four years. Worked during the day and attended lectures at New York University at night. She became involved with a subversive, Indian nationalist group, Friends of Freedom for India, operating in violation of current U.S. laws. Smedley kept their correspondence, their codes, and foreign addresses, a significant early trend.

1915: Attended summer school at the University of California.

1918: Smedley was arrested (18/19 Mar.) with Salindranath Ghose, an Indian political agitator, on charges of action as an agent of a foreign government and aiding and abetting such actions in violation of Section 3, Title 8 of the Espionage Act and Section 332 of the U.S. Criminal Code. She was released on bail May 7th and the case was never brought to trial. A significant facet of this case was the appearance of German funds, reaching Indian nationalists groups. Smedley was aware of the nature of these funds. It must be recalled that in those critical war years the German General Staff was notoriously engaged in fomenting subversive political movements throughout the world to damage the Allied war effort. Rebellions flared up from North Africa to India. German secret agents stirred up the Berbers, the Touaregs and Senussi, the Kurds and Afghans. Subversive, nationalistic movements were tailor-made for this purely military enterprise.

On June 11, parallel indictments were returned by a Federal Grand Jury in San Francisco against Salindranath Ghose, Tarak Nath Das, Kulin B. Bose, William Wotherspoon, Agnes Smedley of New York, and Bluma Zalnik, accusing them of attempting to defraud President Wilson through representations that they were on an accredited mission from the Nationalist Party of India. Smedley was not brought to trial in this action either. Wrote her first short stories, *Cell Mates*.

1919: She sailed from New York on a Polish-American freighter as a stewardess. Smedley jumped ship in Danzig and went to Berlin.

1920: In Berlin, she joined Virendranath Chattopadhyaya, an international agitator, with whom she lived informally for eight years. They were never married. She characterized him as the epitome of the secret Indian revolutionary movement and its most brilliant protagonist abroad. He eventually became a Communist party member.

1921: Smedley visited Moscow in June and attended a meeting of Indian revolutionaries held at the Hotel Lux. In commenting on this trip, she admitted membership in the delegation from Germany. In October, Smedley was reported to be in Geneva, Switzerland, and information was received that she was paid the sum of 5,000 marks by the Soviet Legation there for traveling expenses. In the same month, she attended the Congress of German Syndicalists at

Dusseldorf. At this meeting she used among several aliases that of Mrs. Petroikos.

1923: Left Chattopadhyaya twice to rest in the Bavarian Alps and later became very ill. She sought the help of an alienist who gave her psychoanalytic treatments for two years. Smedley then taught an English seminar at the University of Berlin and also lectured on Indian history. She entered the University of Berlin to study for her Ph.D., but lack of scholastic background forced her to drop this project before the end of the first term. Smedley wrote two works on Indian history which were published in German historical journals. She also joined a group of Republican, Socialist, and Communist physicians who were trying to establish the first birth-control clinic in Berlin.

1927: Smedley spent a number of months in Denmark and Czechoslovakia where she wrote her first book, *Daughter of the Earth.*

1928: Broke off her informal liaison with Chattopadhyaya and went to France. She later returned to Germany where she was hired as a correspondent for the *Frankfurter Zeitung.* Smedley made her way to China, stopping in Moscow and then traveling across Siberia. It is pertinent to note that the Soviet master spy, Richard Sorge, also used an assignment as a *Frankfurter Zeitung* correspondent as a convenient cover for his espionage activities.

1929: Smedley arrived in Harbin and after spending three months in Manchuria entered China through Tientsin. She spent some months in Peiping, visited Nanking, and then went to Shanghai. It was here that she began to frequent leftist and Communist groups.

The Sorge trial and Shanghai police records reveal more extensively than her own admissions, the nature of her activities and associations. She acted as a go-between, warning leftists wanted by the police and generally interesting herself in Communist and leftist organizations.

1. *Arrival in Shanghai.* Miss Agnes Smedley, also known as Alice Bird and Mrs. Petroikos, arrived in Shanghai in May, 1929 as a correspondent of the *Frankfurter Zeitung,* the official organ of the German Social Democratic Party. She had traveled from Berlin via Moscow, Harbin, Mukden, Tientsin, and Peiping on U.S. Passport Number 1266 issued June 27, 1928, by the U.S. Consulate in Berlin; she was known to possess an alternate German passport in addition. During her trip across the U.S.S.R. she stopped in Moscow in the period of the Sixth World Congress of the Comintern, held in Moscow in July and August, 1928.

Shanghai Police report that Smedley was in the direct

service of the Far Eastern Bureau (FEB) of the Central Committee of the Third (Communist) International (Comintern), receiving orders directly from the Central Committee (ECCI) in Moscow but maintaining no direct connection with the local Soviet Communists in order to camouflage her activities.

2. *Organizations.* Agnes Smedley arrived in Shanghai when international Communist activities were becoming prominent again after the 1927 split between the Kuomintang and the Chinese Communists and the subsequent rupture in diplomatic relations between China and the U.S.S.R. had caused a breakdown of the Comintern structure. The Comintern already had organized the Pan Pacific Trade Union Secretariat (PPTUS) as its major organ for agitation and propaganda in China, and a variety of collateral subversive organizations received support from this Comintern agency. The Shanghai Municipal Police soon placed Smedley under surveillance, on the ground of being affiliated with the Far Eastern Bureau (FEB) and of having been charged by the Comintern with the establishment of Communist organizations among workers. Smedley's connections with Chinese radical movements, however, were considered more direct than those of the foreign-run Pan Pacific. Police considered her to be a member of the All China Labor Federation (Union Syndicale Pan Chinoise), an ostensibly Chinese labor group which received considerable aid from the Pan Pacific and its parent body, the Shanghai branch of the Far Eastern Bureau.

Smedley was an active member of the Shanghai branch of the notorious Noulens Defense Committee, a world-wide Communist-front organization set up by International Red Aid (MOPR) specifically to free Paul and Gertrude Ruegg, more commonly known as Noulens, the leaders of the Shanghai FEB, tried and convicted for espionage. With Harold Isaacs, she was a member of the China League for Civil Rights, and of the local Friends of the U.S.S.R., a Communist-front group, directed by the Comintern through local agents. When the Anti-War Congress, another front for the Comintern's League Against Imperialism, sent a mission to Shanghai in 1933, Agnes Smedley was listed prominently as one of the local supporters. As an erstwhile member of the Hindustan Association of Berlin and of the Berlin Indian Revolutionary Society, Smedley continued to devote considerable attention to the independence movement in India, a political agitation in which the Comintern took great interest. She was known to have been in touch with anti-British Indians in Shanghai, on several occasions to have edited anti-

British propaganda on behalf of the Shanghai branch of the Indian Youth League and to have given considerable financial support to Indian revolutionary organizations.

3. *Publications.* Agnes Smedley came initially to the attention of the Shanghai authorities through an article published in the *Frankfurter Zeitung* regarding alleged gigantic preparations taken by the Shanghai Municipal Council for the suppression of anticipated Communist disturbances in August, 1929. The article was reproduced in *Izvestia* on December 8, 1929. In addition to acting as correspondent for the *Frankfurter Zeitung,* Smedley contributed articles to the *China Weekly Review,* a Shanghai publication with intermittent leftist trends. An article under her own name entitled, "Philippine Sketches," was published in the June, 1930 issue of *New Masses,* definitive American Communist party organ, and an anonymous article was ascribed to her entitled, "London Behind the Hangman Chiang Kai-shek," which appeared in *Rote Fahne* (Red Flag), the organ of the German Communist Party, September 5, 1931. In 1933 she appeared under her own name in *International Literature,* the foreign language organ of the Comintern International Union of Revolutionary Writers, in an account of the Communist uprising in Kiangsi. Her book *China's Red Army Marches,* an account of the Communist "Long March," was banned both by Chinese and Shanghai authorities shortly after its publication in 1934 because of its violently anti-Kuomintang tone.

4. *Associations.* Agnes Smedley was an associate of C. Frank Glass, who was locally classified as a card-bearing Communist, and of Harold Isaacs who was for some time the editor of *China Forum,* an English-language Communist periodical first published in 1932. Smedley also was in close contact with the German woman Irene Wiedemeyer (Weitemeyer), a secret Comintern agent and distributor of Communist publications, who was involved in the Sorge espionage case. Edgar Snow and his wife, who wrote under the name of Nym Wales, met Smedley both in Shanghai and later in Peiping, where the Snows edited the publication, *Democracy.* Shanghai police authorities knew that Smedley was closely connected with the Soviet propagandist Anna Louise Strong, writing articles for her *Moscow Daily News,* and, with known and suspected Shanghai Communists, often visiting TASS, the Soviet news and propaganda agency at their Shanghai offices. Her secret association with Sorge is specifically covered in the Tokyo records. Her house became the rendezvous of Sorge's ring; it was here that Ozaki and Kawai were given espionage missions and their reports were, in turn, received. The Shanghai police were on her trail, though

they never fully caught up with either Sorge or Smedley, but they came close in the Noulens case, which led straight to the heart of the Far Eastern Bureau (FEB).

Smedley came to the more serious professional attention of the Shanghai Secret Service when an arrested Comintern agent, Joseph Walden, was found to be carrying a typewritten document listing several local persons who were "shadowed by detectives of the Settlements," evidently a protective warning list. Agnes Smedley's name led a column of twelve.

The police linked Walden, alias Maxim Rivosh, with an American, G. Kennedy, who was known in leftist circles in Shanghai in the early thirties. Kennedy's post-office box was permitted to remain in his name after he left Shanghai and Walden and the clandestine fraternity used it as cover. This may have been a careless coincidence, but it is suggestive of the dangers which association with the wrong company may sometimes entail.

1930: She visited the Philippines and Canton where she professed to be concerned at the plight of workers in the silk industry. She was arrested in Canton at the insistence of the British Secret Police under a charge of traveling on a false passport and being a representative of the Communist International. Apparently she was released after protests were made by the German Consul. Back in Shanghai, Smedley was introduced to Ozaki Hozumi, protagonist of the Sorge Spy Ring, by Irene Wiedemeyer (Weitemeyer), owner of the Zeitgeist Bookshop, a Communist front and mail drop for Comintern spies. At Smedley's request, Ozaki agreed to supply her with information. Later she became associated with Richard Sorge when he arrived in China and introduced him to Ozaki. Smedley became a member of the Soviet Spy Ring headed by Richard Sorge and became one of his principal and most trusted assistants. Her house was often used as a rendezvous for Sorge's agents.

1931: Active in aiding labor representatives in trouble with the Shanghai police. In this period the *Shanghai Evening Post and Mercury* branded her a "Bolshevik" and other publications openly charged that she was in league with the U.S.S.R. Local comments, based on intimate observations on the spot, are significant. The police records were simply confirmatory. She left the *Frankfurter Zeitung,* allegedly at the request of the British and other foreign interests in China. She was introduced by Ozaki to Kawai Teikichi and Smedley persuaded him to become a member of the Shanghai spy ring. She joined the Noulens Defense Committee which was organized in behalf of Paul and Gertrude Ruegg (alias

Noulens). Associated with Smedley on the committee was Harold Isaacs, as well as many other prominent leftists.

The leading agitators in the movement were under orders of Moscow. The frantic efforts in behalf of the Noulens were, of course, inspired by and with the intervention of International Red Aid, the Soviet agency for the assistance of secret operators in trouble. What looked like a humanitarian gesture by the foreign colony in Shanghai was a brazen rescue scheme ordered by the Comintern. In this period she also published an article on the Communist uprising in Kiangsi in *International Literature,* organ of the Comintern's International Union of Revolutionary Writers.

Even had Smedley not been professionally trained or skilled as an agent or associate of agents, her experiences in Shanghai with the police would have made her especially cautious in covering her tracks. Following is a digest of some of her experiences in this connection (*Battle Hymn of China*):

". . . I had been arrested by the Chinese police of Canton, acting upon a secret official document sent them by the British police of Shanghai; the document charged that I was a Russian Bolshevik traveling on a false American passport. When the German Consul General intervened, the Chief of Police showed him the document from Shanghai. The American Consul General also saw it, but equivocated when I asked about it. . . . For weeks, I lived under house arrest, with armed gendarmes wandering in and out of my apartment at will. If I went out, they followed. . . . This Canton Incident was really the setting of Woodhead's attack on me. . . ."

This disarming frankness is a clever maneuver in that Smedley could not possibly deny a police record. This embarrassing fact is not easily shrugged off. The police surveillance is significant and, as the Kawak testimony shows, amply justified.

1932: Smedley and Isaacs with a group of leftist sympathizers were members of the first League of Civil Rights in Shanghai. This organization seems to have been a failure. Smedley also became a member of the Society of Friends of the U.S.S.R., Shanghai Branch, whose roster included such Comintern agents as Irene Wiedemeyer.

Mme. Sun Yat-sen also had lent the prestige of her persuasive name to many Communist fronts. The old Society of Friends had suddenly mushroomed into a Sino-Soviet Friendship Association, in our day; she addressed an inaugural meeting in Peiping on September 6, 1940—curious index of the fanatic persistence and perennial quality of the Shanghai Conspiracy, 1929-1949.

Smedley also became very friendly with a British Communist, C. Frank Glass, a suspected Comintern agent. With the aid of Ozaki, Smedley set up a spy ring in Peiping and Tientsin and put Kawai Teikichi in charge. This northern espionage organization operated until June, 1933. She also enrolled Funakoshi Hisao and met Nozawa Fusaji in the Shanghai ring.

1933: In failing health, she went to the Soviet Union where she was at the worker's rest center at Kislovodsk in the Caucasus, a concession not usually granted to foreigners. She mentions close associations with Soviet and American Communists. It was here that she wrote her book *China's Red Army Marches*. It seems unlikely that she could have ever gotten the manuscript out of the country, if it had not had official Soviet approval. Her previous books had been translated into Russian and were widely circulated. Smedley remained in the U.S.S.R. for eleven months. She again met Chattopadhyaya in Leningrad where he was connected with the Communist Academy of Sciences. At this time, Smedley served on the staff of the International Union of Revolutionary Writers which had been founded some years earlier in Moscow. Whittaker Chambers had been on the organization's staff in 1933.

1934: Traveled through central Europe and France and then returned to New York where she unsuccessfully sought a correspondent's berth with an American publication. After visiting her family in the U.S., she sailed for China. Her ship, the *President Cleveland*, stopped for a day (Oct. 19) at Yokohama. She called on Ozaki at the *Tokyo Asahi* newspaper offices. He took her to see the Imperial Museum and dined with her. This was the period of Sorge's active operations in Tokyo.

1935: Smedley was back in Shanghai. Her name appeared on a list of twelve persons under Shanghai police surveillance. Amongst other incriminatory documents, the list was found in the possession of Joseph Walden (alias Maxim Rivosh) who was later sentenced to fifteen years in prison for subversive activities.

1936: In the fall Smedley went to Sian and was there when Chiang Kai-shek was kidnapped. Apparently it was here that she made arrangements for her later trip through Chinese Communist territory.

1937: In August, she went to the Chinese Communist capital, Yenan, where she rapidly gained the confidence of top Red Army leaders. Thereafter, Smedley gives every personal, intellectual, and literary evidence of supporting their cause, without reservation. She then went through Sanyuan to Sian where she was treated for a back injury. In October she was in Taiyuan where she met Chou En-lai. By late October, Smedley was with the mobile headquarters of the Communist Eighth Route Army. It was there that she became friendly with Communist Army leaders, Chu Teh and Peng Teh-hwei. She spent early November with units of Lin Pao's First Front Army of the Workers' and Peasants' Red Army from Kiangsi, a unit of the Eighth Route Army. Later in the month Smedley returned to Chinese Communist headquarters. At the end of November she was in Pingyanfu with fighting units. After another stay at Communist headquarters, she started back to Hankow just after the end of the year.

1938: During the early part of the year Smedley was in Tungkwan. Then at the request of Mao Tse-tung, head of the Chinese Communist Party, she went to Hankow to continue her work for the Communist cause. Here she did publicity for the Chinese Red Cross, lectured and wrote urging support for the Communist armies. She left the city before it fell to the Japanese (October, 25) and started toward Chungking.

1939: Smedley visited units of the Communist New Fourth Army and made her way through Central China with various Communist guerrilla groups. She also visited certain Central Government units and finally rejoined the Communist irregulars in Hupeh Province toward the end of the year.

1940: In June she made her way to Chungking where she lectured and worked for increased medical aid for the Communists.

1941: Flew to Hong Kong where she was treated for chronic illness and continued active in collaboration with leftist and Communist elements. She returned to the U.S. in midsummer.

1943: Smedley spent considerable time at Yaddo, Saratoga Springs, N. Y., a retreat for artists and writers. She left to lecture at Skidmore College.

1944: Smedley was working on a play about China and had in mind a revolutionary novel on the same subject.

1945-47: Lectured and wrote for periodicals, many of which were leftist. During this period she became active in the Committee for a Democratic Far Eastern Policy, a Communist-front organization. Smedley became a member of the National Council of the League of American Wrtiers, an affiliate of the International Union of Revolutionary Writers. The League has been branded a Communist-front organization by the Congressional Committee on Un-American Activities and by the Attorney General's Office.

1948: Moved to Palisades, N. Y. She published articles on China in the leftist *New York Star.* Smedley was one of the supporters of the National Writers for Wallace Committee formed under the auspices of the National Council of Arts, Sciences and Professions. Smedley also published an article in *The Protestant,* which is listed by the House Committee on Un-American Activities as a Communist-dominated publication.

1949: Embroiled in a controversy with the Chief, Military Intelligence, Far East Command, Tokyo, over release (by Washington) of a report, dated December 15, 1947, "The Sorge Espionage Case," she threatened to sue for libel, aiming at General MacArthur instead of General Willoughby, who was the responsible head of the department that compiled and prepared the report. Having gained the maximum amount of publicity from tying her name with that of the famous wartime commander, Smedley lapsed into discreet silence and made no motion to pursue her suit, which would have brought to light the voluminous records of this case.

1950: Left for London, on the eve of a summons from the House Un-American Activities Committee, ostensibly to work abroad on a biography of Chu-Teh, Chinese Communist Commander in Chief. She died suddenly in a London Nursing Home.

Her will left all her property, royalties on her books, and her ashes to Chu-Teh. The ashes were shipped to and installed ceremoniously in Peiping, capital of Chinese communism.

Opinions of American, British, and Japanese Lawyers

The inferential repudiation of the original report and the astonishing publicity in favor of Smedley, gave Tokyo pause.

Steps were taken to re-examine every documentary item and to institute expert legal research, scrutiny, and notorization by lawyers of the highest professional standing, including the Judge Advocate General of the Far East Command. These learned gentlemen prepared the material for possible use in American Courts, just in case the mouthpieces of the Reds had the audacity to continue suit for libel. Their opinions and conclusions are very illuminating:

". . . In rendering our opinion, we are primarily concerned with the subject matter of an intelligence report entitled, 'The Sorge Spy Ring,' which is recorded in Periodical Summary, CIS, GHQ, FEC, No. 23, December 15, 1947, and the evidenciary exhibits supporting the statements therein contained. It is neither our intention nor our prerogative to criticize the report as to form or method of compilation, but if its narrative style be considered unusual for intelligence or informational purposes, such could in no manner or ways affect its meaning and intent. However, we are concerned with its contents and it is our opinion that the mass of documentary evidence, including Japanese court records, report of investigation officials, judgments of trial courts, testimony of living witnesses and police records of other nations supporting the report completely justify the general intent and purpose of the report. We are particularly concerned with that portion of the report which deals with Agnes Smedley and Guenther Stein.

". . . Based upon our examination of the documents listed immediately heretofore, it is the opinion of the undersigned that these evidences established proof that Richard Sorge and his associates were espionage agents for the Russian Army, and that Agnes Smedley and Guenther Stein are Communists in mind, spirit and practice, and that they were actively and knowingly connected with the Sorge spy ring in China and Japan; and we are further of the opinion that the strong chain of evidence fully and conclusively supports the intelligence report entitled Periodical Summary, Civil Intelligence Section, GHQ, FEC, No. 23, dated December 15, 1947, 'The Sorge Spy Ring: A Case Study in International Espionage in the Far East.'

"We, the undersigned, fully realizing that certain processes and procedures are necessary for the authentication or verification of documentary evidence before they may be introduced in courts of record in the United States, or be used as a basis for evidence, have examined the methods and procedures used for the authentication and verification of the documents listed in the following six (6) pages, and after having duly considered the testimony of witnesses and having examined their written statements and interrogations, together with their seals and signatures appended thereto, have arrived at the conclusion that the authentication and verification of the documents, including the statements from witnesses, is in accordance with existing laws and procedures.

"We, therefore, certify that it is our opinion that

the authentication and verification of each of the several documents mentioned is legally sufficient to give legal standing to their full use within the scope of the rules of civil procedures for the courts of the United States, or foreign courts adhering to Anglo-American jurisprudence.

It is our further opinion that:

a. The authentications and verifications herein referred to are good, sufficient, and legal identifications of the documents to which they relate.

b. That such records and documents are sufficiently authenticated to permit their full use before any court of record subject to the limitations imposed by the prevailing rules of evidence.

c. That the procedures and methods employed in the authentication of the documents herein referred to are those that are normally used in the preparation of documents to be used for the same identical purposes for which these documents are, or may hereafter, be intended."

J. Woodall Green,
Member, Maryland Bar

> E. V. A. de Becker & R. Usami
> Member, Middle Temple, London
> Member, Inner Temple, London
> Member, Tokyo Bar
> International Lawyers,
>   Tokyo, Japan

Joseph S. Carusi,
Member, Connecticut Bar

> Franklin E. N. Warren,
> Member, Oklahoma Bar
> Member, New Mexico Bar

PART FOUR

THE SHANGHAI CONSPIRACY

Shanghai: The Link with Today

Sorge's story, while often evasive or inherently cautious, nevertheless contained so many leads, pointing to China, as a focal point of the conspiracy, that it aroused the interest of the Tokyo intelligence in Shanghai. The particular part of the Sorge material that seemed especially important was his very brief but suggestive description of various groups, *i.e.*, "apparati" in the Shanghai area; the Lehman Group; The Frolich-Feldman Group; The Comintern Group; The Noulens incident.

The so-called Comintern Group appeared especially significant; it turned out to be the Pan Pacific Trade Union Secretariat (PPTUS). On closer scrutiny, we found that this organization had been directed by one Earl Browder, the former head of the American Communist Party; in due course of time, his successor Eugene Dennis had made his appearance, not to mention such a stalwart of the American party as J. H. Dolson and, last-but-not-least, the elusive, bail-jumping Gerhardt Eisler, as usual beating a customary hasty retreat, when one of his associates, Noulens, was arrested and tried.

Obviously a case has more than historical value if it leads directly to prominent American Communists who are still most active in our midst.

An epic search began to get access to the Shanghai Municipal Police records. I exploited my friendship with the Chinese Ambassador in Tokyo, to apply pressure through his channels. I interviewed former police officials like Mr. Robert Jobez, the former Deputy Commissioner of the French Section and Mr. J. Crighton, former Chief Detective-Inspector, Shanghai International Police. The Central Intelligence Agency entered the picture and rendered brilliant and friendly assistance. We tracked down invoices and shipments from Chinese warehouses, through the progressive flights of the Nationalist government from Nanking to Formosa. Finally, a series of dossiers, not all complete, was assembled and shipped to Tokyo.

The element which intrigued MacArthur's intelligence research was the ultimate and dramatic recognition that the Sorge story did not begin or end with Tokyo, that it was no accident that Sorge served in Shanghai first, and that his later operations, localized in Japan, were only a facet in the general mosaic of Soviet and Comintern international strategy.

Shanghai had been the focal point of Communist espionage and political subversion. Tokyo had been lucky in acquiring substantial parts of the municipal police records. The old files had already been tampered with, especially those bearing on American personalties, but someone had bungled or else G-2 had worked too fast. Enough material remained to present an impressive continuity. Some of the Shanghai police officers were traced to Hong Kong, like Mr. Crighton, former Chief Detective-Inspector, who has a perfect recollection of Agnes Smedley, identified her as a Communist, working with the Communist party in Shanghai, stated that she worked with the Noulens and recalled that her police file was voluminous. His confirmation of the Shanghai files actually acquired by Tokyo is collateral evidence from most authoritative quarters.

Shanghai Police Files Confirm Sorge Records

The miscellaneous records of the British and French Shanghai Municipal Police in the early thirties, open up an astonishing vista on a fantastic array of Communists fronts, ancillary agencies, and the vast interlocking operations of the Third International in China. It is in this particular period that the groundwork was laid for the Communist successes of today.

As in the Japanese Court Records, Smedley now appears in these independent documents, associated with well-known Comintern agents, leftists, and sympathizers; affiliated with or assisting in activities, most of which were Comintern-directed for the ultimate strategic benefit of Soviet Russia.

The role of Shanghai, a veritable witch's cauldron of international intrigue, a focal point of Communist efforts, already becomes apparent in the records of the Sorge trial and collateral testimony. The Zeitgeist Bookshop, rendezvous of Sorge and Ozaki, and its astute owner, Miss Wiedemeyer (Weitemeyer), appear again, viewed from a different angle, recorded this time by a reputable international police body. Smedley had attacked the Japanese Court material as "obtained under torture and duress"; this claim is, of course, a typical "red herring" and the customary smear-defense expected of a cornered individual. On the other hand, the files of the Shanghai International Police can hardly be impugned as obtained under torture and duress, which Smedley slyly attributed to the "Japanese Fascists who were enemies of the United States." Communist strategic defense is often brilliant. This innuendo is a clever but futile defense maneuver.

There is more to the Shanghai Municipal Police files than an inferential accusation against Smedley. Smedley manipulated both time and space. In Shanghai, in the early thirties, we are not dealing with the period of our uneasy alliance with the Soviets (1941-45), but with the prewar years of 1930-39, in the heyday of the Third International, prelude to the infamous Stalin-Hitler Pact, sole factor that made World War II at all possible. We are dealing here with a conspiratorial epoch in the history of modern China. Shanghai was the vineyard of communism. Here were sown the dragon's teeth that ripened into the Red harvest of today, and the farm labor was done by men and women of many nationalities who had no personal stakes in China other than an inexplicable fanaticism for an alien cause, the Communist "jehad" for the subjugation of the Western world.

American Communists in China

The greater design of the Soviet conquest of the East is already clear in the confession of Sorge, Soviet master spy. It is again recognizable in the intricate pattern of the Third International "apparatus." Shanghai was the focal point of sabotage and subversion, and to this "Mecca" flocked the Communist operators of the world for training, for experimentation, for career investments.

In 1927, a conference was held in Hankow under the auspices of the Third International and attended by Tom Mann (Gt. Britain), Earl Browder (U.S.A.), Jacques Doriot (France), Roy (India), and a number of others. It was decided that Communist work in this part of the world would be conducted by the Pan Pacific Trade Union Secretariat, of which Earl Browder was made secretary. He soon afterwards became active in this work in which he was assisted by Katherine Harrison alias Alice Read, considered by the police as a convenient *ménage-a-deux*. Earl Browder and his female assistant continued their work in the following year (1928) and spent most of their time in Shanghai. They were joined that year by one W. A. Haskell who also was assisted by a woman named Emerson, presumably his wife.

One of the police dossiers states: "During 1929 W. A. Haskell and Miss Emerson left Shanghai, but the ranks of foreign Communist agents, in that city, were by no means reduced, for Gerhardt Eisler who lived in Wong-Shaw Gardens, between March 20th and November 30th, George Hardy and J. H. Dolson also visited Shanghai one after the other. . . ."

Guenther Stein and the Institute of Pacific Relations

Guenther Stein is another link with the present. A notebook confiscated from Sorge listed six members of his spy ring, together with their aliases, and Stein was listed among the six. An intercepted radio message from Moscow referred to his code name, that means that his identity was known, that he was listed in the personnel records of the Soviet Army Intelligence. There is testimony by Klausen and Sorge, that the wireless technician erected a transmission set in Stein's house; Stein not only was living on the premises, at the time, but gave his consent. Stein acted as a courier for the ring and carried photographs and microfilm to Shanghai where they were delivered to a liaison agent from Moscow, at the Hotel Metropole. On one occasion, Stein was instructed to and did bring back from Shanghai a smoking pipe of extraordinary design, a woman's shawl, and a brooch. These items were later used by Anna Klausen for identification purposes, when she was sent to Shanghai to deliver 20-30 rolls of film to another Moscow agent.

When the story broke, on February 10, 1949, Stein was in New York. Two days later, he turned up in Paris. The trail of Guenther Stein is calculated to raise many questions. Who sponsored his entry into the United States late in 1944 in view of our laws barring alien Communists? Stein was an official participant in a conference of the Institute of Pacific Relations at Hot Springs, Virginia, lasting from January 6 to January 17, 1945. The meetings significantly were closed to the press. Stein was there as a member of the British delegation. The Americans' representatives at this super-secret conference must have observed Stein in action. Edward C. Carter was Stein's chief when the latter served as correspondent for the Institute in Chungking. Henry Wallace, Carter Vincent, and Owen Lattimore saw Stein in Chungking.

Another contact between the Institute of Pacific Relations and the Sorge espionage ring was found in the redoubtable

Hozumi Ozaki, who died with Sorge on the gallows. He came to the United States in 1936 to attend an Institute Conference in the Yosemite Valley in California. There, according to Miller Freeman, Seattle publisher and former naval intelligence officer, he made the contact to secure permission for the Japanese Navy to survey the Aleutian Islands under the guise of a scientific fisheries survey. When the Japanese got around to attack the islands, they had pretty detailed topographical and geodetic information.

Finally, Saionji Kinkazu must be mentioned to link the past with the present. He was picked up in the Sorge group, found guilty of passing secret information to Ozaki, and was given a sentence of three years' imprisonment with stay of execution. However, Saionji has been affiliated with the Japan Council since its start in 1923. He has been an intimate of Ozaki, Ushiba, and Nawa. Ushiba Tomohohiko was at one time General Secretary of the Japan Council. Like Ozaki, he was one of Prince Konoye's secretaries or "bright young men"; while not as important a figure in the Sorge ring as Ozaki, he was arrested in the general roundup of suspect individuals.

The Japan Branch of the Institute of Pacific Relations

These men are back plying their trade: the Japan Section of the Institute of Pacific Relations. I cannot speak with any degree of authority on the American Section of this Institute, but I am familiar with the Japanese operations, in the twilight zone of fellow traveling, that broad color zone which ranges from innocuous rose to deep red, from intellectual flirtation to treason.

This also involves the matter of relationship between the Japan Council and other organizations, usually maintained through a series of interlocking directorates. One rather good example is the China Research Institute headed by Hirano Gitaro. This gentleman is an intimate of the Soviet Mission in Tokyo, and the Institute has a wide reputation as a "front"; I have classified it as a Communist party "apparatus." Many of the directors of the China Research are also directors of the Japan Council of the IPR. The head of the China Research is a strong Communist sympathizer. Nawa, above referred to, is head of the Kyoto branch.

The American contacts of the China Research Institute are very interesting; among them are such names as William C. Johnstone, Karl Wittvogel (testimony in the McCarran Committee, Paul Kattenburg, Andrew Roth (Amerasia),

Jerome B. Cohen, Raymond Dennett, T. A. Bisson, Bruno Lasker, Franz Michael, and Philip Jaffe (Amerasia).

There are other associated organizations which fit into this same general design; among them are known fronts like the Political and Economic Research Institute, the Sino-Japanese Friendship Society, the Japan Friendship Society, the Sino-Japanese Trade Promotion Society, and others.

Here again, a pattern: our Congressional committees and the Attorney General have listed many American groups, as fronts; one has only to eliminate the references to Japan and virtually the same names of organizations appear in the American scene.

Earl Browder: American Communist in China

There were plenty of other leads in the original G-2 report, pointing at American Communists principally on the Pacific Coast. Eighteen names of Communist agitators, agents, and suspects were reported as connected with the Sorge case as covered in the trial records in this connection.

The Honorable Walter H. Judd of Minnesota said as follows in the House of Representatives on Tuesday, July 18, 1950:

". . . *The Daily Worker* of September 7, 1937, reproduced three letters written to Earl Browder, then head of the Communist Party in America; one was from Mao Tsetung who signed himself as President of the Chinese Soviet Republic; one from Chu-Teh, leader of the Chinese Red Army, and one from Chou En-lai, now Prime Minister of the Communist regime in China. These men had written to him shortly after the outbreak of the Japanese all-out war against China in 1937. They were appealing for help from their Communists brethren here. Chou En-lai began his letter to Browder:

"'. . . Comrade, do you still remember the Chinese who worked with you in China ten years ago? We feel that when we achieve victory (in China), this will be of considerable help to the struggle of the American people for liberation . . .'

"Now, what had Earl Browder been doing in China in 1927? He was there with other leaders of the Communist hierarchy from all the world to help the Reds seize complete control of China as the Bolsheviks had done in Russia in the October revolution just ten years before. Chiang Kaishek in China was scheduled to be what Kerenski had been in Russia—an interim leader to be overthrown by the Reds as soon as he had defeated the war lords. . . ."

Congressman Judd is about as well informed on China

as any man living and his exceptional knowledge is far superior to the knowledge of the spurious experts of the Institute of Pacific Relations or the Committee for a Democratic Far Eastern Policy. He justly points out the very suggestive fact that the then head of the American Communist Party was in intimate correspondence with the leaders of Red China, the same men who now have thrown their murderous hordes against American soldiers in Korea.

The J. H. Dolson who operated in Shanghai is none other than the Cincinnati Communist, recently arrested by the FBI in their roundup of the so-called second-string American Communist leaders. The elusive bail jumper, Eisler, belonged to the Shanghai group in 1935, and his Attorney Carol Weiss King would have had more difficulty in defending him in 1949, had the jury known something about his slippery antecedents.

Eugene Dennis, Alias Paul Eugene Walsh

It was an almost foregone conclusion that Eugene Dennis, Browder's pupil, secretary, and successor, would sooner or later make his appearance in Shanghai, the proving ground of Red conspirators.

Time in its issue of April 25, 1949 featured Eugene Dennis, the boss of the American Communists, then on trial in Judge Medina's Court. There is no particular point in repeating this terse, well-written story of the efforts and world itinerary of a Soviet agent; important, however, are certain connecting links with the Sorge report. Dennis, who used to be Francis X. Waldron, obtained a fraudulent passport as "Paul Walsh" and traveled via Europe and South Africa to China. The world-wide ramifications of the Third Comintern, with Shanghai as the Far Eastern operating center, is reflected in the itinerary of this American disciple. Paul Eugene Walsh, alias "Paul" or "Milton," suddenly appears in the records of the Shanghai Police; his police card states:

". . . From Dec. 1, 1933 until June, 1934, he resided at Flat 6, Gresham Apts. No. 1224 Avenue Joffre. On May 30, 1934, the lease of Flat 34 D Foncim Apts., No. 643 Route Frelupt was transferred to his name from Harry Berger, with whom he was obviously on terms of good friendship. Walsh resided at the latter address from June 1, 1934 until October 9, 1934 when he secretly left Shanghai for Trieste on the SS *Conte Verde*. It has been established that Walsh was one of the masterminds of the local machine of the Komintern and as such was responsible for the collation of many important documents relating to the propagation of Communist ideas in the Far East. . . ."

The Shanghai police classification ties in neatly with related fragments in the Sorge case; Sorge's assistants operated habitually under aliases or codes, usually their Christian names, viz., Paul, Max, Alex, John, etc. Significantly, a Comintern agent, under the code name of "Paul" took over the Shanghai station after Sorge's transfer to Japan.

At any rate, the police card reference to "the local machine of the Komintern" points to Browder's creation, the Pan-Pacific Trade Union Secretariat. This Red front dabbled in labor organizations and water-front trouble, but it also did a lot of other things under orders of the Soviet Army Intelligence. Sorge is quite specific defining its mission:

"The Comintern Group (FEB) consisted of two branches, the Political Branch (headed by Gerhardt Eisler) and the Organization Branch (headed by Noulens); in the light of the current China debacle, the operational missions were significant: liaison between the Comintern (Soviet) and the Chinese Communist Party; political policy (decided upon by the Comintern) with respect to the Chinese Communist Party; exchange of information between the Chinese Communist Party and the Comintern; financial liaison between the Comintern and the Chinese Communist Party; the movement of personnel between Moscow and the Chinese Communist Party."

In 1930 a large host of agents of the Third International came to Shanghai and became associated with the Pan-Pacific Trade Union Secretariat, and another important organ of the Third International, called the Far Eastern Bureau. The new arrivals included Hilaire Noulens (or Paul Ruegg) and Mrs. Noulens, of unknown nationality; A. E. Stewart, Margaret Undjus, and Judea Codkind, Americans; and Irene Wiedemeyer (Weitemeyer) who was German.

Smedley was an associate of Irene Weitemeyer (Wiedemeyer) who operated the Zeitgeist Bookshop in Shanghai, rendezvous of Communists and "mail-drop" for espionage agents. Ozaki, Sorge's right-hand man, was introduced by Smedley in Weitemeyer's place. Sorge testified:

". . . As previously stated I first met Smedley in Shanghai, acquired her as a member, and through my recommendations, she was registered with Comintern Headquarters. I do not know as to whether she was affiliated with the American Communist Party. Ozaki was also acquired in China. I re-established contact with him after arriving in Japan, worked with him, and recommended him to Comintern Headquarters for registration. Thus I recommended both of them and offered myself as one of the two sponsors required for each new members. A member in Moscow consented to be the other sponsor on the strength of my recommendations and reports. . . ."

The Shanghai police card on Smedley states:

". . . Agnes Smedley alias Alice Bird and Mrs. Petroikos. . . . Member of the following societies: Friends of the USSR, Hindustan Association in Berlin, Berlin Indian Revolutionary Society, Noulens Defense Committee, All China Labor Federation, and the China League for Civil Rights. . . . In possession of two passports German and American. Arrived in Shanghai in May, 1929 from Berlin as the correspondent of the German newspaper *Frankfurter Zeitung*. She is in the service of the Eastern Branch of the Central Committee of the Communist International and is definitely known to have assisted local Indian seditionists on several occasions . . . her chief duties comprise the supervising of Communist organizations among workers, and that she receives orders direct from the Central Committee of the Communist International in Moscow. . . ."

The Shanghai police observed and recorded these furtive men and women, often without making direct accusations. Such things are a matter of cumulative surveillance, but dossiers are never opened without a good reason.

The Case of Hilaire Noulens, Alias Paul Ruegg

The case of Hilaire Noulens, alias Paul Ruegg, is both interesting and typical: The clandestine fraternity, working under the aegis of the Comintern, or the Red Army, could always count on a variety of front organizations to rally to its defense whenever it was in trouble. The principal agency was The International Red Aid (MOPR), created in 1922, known as International Labor Defense in America. Inferentially, whenever the defense swung into action it was a foregone conclusion that the chief protagonists were under orders of the Comintern. To the gullible outsider, the defense action might look like a legitimate civil liberty move with some sentimental appeal; however, to those in the know it was just another Red front mobilizing pink lawyers, agents, and fellow travelers.

Noulens arrived in Shanghai in 1930 under cover of a stolen Belgian passport as Fred Vandercruysen to head the Far Eastern Bureau. Fifteen months later, he was arrested for Communist activities linked with a French Communist, Joseph Ducroux, alias Serge LeFranc, then operating in

Singapore. During the trial that led to Noulens' conviction, the authorities learned of his importance in the Comintern apparatus. This group operated on a considerable scale; they maintained seven bank accounts, rented fifteen houses or apartments—a veritable political rabbit warren; Ruegg-Noulens used at least twelve names in Shanghai and carried one Canadian and two Belgian passports, while his wife used five names and two Belgian passports.

Here again the *Time* article furnished an interesting clue to identities; in a subparagraph headed: "The Little Kremlin," it said:

". . . All but the most secret Communist operations in the U.S. were and still are, directed from the ramshackle, nine-story loft building, on 36 E. 12th St., not far from Manhattan's Union Square. To its top-floor offices came the Communists' international 'Reds,' the shadowy men with the changeable names like P. Green, G. Williams, A. Ewart, H. Berger . . . which in a wink of the eye might become Drabkin, B. Mikhailov, Braun, or Gerhardt Eisler. These were Moscow's agents. From the ninth floor the word which they brought from Moscow was passed along to the faithful, to the party hacks on the *Daily Worker* and Yiddish-language *Freiheit,* to the cultivators of organized labor's vineyards, to men like Christoffel in Milwaukee. . . ."

The interesting thing about *Time's* shadowy men with the changeable names like A. Ewart, H. Berger, or Gerhardt Eisler, is that these same names and identities appear both in the Sorge records and the Shanghai police files. Their crooked paths meander on into the forties and into the United States.

A man of many aliases, when Paul Walsh appeared, it was Berger who rented his Shanghai apartment to him; Flat 35 D Foncim Apts. No. 643 Route Frelupt. Berger left Shanghai for Vladivostok July 19, 1934, on the S.S. *Yingchow* because of police raids on No. 38 Race Road, which netted incriminating Communist documents.

He appears in the Canadian espionage case as an "Agent in the U.S."; Fred Rose, Communist member of the Parliament in Canada used Freda Lipshitz as go-between himself (cover name Debouz), Berger, and others in Washington.

Most of the old wheel horses of the Communist party operated in Shanghai during one period or another, the professionals of the clandestine fraternity as well as the acolytes and dupes, who flirt with the Red menace. In the bistros of the French Concession, in the furtive rendezvous of the Shanghai conspirators, you can invariably detect the metallic tinkle of thirty pieces of silver.

Another familiar name is that of the bail-jumping Eisler. Sorge reports on him as follows:

"The Comintern Group in Shanghai consisted of a Political Branch and an Organization Branch. The Political Branch was in charge of Gerhardt (Eisler) whom I had known in Germany and worked with in my Comintern days.

"With the arrest of Noulens, Gerhardt's status in Shanghai became precarious and he decided to return to Moscow in 1931. . . ."

The tendrils of Mr. Eisler's operations reach into far places. He next appeared as Communist International Representative in the U.S. in 1936. His first wife was Hede Gumperz. Eisler was later transferred to Europe. His second wife, Hede's sister, Elli, whom he married in 1931, said she was still his wife in 1946. He returned to the U.S. with another woman, whom he apparently married in 1942. The amorous exploits of Comintern agents appear to be as complicated as their professional involvements. Hede Gumperz was in charge of an underground Communist "apparatus" in Washington. She broke with Stalin later on. She said she knew Alger Hiss and talked with him in an apartment of Noel Field, State Department official who was a member of her "apparatus."

A great many young American soldiers died in the war period 1941-45, while Gerhardt Eisler was pursuing his business of treason and sabotage in the comparative safety of the United States. He found Europe too hot for him in 1941. Needless to say, he never came closer to the United States services than perhaps an attempt to subvert some government employees. Eisler's spectacular arrest in New York and subsequent escape to London dovetail accurately with the general pattern of his career. He had left Shanghai in 1931 in as much of a hurry and for the same reasons.

The Comintern Apparatus and Shanghai Affiliates

Other individuals, implicated in varying degrees, definitely committed or not to the Communist movement, who are covered elsewhere are understandable only in terms of their subservience to a foreign master. It is a relationship that requires a background examination of the formidable worldwide machinery of the Comintern "apparatus," a Machiavellian tool of the imperialist expansion of the Soviets, who have made progress beyond the wildest dream of Czarist ambition.

The Moscow Headquarters of the Third (Communist) International (Comintern) during the 1930's paralleled the organizational structure of the Soviet government. Led by a World Congress of Soviet and foreign Communists, who met at intervals between 1919 and 1935, the Comintern was actually controlled by the U.S.S.R., because of its leadership in the world Communist movement and a Comintern organizational ruling which gave the largest representation to the nation playing host to the Congress—in every case the Soviet Union. The executive functions of the Comintern were vested in the Executive Committee of the Communist International (ECCI), which claimed several foreign members but in reality was controlled by its predominant Soviet representation. Like the World Congress, the Committee met periodically, primarily to determine general lines of policy, but final control of the Comintern rested in the Praesidium, which was made up, among others, of a Politburo, several standing Commissions, and a political secretariat. Under the Praesidium there were several training schools, sectional or regional secretariats and auxiliary departments, which were concerned with generalized work in specific fields and, finally, certain auxiliary organizations which worked directly and specifically with foreign Communist or Communist-front groups.

The Comintern was the nondiplomatic foreign arm of the Soviet. Organized at Moscow in 1919, the Comintern was, until its alleged dissolution in 1943, a quasi-governmental body aimed largely at fostering Communist and Communist-front groups in the capitalist world in order to carry out such Communist strategy as the Russian government considered essential to the promotion of world revolution or, as conditions required, the protection of the Soviet Union.

Only a few of the Moscow auxiliary organizations are of immediate concern here, although all of them, numbering about thirteen, had variable interests in Shanghai, operating through an extraordinary variety of channels.

Before listing the Chinese—or Far Eastern fronts, some general presentation of the nature and purposes of the organizations should be given for the benefit of those who are not familiar with the highly important adjuncts to international communism. The Communist front is an organization whose members are, for the most part, not Communists and who are possibly quite innocent of the carefully concealed alien control of the organization. Some fronts are conceived, created, and operated by the local party. Others are originally non-Communist groups that are infiltrated until Communists assume positions of parliamentary control from which they dominate every activity of the group.

The whole front system was conceived in the Soviet Union. Karl Radek, Otto Kuusinen, Willie Muenzenburg—who flits in and out of the Far East, though resident in Berlin—and Georgi Dimitrov who seemed to be equally at home in Prussia and Bulgaria, were the founders of the Communist front concept as a part of the international Communist solar system; their instructions to foreign national parties may be found in the directives and statutes of the Third Comintern and in the decisions of the Comintern's executive committee.

As in Shanghai, through this system of fronts, the party has achieved variable success in penetrating almost every phase of American life. On the labor front, in our educational institutions, in the motion picture industry, in the newspaper world, in certain facets of the federal government, in scientific and research circles, in the administration of welfare and relief—in fact in a nationwide cross section of civic enterprises, we find a host of front organizations actively functioning and actually controlled by the Communist Party of the United States.

Fronts are used as media for recruiting lush crops of liberals who are under the illusion that they are enlisting in an international crusade against fascism; they are used to adapt American public thinking to the international Communist party line, and they are also used for the purpose of keeping a steady supply of money flowing through the various fronts and eventually into the treasury of the Communist party itself.

There have been fronts to promote peace, Kremlin style; fronts to turn us away from and smear Chiang Kai-shek and to induce support for the Communist People's Government; fronts to protect refugees from fascism, usually subversive riffraff with not the slightest pretense to civic responsibility; fronts to protect such international Communist agents and operators as Gerhardt Eisler; fronts by which the Party seeks to divide our people and whip up racial antagonisms such as the Citizens Committee for the Defense of Mexican-American Youth; fronts to foment and run strikes; fronts to keep a steady barrage of smears and criticisms leveled at our courts, our law enforcement agencies, and the Federal Bureau of Investigation. The impact of hundreds of these organizations on our American way of life is incalculable: it represents the corrosive prostitution of moral and civic values. It has been found that the most successful weapon through which these organizations can be fought is public exposure through carefully documented evidence such as the Sorge record; exposure of this type drives non-Communists and joiners away from the infantile temptation of affiliating with these organizations, and ultimately reduces them, we hope, to a weak and relatively impotent position.

In analyzing individual affiliations with these various groups many factors must be considered with great care to avoid injustices; thus many people who opposed General Franco as a type of totalitarian ruler were drawn into various Spanish loyalist fronts during the period of the Spanish Civil War; many Jewish people were lured into the Anti-Nazi League when Hitler was persecuting the Jews in Germany; most of those who affiliated with these organizations quietly dropped out when they became aware of the hypocrisy of Communist control.

On the other hand, there are certain fronts so patently Communist in character that one must be naïve, indeed, to join them innocently and moronic to remain a member for any length of time without realizing precisely what is going on. Typical of this type of front are the American-Russian Institute, the Civil Rights Congress, and the Joint Anti-Fascist Refugee Committee, etc. The Communist schools in various states are so much an integral part of the Party "apparatus" that they cannot be classified as merely front organizations. In California, for example, these institutions were known as "Workers' Schools" and no effort was made to disguise their Communist status; in San Francisco the Workers' School became the Tom Mooney Labor School and finally the California Labor School; under the direction of Holland Roberts, formerly a professor at Stanford University. In Los Angeles the Workers' School took on the label of Peoples' Educational Center and now it functions as the Southern California branch of the California Labor School.

The interlocking ramifications of these enterprises, on a state or national plan, can be traced on a global basis as well. This concept, of course, implies the existence of a sort of administrative general staff; we might as well accept the unpleasant fact that it exists and that its headquarters are in the Kremlin. When Sorge wanted assistants in Japan, they were summoned from all the corners of the world; when the Kremlin wanted to organize Chinese labor, British, American, French, and Indian top-flight experts converged on China; when Smedley needed protection, the pink press sprang raucously to her defense; her false protestations were printed, simultaneously in New York and Hong Kong. Perhaps the most striking instance is contained in the slippery meanderings of Gerhardt Eisler, almost caught in Shanghai and almost caught in New York; though fifteen years and 10,000 miles apart, Red mouthpieces then and later were ready to match their tainted skill against the judgment of government officers.

Kremlin International Master Fronts

1. Profintern. The Red International of Labor (Profintern) was created in 1919 in order to counteract the influence of the International Federation of Labor Unions of the Second (Socialist) International. The Profintern consisted of a headquarters apparatus controlled by the Praesidium and of affiliated sections which in most countries outside the U.S.S.R. took the form of Red Trade Union Opposition. In the field, the Profintern organized International Propaganda Committees for work among specific trades. In addition, the Profintern sponsored the creation of parallel labor union federations of which the Pan Pacific Trade Union Secretariat (PPTUS) and the All China Labor Federation were important examples.

2. Krestintern. The Red Peasants International (Krestintern) was founded in 1923 to break the resistance to communism of the peasantry in various countries. Although it enjoyed far less success than organizations devoted to the laborer and the intelligentsia, it directed local Communist groups which organized so-called peasants' unions including the Chinese Peasant League.

3. VOKS. The Society for Cultural Relations with Foreign Countries (VOKS) was established in Moscow in 1923 to promote Soviet culture abroad as an instrument of political propaganda. The cultural attaché of each Soviet embassy abroad was in direct charge of VOKS objectives and, as such, was charged with liaison with the ECCI in Moscow and with the formation of the so-called friendly societies. The activities of VOKS can be gauged from the sections of its headquarters: Foreign Relations; Reception of Foreigners; International Book Exchange; Press; Exhibitions, etc.

4. MOPR. International Red Aid (MOPR), created in 1922, has been characterized as the Red Cross of the Communist International, designed primarily to assist political prisoners, secret agents caught red-handed and other "victims of bourgeois reaction." International Red Aid, which functioned legally and illegally in 67 countries, was complemented by Workers International Relief, both directed for

many years by the German Communist Willi Muenzenberg. Abroad not only International Red Aid itself but separate Communist-front groups organized for the defense of a particular case have played the leading role in assisting individual Communists jailed for subversive activities.

With calculated skill international communism long ago subverted semantics to confuse the slogans and concepts of capitalist society; the universal sentimental appeal of the historical Red Cross and its protection of the weak and oppressed was bound to be exploited. As the legal arm of the international Communist conspiracy, International Red Aid, or MOPR, functioned as a subdivision of the Comintern as early as 1922. The initials MOPR represent the Russian words for "International Class War Prisoners Aid Society"; it was described by Gregory Zinoviev, then head of the Comintern, as follows: ". . . The Executive Committee of the Comintern regards the International Red Aid as one of its branches and indeed as one of the most important of them. . . ."

Under the direction of Klara Zetkin and Willi Muenzenberg, MOPR flourished and developed internationally at a rapid pace and also expanded in the United States under the leadership of James B. Canon, a charter member of the American Communist Party.

MOPR and its American Tendrils

In this country MOPR has operated under the name of International Labor Defense (ILD) since about 1928, though it was formerly known simply as International Red Aid. Louis Coleman correlated the nation-wide activities of the organization from his office at East 11th Street in New York City. The California headquarters was located on 1006 Market Street, San Francisco, and on 127 South Broadway in Los Angeles. It is significant to note that the Communist party district of which California was a part was District 13 comprising the States of California, Arizona, and Nevada, and that the International Labor Defense was also divided into National districts and California was in District 13 which was identical with the geographical limits of the Communist party district which bore the same number. Sam Davey headed the District in the critical China period. The ILD was operated under the direction of such veteran Communists as Elaine Black, Ida Roth, and Leo Gallagher. The District furnished Miyagi for the Sorge operations in Japan.

Documentary sources show that there was a constant and

intimate liaison between the ILD and the American Civil Liberties Union in California; Leo Gallagher, chief counsel for the ILD, was also an officer in the Southern California chapter of the Civil Liberties Union in 1935 and naturally did his utmost to further the Marxian class struggle concept in both organizations simultaneously.

Carol Weiss King, in 1917 a research worker in the Civil Liberties Union in New York, has played an exceedingly important role in the organization and direction of a wide variety of Communist legal aid fronts in this country. The high level on which this lady operates is indicated by the fact that she has acted as counsel for Earl Browder, Israel Amter, Robert Minor, Sam Carr of the Canadian espionage apparatus, Harry Bridges, Jay Peters, and the Eisler brothers—Hans and Gerhardt. She also was a contact for Hede Massing when the latter was a Soviet agent in New York.

Mrs. King and her law partner, the late Joseph R. Brodsky, helped organize the International Labor Defense in this country; all lawyers for the ILD are guided by an extraordinary directive, viz., ". . . transform the prisoners' bench into a revolutionary platform. From the defendant, become the accuser. Organize mass defense to mobilize the masses against bourgeois Fascist justice."

Brilliant Exposé in The Saturday Evening Post, February, 1950

In *The Saturday Evening Post* for February 17, 1950, in an article "The Commies' Dearest Friend," Mr. Craig Thompson traces the activities of Mrs. King and points out that "if all lawyers followed the directives of the ILD, all legal process would become a shambles and courtrooms propaganda rostrums, which is, of course, what Red Aid wanted."

I read Craig's article into the Senate and House Hearings, in August, 1951, as one of the most profound and brilliant analyses of the genealogical evolution of a subversive series of interlocking agencies, in a shocking *mésalliance* of the juridical immunities of a civilized country and the callous prostitution of its laws. The article was devastating since its lead photograph showed a smiling Carol Weiss leading Gerhardt Eisler by the hand. Fifteen years ago, in Shanghai, when his colleague, friend, and associate, Hilaire Noulens, was caught under espionage charges, some other lawyer told Eisler to beat it, to jump bail, to live and connive another day. It seems unlikely that Carol Weiss was unaware of this slippery client's antecedent.

As the party goes deeper and deeper underground its so-called "defense" fronts become correspondingly more important. These organizations of sympathetic lawyers have always been of the greatest practical support to the party. In the United States many attorneys are devoting their entire time to the affairs of the party members and front organizations and to the Communist-dominated trade unions. An entire report might well be written about the disruptive techniques employed by these officers of our courts.

Chameleonlike, the pseudo-legal fronts changed coloration and objectives. Weiss created an International Juridical Association (IJA) which later merged with the National Lawyers Guild (NLG). The defense of the Scottsboro case was a Brodsky-Weiss project. She had other successes based on American indifference, legalistic quibblings, and plain ignorance. The Supreme Court upheld an ILA brief to "permit picketing in the absence of a strike." The charge of mutiny against the crew of the S.S. *California,* a famous case of a "strike at sea" was retracted. Legal sanction for mutiny is a great help in the "class struggle." Meanwhile the Labor Defense has become the Civil Rights Congress. The finances of this organization recently became a public issue. Thompson reports sizeable fees paid to defense lawyers. Weiss got $5,877.44; A. J. Isserman, $2,000; more than $15,000 went to lawyers in a five-month period. While he remained in the States, Gerhardt Eisler drew living expenses and when he jumped bail, the Congress paid $23,500. Mrs. Weiss entertained the Eislers in her home. She got the Eislers into the country in the first place. Hans was held up in Cuba, as a known Communist. An appeal was made to Mrs. Roosevelt, who appealed to the State Department. When the Consulate in Cuba remained firm, he was moved into Mexico and got in through that easy gateway. In Gerhardt's case, to pay his fare from a Spanish refugee camp to New York, Weiss employed the American Rescue Ship Mission, another front which she organized and which later became the notorious Joint Anti-Fascist Refugee Committee.

I have touched on the absorption of Weiss's International Juridical Association by the National Lawyers Guild. This Guild had respectable antecedents but it has fallen into Red hands. Since 1939 the Guild has opposed all legislative committees investigating communism, has taken a position against the federal loyalty program, has provided legal counsel for Communists, fellow travelers, fronts, and Soviet spies, has directed torrents of abusive criticism against the Federal Bureau of Investigation and its director. Hoover quoted a Guild member as having declared, "If we keep up the constant criticism of the FBI and of Hoover, and if this criticism is systematically kept up and followed all the time, particularly by organizations, it can and will weaken the power of the FBI and hamper them very effectively. . . ."

The National Lawyers Guild has assiduously followed the Communist party line since 1939, even making an overnight complete switch on June 22, 1941, so definitively illustrated by comparing *Daily Worker* articles immediately before and after that highly significant date. The Guild has opposed fingerprinting aliens; supported Harry Bridges; urged abolition of the Congressional and California Committees on Un-American Activities; protested trial of the Communist National Committee members at Foley Square; protested contempt proceedings against the defiant Hollywood witnesses; protested against the Federal Government's loyalty progress; opposed the non-Communist oath provision of the Taft-Hartley Act; opposed universal military training; protested against the Voorhis Act which required registration of organizations that are under foreign control; advocated withdrawal of all U.S. troops from China and urged American aid to Communist China; opposed the European recovery program; and denounced the United States for insisting upon maintaining secrecy in connection with atomic weapons research. The Congressional Committee's report on the National Lawyers Guild and the Communist party line demonstrate clearly how the two coincide.

The American Civil Rights Congress

To me, as a federal security officer, the repetition of the international pattern was tremendously important. As I touched upon the Noulens case in Shanghai, and the Communist agitation in its wake, the similarity in procedure was striking. The bail jumper Gerhardt Eisler was a link; the connivance of legal talent to protect him was another. The threads from the Kremlin MORP through the China League for Civil Rights lead inevitably to the American Civil Rights Congress with only a slight difference in wording. This Congress which forfeited Eisler's bail bond—and that of the fugitive Communist leaders—is worthy of close attention as a laboratory sample of how a Kremlin blueprint becomes an American reality.

When a Communist or a front organization runs afoul of the law or is brought before a legislative investigation committee, the Civil Rights Congress immediately provides legal talent, financial support and propaganda. This powerful front is officially listed as Communist controlled by the Attorney General of the United States, and, like the National Lawyers Guild, is vital to the Communist party.

The Civil Rights Congress resulted from a merger of the International Labor Defense and the National Federation for Constitutional Liberties. These two organizations simply disappeared and were replaced by the Civil Rights Congress and several less important front organizations that functioned on a lower level.

In April, 1946, a National Congress on Civil Rights was convened at Detroit at the behest of Carey McWilliams, Norman Corwin, Paul Robeson, Dr. Kirtley F. Mather, the late Colonel Evans Carlson, Elizabeth Gurley Flynn, Vito Marcantonio, and others. Such congresses are typical maneuvers through which the Party launches its front activities such as the Writers Congress, the Congress of American Women, the Congress of Spanish-Speaking People, the Congress for Social and Unemployment Insurance, etc.

The Civil Rights Congress opened national headquarters at 205 East 42nd Street, New York City. It now boasts at least 75 chapters in 15 states; among those who have served on the national board are such chronic Communist fronters as Paul Robeson, Dashiell Hammett, John Howard Lawson, Hugh Bryson, Charlotta Bass, Philip M. Connelly, Max Yergan, Herbert K. Sorrell, and Carol Weiss King.

A distinction between the functions of the National Lawyers Guild and the Civil Rights Congress must be made clear. The prime purpose of the Guild is to recruit liberal lawyers to the Red cause. The Congress is much closer to the party. It provided funds for notorious international Communist operators like Gerhardt Eisler; it provided bail for persons convicted of contempt; it waged a constant fight against "police brutality" which is automatically charged upon the arrest of racial minority members or Communists; it maintained liaison with high-ranking Soviet officials. It also whips up mass picketing and hysteria, as it did in Los Angeles on August 7, 1948.

At noon on that date, following some preliminary publicity in the *Daily People's World*, about 100 people assembled in front of the Federal Building in Los Angeles. Anne Shore, well known in connection with affairs of this kind for many years, arrived in a 1936 Ford sedan, which bore California license number 7V105. This car was registered to Frieda Rapoport, 5331 Baltimore Street, Los Angeles, who is an old hand at these demonstrations but prefers to work in the background. The car was loaded, not only with Miss Shore, but with leaflets, placards, circulars, picket signs, and other propaganda material.

A picket line was formed in a circle in front of the entrance to the Federal Building, and on the first lap each picket was handed a placard. So quickly was this affair staged that one Negro made two rounds carrying a sign which read: "We of the American-Jewish Congress protest the Foley Square persecution"—before the mistake was rectified.

Prominent among the pickets were Leo Gallagher, attorney (ILD), Louis Schwartz, of the *Downtown Forum,* and Ted Kalman, of the *Daily People's World.* The particular public nuisance, staged with considerable aplomb, is typical of Civil Rights Congress activities.

The Shanghai police reports of fifteen years ago describe identical, parallel operations, especially the demonstrations on the occasion of the arrival of Lord Marley; these are special techniques and it must be clear by now, that Shanghai was a sort of "field laboratory."

IURW

The International Union of Revolutionary Writers was organized in 1925, probably under VOKS auspices, to enlist sympathetic literati abroad for the promotion of pro-Soviet and anti-Fascist and antiwar themes. In Moscow the IURW was responsible for the publication of the English-language *Moscow Daily News* and *International Literature,* a periodical devoted to the promulgation of Communist ideology abroad. At one time an American, Walt Carmon, was an assistant editor of *International Literature.* Carmon is listed in the "Fourth Report, Un-American Activities in California, 1948," as a member of the League of American Writers and affiliated with its Congress.

Langston Hughes, the American Communist poet, and Agnes Smedley were contributors. Anna Louise Strong for years was editor of the *Moscow Daily News,* while another American, Fred Ellis, was employed as a cartoonist on the staff of *Trud,* the official organ of the All Union Council of Soviet Trade Unions. The printing of these foreign language periodicals was done by the State Publishing House (Gosizdat) in co-operation with the International Book Publishing Association (Mezhkniga), both Soviet government enterprises.

We have already had a typical sample of Hughes's poetic style. It requires no imagination to know what would happen to the Christian churches in America if men of his ilk were ever to get the upper hand. All anyone has to do to visualize the blood bath which they would stage is to refresh one's memory about the pattern of the Soviet purges or the calvary of the Catholic Church, from Bucharest to Warsaw. That story has been told again and again—and yet, there are supposedly well-meaning joiners who flock to the spurious banners of treason, under the guise of Communist-front organizations.

From the point of view of Tokyo, the trend of Communist, Red or pink newspapers, magazines, book reviews, etc., was an established fact; there is an organized literary liaison between these publications and Communist writers. It is no accident that Smedley appeared in some of them and that, in turn, she received immediate and co-ordinated support, in 1949. Even later, Hugh Deane, well known to the counterintelligence of Tokyo, has run a series of articles in the *Compass* on the Smedley-Sorge story plainly timed and designated as a counteroffensive and smoke screen, to offset the Senate and House Committee hearings, in August, 1951.

The so-called Committee for a Democratic Far Eastern Policy is a typical front, and came to our notice as a proponent of a particularly violent anti-Nationalist editorial trend. From its virulent and generally senseless attacks against Chiang Kai-shek, it was only a step to an assault on MacArthur. The timing—October, 1950—too, was most significant. The Eighth Army had just completed the destruction of the North Korean Army and raked in over 130,000 prisoners of war, after the brilliant tactical maneuver of Inchon—a master stroke by MacArthur. The Army was on its way north, in pursuit of the remnant of North Koreans. The Chinese were massed along the Yalu and threatened with intervention of "volunteers." They were to find carefully co-ordinated "literary" support in the American and world Red press.

The Committee publishes a slick monthly called *Far East Spotlight,* sold in all Communist bookstores for twenty cents a copy or three dollars for a year's subscription. The issue for October, 1950, listed the national officers as follows: Maud Russell, Executive Director; Leonard Leader, Assistant Executive Director, Philip O. Keeney, Treasurer; William Kerner, West Coast Director; Executive Committee: Hugh Bryson, Abraham Chapman, Rev. John Darr, Jr.; Morris Davis, Hugh Delacey, James Durkin, Taletha Gerlach, Ira Golobin, C. E. Johansen, Rita Judd, Rev. J. Spencer Kennard, Paul Robeson, Nathan Rook, Arthur Schutzer, Chu Tong, Jeannette Turner, Jeffry Van Clief, and Susan Warren. Contributors to the publication have included: Herbert Aptheker, Hugh Bryson, Shuji Fuji (former editor of a Japanese-Communist paper in Los Angeles), Victor Perlo, Martin Popper, Mrs. Paul Robeson, Agnes Smedley, Professor Dirk J. Struik, and Henry Wallace. An interesting name in this line-up is Mr. Keeney. He was once employed in Tokyo in the public library service of the Civil Education Section and since that time never fails to remind the public of this creditable association. He is careful, however, not to mention how precipitately he left that service.

The October, 1950, issue is typical of the propaganda line of this publication. It heaps abuse on Chiang Kai-shek while praising the Chinese Communists; it tells us to take our troops immediately out of Korea; once again providing irrefutable though indirect, testimony that General Douglas MacArthur is an American bastion of strength in the path of the Kremlin plan for complete domination of the Far East, this issue vehemently advocated the General's dismissal and attempted to undermine him by the usual smear attacks against him, culled from the world press:

". . . Gen. MacArthur confirms the view that he is not a fit and proper person to be in charge of responsible military operation. . . . When MacArthur allows Chiang Kai-shek to talk of reconquering China with American help, we wonder whether the American people are now so completely the victims of war propaganda that they can be bamboozled into so wicked and disastrous an imperialist venture. We cannot believe that the British commonwealth will allow itself to be dragged by Gen. MacArthur into an 'intervention' which would drive all the Asiatic peoples into the Communist camp. . . .

". . . urging that the United Nations Security Council reconsider its refusal to hear representatives of China, the conservative *Sunday Observer* declared September 3: . . . Even our Allies who do not recognize the Chinese government have an urgent practical interest in meeting its representatives on neutral ground, and thus establishing some contact. . . .

"The Liberal party's *London Star* ribbed MacArthur as a man who 'fancied himself as an orator,' scholar and corncob-smoking father of all GI's. Then more seriously, it warned that 'In a democracy, the government makes policy and the business of military commanders, as of diplomats and civil servants, is to carry it out. . . .'

"The *Sunday Pictorial* with four and a half million circulation, has said simply: 'America must recognize, as Britain has done, the Red Victory in China. She must disown the corrupt regime of Chiang Kai-shek and withdraw her protection from Formosa. . . .'

"The Labor Party newspaper *Daily Herald* showed its

concern with America's policy on Formosa in a peace head-line: 'The Menace of MacArthurism.' Wrote member of Parliament Michael Foote: 'MacArthur believes that communism can be fought with the weapons of old imperialism. . . .'

"The authoritative *Manchester Guardian* rapped MacArthur's suppressed statement on Formosa as 'deplorable.' For particular criticism, it singled out his statement that America's frontier has 'shifted to embrace the entire Pacific ocean which can become a peaceful lake only if dominated by the U.S. But does Asia desire that the Pacific should be an American lake? Are these arguments to advance in the middle of a United Nations campaign?'

"The London *Daily Mirror* with a circulation of four million pointed out wryly that MacArthur is not just a U.S. Military man 'who has over reached himself meddling in foreign policy' but that now he operates under the U.N. flag. It is profoundly shocking that he should risk entangling the U.N. elsewhere by his ill-advised and provocative claims concerning Formosa. . . .' "

The foregoing extracts from a publication issued by a known Communist-front organization, one so classified by the Department of Justice, show how carefully the Communist party line pinpointed its attention on the undermining of General MacArthur and how effectively it used statements by well-meaning dupes to bolster the Party line. I am in no position to know what effect, if any, this type of Red propaganda had on American thinking in high places. The Congressional committees are more than justified in tracking down the secret motivations of our American policy in China. The role played by Communist publications is an important facet of this complicated record. There is little doubt that the communization of China was an objective toward which all active Communists were frantically driving within the limits of their specialties, nationality, or positions. Pattern and purpose were just as clear and as determined in the thirties in Shanghai as they were later in North Korea or Indo-China.

Chinese Organizations and Communist Fronts

On a national and sectional level the organs of the Comintern often lost their obvious coloring, becoming Communist-front groups in a host of forms. However, each auxiliary organization of the Comintern was represented abroad, often by apparently unconnected groups, which ranged from outright Communist to pseudo-liberal associations which were organized or infiltrated by Comintern agents. In many cases, these national organizations could be traced to more than one Moscow group. Often they were temporary organizations or local movements designed to gain popular or mass support for an immediate aim; just as often, however, they were serious long-term projects. As these groups touched the Shanghai scene during the period of Smedley's residence there, they formed an interesting and complex web which deserves detailed treatment.

1. *PPTUS: The Pan Pacific Trade Union Secretariat.* PPTUS and its parent organization, the Shanghai branch of the Far Eastern Bureau, were the most important and highly organized apparatus for Comintern labor activities in the Far East during the late 1920's and early 1930's. The PPTUS was set up in 1927 at a conference in Hankow, attended by several prominent Comintern leaders, including Lozovsky, a Comintern agent who rose from secretary of the Profintern in 1928 to a transient position as leader of the Soviet labor movement.

Another member of the Hankow conference who later became first head of the PPTUS was the American Communist Earl Browder, who was assisted in his work in Shanghai by an American woman, Katherine Harrison. Other Americans, including a journalist James H. Dolson, one Albert Edward Stewart, and Margaret Undjus, were prominent in the affairs of the PPTUS as was the German woman Wiedemeyer. Richard Sorge himself was suspected by the Shanghai police of having come on a mission for the PPTUS when he arrived in Shanghai in 1930.

Set up for Comintern work in China, Indo-China, Malaya, Japan, Formosa, Korea, and the Philippines, the PPTUS had no direct connection with the ECCI or the Praesidium in Moscow although a chain of liaison existed to the Profintern and some instances of direct connection between Moscow and Shanghai were substantiated. In that particular period and primarily for security, the PPTUS derived its authority from a Comintern subsidiary in Berlin, the Western European Bureau (WEB), and from the WEB through the Far Eastern Bureau (FEB) in Khabarovsk and Vladivostok. This is confirmed in a report by Deputy Commissioner of Intelligence in the French Municipal Police. "Simultaneously with the establishment of the Far Eastern Bureau of the III International, the Profintern established in Shanghai, a branch of the Pan-Pacific Trade Union Secretariat, an auxiliary organization of the Profintern charged with directing the militant syndicalist movement in the countries bordering on the Pacific and with headquarters in Vladivostok since 1929. . . ."

The Western European Bureau, largely an organ of the immensely powerful and well-organized (pre-Hitler) German Communist Party, went far beyond its stated function of maintaining contact with the sections in Western Europe; in fact, the WEB appears to have been, for a time, almost a peer of the ECCI, operating often independently. From the WEB authority went to the Far Eastern Bureau in Shanghai. There was also an FEB (Delburo) in Khabarovsk (later transferred to Vladivostok) which maintained direct contact with both the illegal FEB in Shanghai and the Praesidium of the Comintern in Moscow. Instructions and cash subsidies for distribution by the FEB were transmitted from the WEB in Berlin through courier channels to an import business in Shanghai dealing in wines, perfumes, and other luxury articles. Comintern agents in the import company passed on these funds and instructions to the staff of the FEB (Shanghai) which consisted of eight or nine Europeans and several Chinese. Funds of the FEB were deposited in no less than seven Chinese banks from which they then were withdrawn as needed. The FEB was a regional organ of the Comintern, responsible for the dispatch of students for training in Moscow and for payments to Chinese organizations led by the PPTUS. The size of the payments, at least $500,000 annually, gives some indication of the importance attached to China alone by the Comintern strategists of the early 1930's.

The operational unit of the FEB, although preceding the parent body in date of formation in Shanghai, the PPTUS (also known as TOSS) was staffed largely by the same personalities although direct PPTUS work was done by three foreigners aided by Chinese translators. Two of the foreigners working for PPTUS during the early 1930's are known to have been Albert Edward Stewart and Margaret Undjus, while the third was James Dolson, all Americans. When Earl Browder left Shanghai in 1929 or 1930, Gerhardt Eisler is reported to have taken his place as secretary of the PPTUS. It is certain that Eisler was in Shanghai in 1929 in connection with the PPTUS. The interlocking evidence of the Sorge Records settle this point beyond a doubt; the FEB was divided into an organization section under Noulens and a political branch under Gerhardt Eisler. When Noulens was arrested, Eisler fled and other operators went underground. Conversely, this fact puts the Noulens Defense Group in a proper light: Soviet agents staging a defense rally for another agent caught in the act.

The most famous of the Comintern agents connected with the FEB and PPTUS were Paul and Gertrude Ruegg, more widely known as Mr. and Mrs. Hilaire Noulens. Noulens, traveling on a stolen Belgian passport as Ferdinand Vandercruysen, arrived in Shanghai March 19, 1930 to head the FEB. Fifteen months later, on June 13, 1931, he was arrested for Communist activities as a result of a cable address found on a French Communist, Joseph Ducroux, alias Serge Lefranc, when the latter was arrested in Singapore on June 1, 1930. The French report previously quoted has this to say:

"Two sheets of paper were found on Lefranc, one bearing the address: 'P.O. Box 208, Shanghai' and the other, 'Hilonoul, Shanghai' . . . Raids were immediately made on the other houses rented by Noulens under various names. They resulted in the seizure of large quantities of Communist literature and of numerous documents in different languages relating to Communist activities in the Far East, as well as in the arrest of Noulens' wife, also known as Madame Vandercruysen, Motte, Ruck, etc. . . ."

Following Ruegg's arrest, trial, and conviction, authorities learned that he and other members of the FEB and PPTUS, in addition to seven bank accounts, had rented 14 or 15 houses and apartments while in Shanghai, seven of which were known to have been maintained concurrently. Ruegg himself used at least 12 names in Shanghai and carried one Canadian and two Belgian passports and his wife used five names and also carried two Belgian passports.

The All China Labor Federation, of which Smedley was a member, was one of the recipients of the FEB subsidies, receiving $1,800 monthly from the PPTUS.

2. *Noulens Defense Committee: International Red Aid.* MOPR, as stated, has taken various forms abroad. In Shanghai it played its most spectacular role during the early 1930's. When Paul and Gertrude Ruegg were arrested June 13, 1931, the International Red Aid took charge of their defense. Willi Muezenberg, German Communist wheel horse and one of the Comintern's most efficient organizers of both Communist and front groups, formed a defense unit first known as the Noulens' Defense Committee, * the Shanghai

---

* J. M. Jobez, the former Deputy Commissioner of Intelligence in the French Municipal Police, Shanghai, again provides collateral information on this notorious case: "On August 19th and 20th, 1931, Madame Sun Yat-sen who had just returned to Shanghai from Berlin received from various radical groups and organizations in Europe a number of telegrams demanding that she intervene in the Noulens' case

branch being led by the Harold Isaacs and boasting among its members Agnes Smedley, Irene Wiedemeyer (Weitemeyer), and Madame Sun Yat-sen; the group continued efforts to free these Comintern agents for several years after they were finally sentenced.

The Rueggs, when arrested, posed as Belgian citizens named Herssens, and had used many aliases, such as Vandercruysen, although the man had previously been known in Shanghai as Hilaire Noulens. Their claim to Belgian protection was disapproved and the couple was handed over to the Chinese authorities for prosecution as Communist agents. The League Against Imperialism and other Comintern groups protested that Noulens, as he was then known, was merely the paid secretary of the PPTUS, possibly a more easily defensible position than his actual position as leader of the FEB. Later in 1931, a collateral English defense group, apparently inadvertently, referred to him as "Ruegg." The ensuing investigation disclosed that Paul Ruegg was an active Swiss Communist who had been prominent a decade earlier in Switzerland and had come to police notice only sporadically after he had gone to Moscow in 1924. After the disclosure of Ruegg's identity, the international committee adopted his real name for their Committee for the Defense of Paul and Gertrude Ruegg. The committee attracted or solicited known Communists, incidental sympathizers, and non-Communist humanitarians, listing Lion Feuchtwanger and Albert Einstein as German members of the Committee, and several sentimental Americans then at the height of their fame, including Floyd Dell, Sinclair Lewis, Theodore Dreiser, John Dos Passos, and Oswald Garrison Villard.

Despite MOPR efforts, the Rueggs were found guilty of seditious activities and imprisoned in Nanking. With the release of many political prisoners, when Nanking fell to the Japanese, the pair were liberated in September, 1937 and have since disappeared. Ruegg is reported to have entered the U.S. in 1939 as Naum Katzenberg and another report

and advocate the liberation of the defendants. Among the senders of such telegrams were German artists and writers, a Communist member of the German Reichstag, Clara Zetkine, who died toward the end of June, 1933, in the U.S.S.R., a group of Labor Party members of the British Parliament, Spanish writers, artists and scientists, the Central Committee of the League Against Imperialism, the Central Committee of the International Workers Relief, Romaine Rolland, Henry Barbusse and others. . . . Early in September, 1931, in their turn, the foreign radical circles in Shanghai formed an aid committee of the Pan-Pacific Trade Union Secretariat. Among the members of this committee were Madame Agnes Smedley, an American anarchist syndicalist well known in Shanghai's radical circles; G. B. Powell, editor of the *China Weekly Review;* Edgar Snow, H. Isaacs, radical American journalists . . ."

claims that he again visited Shanghai in 1939, Chungking in 1940, and the Philippines in 1941.

3. *Friends of the U.S.S.R.* The Society of Friends of the U.S.S.R., Shanghai Branch, was founded in 1932 by Edmond Egon Kisch, a Czechoslovakian journalist long known as a Comintern agent. The Shanghai branch of this pro-Soviet Communist front was one of a series of typical overseas societies for cultural relations between the U.S.S.R. and a given country, the autonomous and ostensibly independent branch in the U.S. being known as the National Council of American-Soviet Friendship, the successor to the (American) Friends of the Soviet Union and the American Council on Soviet Relations. The purpose behind the formation of these groups * is to gain support for Soviet foreign policy objectives through highly publicized participation in these front organizations of liberal elements who were presumed to believe sincerely in the altruistic nature of Soviet policy.

The names of some of the more important members of the Shanghai branch are known and include among others in the early 1930's Agnes Smedley, Irene Wiedemeyer (Weitemeyer), and Harold Isaacs. Communism unmasks boldly when successful. The character of this Society is made plain by its sudden revival in our days in the wake of the Communist conquest of China. A new label appeared, China-Soviet Friendship Association, and opening meetings were attended by Communist big-wigs like Chou En-lai and Liu Shao-chi. Madame Sun Yat-sen was listed as one of the sponsors of the organization which proclaimed its mission as "the establishment and consolidation of the cultural, economic and other relations of China and the Soviet Union."

4. *Friends of China.* Outside the original range of the friendly societies, but similar to foreign cultural groups for the support of countries presently within the Soviet orbit, the International Friends of China was a front organization which capitalized on Western sympathy for China and its defense against Japanese aggression, in order to promote the ends of the Chinese Communists. Like individual fellow travelers, the Friends of China, founded in 1934 with offices in New York, London, and Paris, gave sole credit for Chinese resistance to the Chinese Communists and attempted

* Membership in a Soviet friendship society is not grounds for accusation or proof of Communist party membership. Affiliation could be classified as misplaced sympathy. However, when association is combined with more obviously Communist groups, membership in a friendly society becomes a practical indication of strong support of Communist world objectives. Thus the imperceptible evolution of the fellow traveler.

to divert normal sympathy to their support. Although its stated aims were lofty, the society tipped its hand when it claimed to have "done much to expose the collaboration of Chiang Kai-shek with the Japanese, British, and American imperialists." Although the London and Paris branches engaged in relatively little activity, European members then included such respectable fronts as the Labour Party's chief whip in the House of Lords, Lord Marley; and Bertrand Russell, long known for his interests in China; along with Edmond Egon Kisch, classified as an active Comintern agent; and other known Communists. The New York branch, the American Friends of China, which included Earl Browder in its membership, was the most active. Affiliated with the Communist-front American League Against War and Fascism, the American Friends of China published its own monthly magazine *China Today* which was pro-Communist. The American group also sponsored a Shanghai publication of similar nature, *Voice of China,* published by Max and Grace Granich. This paper, published from March, 1936 until the latter part of 1937, although not overtly a Communist publication, portrayed the Chinese Communists as the only defenders of China's independence and resistance to the Japanese. The magazine was suppressed after more than eighteen months of existence and the Graniches returned to the United States on December 21, 1937.

5. *China League for Civil Rights.* The China League for Civil Rights remained in a twilight zone of respectability inclined toward becoming a Communist-front organization. The group was initially organized by such liberal Kuomintang members as Madame Sun Yat-sen, who, despite her sojourn in Moscow and her acceptance by the CCP, was not then regarded as a Communist; Hu Shih; Lin Yu-tang; and Dr. Tsai Yuan-pei at the height of the Kuomintang persecution of dissident opinion. As a Communist front during its comparatively short existence, it was a perfect example of such an organization. Objected to for obvious reasons by Kuomintang authorities, who closed its Peiping branch, the parent organization capitalized on the high position of the Chinese leaders in Shanghai which precluded any direct action against the League by the Nanking authorities until the organization finally liquidated itself after complete failure to attain its objectives.

6. *League Against Imperialism.* The League Against Imperialism was a relatively early Comintern body, founded by German Communists and various colonial nationals as the League for Struggle Against Colonial Oppression. While it

existed outside any of the auxiliary groups of the ECCI, its direct connection with Moscow and its motives were obvious. It was based on Article 8 of the Conditions of Admission to the Comintern, making it obligatory for Comintern sections in countries with colonies to advocate and support the liberation of colonial populations. At a 1927 Congress in Brussels, the notorious Willi Muenzenberg formed the League Against Imperialism as a front or so-called innocents group, which would serve as a rallying point for anti-imperialist national revolutionary movements and promote the U.S.S.R. as the champion of the liberty of colonial people. Agnes Smedley, during her Berlin days admits having been present when her Indian friends participated with the Communists in founding the League and took an active part, shortly after her arrival in Shanghai in May, 1929, in organizing the China League Against Imperialism. The Chinese branch, along with its Western counterpart, took an active part in attempting to create mass pressure in the Noulens case and participated in several anti-foreign movements, later becoming involved with the Anti-War Congress.

Typical of the Communist-front organizations in seeking respectable stooges, the Anti-War Congress boasted Ellen Wilkinson, the Labour MP, and Lord Marley as leading names. Following a congress in Amsterdam in August, 1932, Lord Marley and a party of foreigners sailed for Shanghai to attend an Asiatic Congress Against Imperialist War. The Chinese Communists had no illusions about this group, despite its liberal front, often referring to it as the Barbusse Mission for one of its members, Henri Barbusse, a prominent member of the Comintern and publisher of the French Communist organs *L'Humanité* and *Le Monde*. The Anti-War Congress presumably was to gather data on Japanese aggression, the Comintern having denounced the 1931 Lytton Mission as a whitewash by the imperialist organ, the League of Nations. Madame Sun Yat-sen, China representative of the World Committee Against Imperialistic War, headed the welcoming committee and a host of organizations in China publicized the mission, organizing mass welcome demonstrations but always attaching to the visit the necessity for the extension of the revolutionary struggle. Joined with these ostensibly Chinese problems were demands to oppose the imperialist attack on the U.S.S.R. as well as to celebrate the recent victories of the (Chinese) Red Armies and to oppose Christianity and fascism. On hand to welcome the mission were Agnes Smedley and delegates from America, Canada, and Australia. It appears, however, that the Anti-War Congress accomplished nothing: Lord Marley spoke at a few meetings, was shocked when taken through a colony of laborers' hovels, and departed Shanghai less than two months after his arrival.

7. *Communist Rendezvous.* The Zeitgeist Bookstore, established by Irene E. I. Wiedemeyer (Weitemeyer), in November, 1930, was part of a widespread and elaborate Comintern network operating from the International Union of Revolutionary Writers in Moscow. Prior to the advent of Hitler, the Zeitgeist Buchhandlung in Berlin, with a branch office of its own in Moscow, was an important Comintern cultural outlet, part of a syndicate headed by Willi Muenzenberg, who was also the German head of the League Against Imperialism, of the Comintern's own bank in Paris, the Banque Commerciale Pour l'Europe du Nord, and of a vast number of other Comintern organizations and enterprises until he was read out of the Comintern in 1938, two years before his suicide. The Shanghai branch of the Zeitgeist Bookstore was set up as a focal distribution point of the International Union of Revolutionary Writers, stocking Communist publications in German and English as well as more legitimate literature, mainly in German. The amount of business transacted by the Zeitgeist Bookstore was small and the shop closed in 1933, ostensibly due to its poor finances. A more likely reason was the destruction of the legalized German Communist Party. After a trip to Europe in the autumn of 1933, Irene Wiedemeyer returned to Shanghai on September 9, 1934 to set herself up in the book business again, this time as the Shanghai representative of International Publishers of New York. The latter organization has long been the publishers of American Communist Party writings and the American distributor of International Literature.

Although Miss Wiedemeyer acted as the agent of International Publishers, another Shanghai group was also known as the authorized agents for International Literature. Mrs. V. N. Sotoff (Sotov), the wife of the head of the Shanghai agency of TASS, operated the American Book and Supply Company, which sold International Literature; it is significant, however, that the American Book and Supply Company and Miss Wiedemeyer's agency occupied offices in the same building at 410 Szechuan Road.

Miss Wiedemeyer had had some ties with the Third International although there are gaps in the information about her activities in Shanghai. She had married Wu Shao-kuo, a Chinese Communist, in Germany in 1925 and had studied the principles of revolutionary movements in Asia at the Sun Yat-sen University in Moscow in 1925-27. In Shanghai she knew Agnes Smedley well and was a member of the

Noulens Defense Committee and the Society of Friends of the U.S.S.R. She, as well as Smedley and Isaacs during 1932, were reported to have been in close contact with John M. Murray, an American correspondent for the Pacific News Agency, a Vancouver organization listed as an outlet for the Comintern and possibly a front for the League Against Imperialism and Colonial Oppression of Canada. In any event the particular role of the leftist bookshop was to operate as an outlet for revolutionary literature, and as a rendezvous of espionage partisans and fellow travelers. The little bookshop had done its part as a recruiting station for the 4th Bureau of the Red Army.

8. *Ancillary American Factors.* The interlocking court records of the Sorge Case and the files of Shanghai Municipal Police show a very considerable traffic of shady international characters, over a long period of years. Their clandestine operations in the thirities have paved the way for the collapse of Nationalist China in later years. The recent State Department "White Paper" throws some flickering light on this complex, general problem:

> . . . The combined force of overpopulation and new ideas set in motion the Chinese Revolution, first under the leadership of Sun Yat-sen and later Generalissimo Chiang Kai-shek. It should be remembered that Soviet doctrine and practice had a measurable effect upon the thinking and principles of Dr. Sun Yat-sen particularly in terms of economics and party organization and that the Kuomintang and the Chinese Communists cooperated until 1927, when the IIId International demanded a predominant position in the Government and in the Army. It was this demand which precipitated the break between the two groups. . . .

This is an oblique admission that the infant Republic was weaned on "Soviet doctrine and practice"; it easily explains the widow Sun Yat-sen as a front for many Communist efforts and it concedes naïvely, that the Chinese Communist Party came under the orders of the Third International, the recognized Soviet tools of international sabotage and subversion.

While the "White Paper" apparently skirts the conspiratorial underground, it confirms the impact of the Comintern apparatus, amply demonstrated in the Sorge and Shanghai documents; it can at once be stated that individual propagandists and operators like Smedley and Stein, and the horde of saboteurs, agents, fellow travelers, and dupes, unleashed by the Comintern, represent the major element in this Oriental disaster, and their nefarious work must be considered a contributory and even decisive factor. The intervention of American Communists in the Shanghai situation has been amply demonstrated.

On the other hand the Shanghai police records contain many instances in which American diplomatic and consular officers had attempted to stem the Red tide, by denying the protection of the International Settlement or American pseudo-citizenship to such operators; a classical case is the intervention of the American consul to stop the publication of *The Voice of China.*

Conclusion

Almost twenty years ago, as stated in the opening pages of this book, His Britannic Majesty's Consul General in Shanghai defined the purpose, justification, and usefulness of security investigation and research, as exemplified by the work of the FBI in the United States and our military and civil security agencies in the Far East:

". . . The function of the Comintern (now Cominform) is to act as the mainspring of an illegal conspiracy against international law and order. Members of the Comintern, like Eugene Dennis (Walsh) are highly trained. Their number is not legion. The Comintern is concerned with guarding their identities. If their function on the spot can be ascertained, then knowledge of their methods becomes available, the ramification of their apparatus becomes known and the chances for internal security are enormously increased. . . ."

The purpose of the Tokyo investigations can hardly be stated more clearly. The thefts of our atom secrets—the fruits of American technical ingenuity—were made possible by a naïve tolerance of Communists and their front organizations, of the saccharine vagaries of fellow travelers and prostituted liberals. Unless we learn the art of self-defense in international terms, we will have the suicide of Western civilization on our conscience.